THE
HOME HARDWARE
HANDBOOK

AN ILLUSTRATED USER'S GUIDE
TO COMMON TOOLS, MATERIALS, AND SUPPLIES
BY THE EDITORS OF MOTHER EARTH NEWS
INTRODUCTION BY BERNARD GLADSTONE

F
FIRESIDE

A FIRESIDE BOOK
PUBLISHED BY SIMON & SCHUSTER, INC.

NEW YORK   LONDON   TORONTO   SYDNEY   TOKYO

Fireside
Simon & Schuster Building
Rockefeller Center
1230 Avenue of the Americas
New York, New York 10020

FIRESIDE and colophon are registered
trademarks of Simon & Schuster, Inc.

Designed by Julia Gran and Michael
Dowdy
Manufactured in the United States of
America

10 9 8 7 6 5 4 3 2 1

Library of Congress Cataloging in Publi-
cation Data

ISBN 0-671-65789-5

Acknowledgments

Although it's constructed of paper and glue rather than wood and nails, building a book differs in no essential way from assembling a house. Either job can be completed solo, but the varied skills brought by a team produce a finish that shines. Luckily for us, we've had some of the best hands around beside us on the scaffolds putting together *The Home Hardware Handbook*.

For their contributions and advice born of decades of experience in the grit of things, we're indebted to Jan Adkins, TJ Byers, Ernie Conover, Bernard Gladstone, Clarence Goosen, Terry Krautwurst, Daniel Mack, Don Osby and Dave Petersen. Design consultation was provided by Will Hopkins and Ira Friedlander; art direction, the windows of the book, came from Michael Dowdy and Julie Gran. They were ably assisted by Nazan Akyavas, Linda Patterson Eger, Bill Lessner, Sandra McKee, Kathleen Seabe, Genia Gould, Robert Graf, Peggy Allen, Michael Soluri and Kay Holmes Stafford.

Apt editorial assistance—the task of protecting us from the "blue thumbs" of spelling, punctuation, grammar and electronic vagaries—was supplied by Assistant Managing Editors Christie Lyon and Liz Brennan, as well as Klara Blair, Julie Brown, Wilma Dingley, Judy Gold, Judy Janes, Lorna K. Loveless, Betty N. Mack, Karen Murray, Rita Norton and Carol Taylor. For coordination and organization, we thank Alfred Meyer and Kate Stuart. Finally, special kudos are well deserved by the ever-clever Dennis Burkholder, *Mother Earth News* Researcher, without whom we'd be short about half the subject matter of this book, and Tim Watkins, Managing Editor, *Mother Earth News*. They are, respectively, the inspiration and driving force that have brought *The Home Hardware Handbook* to print.

Richard Freudenberger
Research Coordinator, Mother Earth News
David Schoonmaker
Technical Editor, Mother Earth News

Contents

Introduction

During the more than 30 years that I served as Home Improvement Editor of the *New York Times*, I attended many hardware shows and exhibitions put on by tool manufacturing companies and other segments of the hardware industry. At one such gathering many years ago—in the days when "do-it-yourself" was a relatively new expression—I was asked if I could explain the tremendous growth in this comparatively recent trend: the fascination among homeowners with learning more about how-to techniques and the tools and materials that went along with them. I answered that in my opinion there were at least three major reasons for this growth:

1. The disappearance of the local handyman, the jack-of-all-trades who could be counted on to show up when needed. This person, who could be trusted to complete repairs and improvements at a reasonable cost and without a lot of haggling, was becoming harder and harder to find.

2. The rising cost of living combined with steadily increasing lifestyle expectations was putting an economic squeeze on many young homeowners. The pinch left them with much less money to spend on hiring others to do home repairs and improvements.

3. Last, but far from least, throughout the country many homeowners were feeling renewed interest and pride in being more self-sufficient and less dependent on others, especially when it came to taking care of their homes. When this spirit of adventure was considered alongside the "can-do" attitude so prevalent in the 1950s and 1960s, it seemed to me that the do-it-yourself trend was almost guaranteed to keep on growing.

Since then, this movement has done more than just continue to grow steadily; it has burgeoned. In fact, most people no longer think of home repair and improvement activities as merely pleasant pastimes or hobbies. Hands-on work has simply become an accepted part of home ownership.

Though active do-it-yourselfers are now found in nearly every walk of life, probably the fastest growing group is the affluent baby boomers. These are people who enjoy working with their hands in their spare time and find it to be a great way to relieve workaday tensions. These enthusiasts really do not *have* to do their own work. They do it simply because they get a great deal of pleasure out of using tools and building things, not to mention the pride of pointing to a successfully completed project.

This book is directed toward all do-it-yourselfers, though it will also appeal to people who are not participants—at least not yet. Some will enjoy reading (and dreaming) about tackling the kinds of projects described in these pages, storing away know-how for the future when they may have more time. Others will find it satisfying to learn all they can about good craftsmanship—how it *should* be done—perhaps because they want to know what to look for when they hire professionals. All readers who are interested in and intrigued by how things work will profit from this book. For them it will be an invaluable reference that they will look to time and again.

Based largely on the do-it-yourself articles and how-to instructional material published in the pages of *Mother Earth News* magazine over the years, *The Home Hardware Handbook* taps the combined experience of that magazine's knowledgeable editors. Like the periodical from which it sprang, this compendium is for men and women who are interested in taking more control of their lives. Making repairs, working with tools and crafting individualized projects from wood are all ways to increase self-reliance.

The Home Hardware Handbook is a friend you can trust for good advice in these pursuits. Browsing through its pages is like turning the clock back to the days when you could walk into your local hardware emporium and absorb endless hours of wisdom from the all-knowing store owner, as well as from the neighbors and local craftsmen who often gathered there. They were always willing to share "trade secrets" and the time- and work-saving pointers passed down from one generation to another.

Within the pages of this book you will find clear, detailed drawings accompanying text written in an understandable yet entertaining style. From discussing basic hand and power tools to designing and outfitting a complete workshop, *The Home Hardware Handbook* goes on to unravel the complexities of selecting fasteners, hinges, lumber and trim, plumbing fittings and other materials necessary to make your home as livable, functional and attractive as possible. The last part of the book consists of a series of chapters devoted to applying newfound knowledge by building ten different woodworking projects. These include a cedar chest, a child's play center, a high chair, a Shaker lap desk, a butler's tray table and various other pieces of furniture. Each project includes comprehensive drawings that give all needed dimensions and cutting outlines, and the text tells the reader how to fabricate the various components and assemble them.

—*Bernard Gladstone*

PART ONE

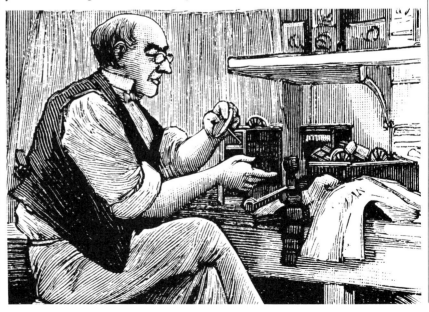

Browsing

One of the joys of living
in America is that there is a tool
for every task (or seems to be),
no matter how arcane.
This can lead to a delicious
sense of mastery.

Hardware Romance

You can find it in every city, every town. Even in the mail.

There is a hardware store in Columbus, Ohio, called Columbus Hardware. It is a high-ceilinged storefront downtown, but when you walk in out of the slicing December wind that scours Columbus, the high, simple space is immediately comforting. It is chiefly the wood that effects that cozy feeling: the worn wood floor, the floor-to-ceiling bank of wooden drawers mounted by ladders that run the depth of the building on tracks and the platoons of wooden tool handles in racks. It must be the wood because the store is not overly warm; the men behind the long wooden counter wear sweaters. They are serious, pleasant men, each with a shirt protector stuck with a ball-point pen and one or two pencil stubs, each wearing on his belt or carrying in his wool pants a tape measure or folding rule. They are usually busy. December, though, is a good time to walk in. Columbus Hardware sends out no Christmas circulars, no phone message pads for customers (I do not believe they advertise), but they do have a Christmas offering: Near the rear cash register is a carton of eating apples from an orchard near Cleveland, perfect scarlet Macs cradled in eggboard separators and square yellow tissues. Beside them is a carton of rolled calendars, the large, shop-wall size, with a print of a country scene, "Cidering" or suchlike, and under it COLUMBUS HARDWARE. (This may be advertising.) You can take an apple, examine the calendar and look around while you reduce the Mac to a thin core. There are table saws, radial arm saws, drill presses and mounted bench tools standing on the floor with their cords coiled. There are outdoor tools: a dozen patterns of shovels, hoes, grubs, peavies,

Johnson bars, scythes, hayforks and some implements you won't recognize. This is no difficulty; someone—not necessarily a clerk—will be glad to name it and explain it. The atmosphere here is like a men's club: relaxed, you need not know someone to speak with him. When a clerk is free he can help you, not always by selling you something. He may listen to you describe your project, nodding, and mount one of the ladders, returning with fittings that may help. You can discuss it with him. He will know. He can compare power tools, discourse on concrete pouring or advise on porch building. He may call in an expert in the form of another clerk. The prices are fair. The inventory is large. In the back, near the alley doors, glass is cut. In the basement are cordage, bulk nails, parts and stock. There is a glass case near the street door: practical knives, reels, micrometers, small tools, tape measures, specialized tools. It is difficult to leave without stopping there.

There are not too many places like Columbus Hardware. It is a reasonable place, a source, a reference, a workable anachronism. My local hardware store is mostly Formica and white pegboard. Its tools and screws and, damn, even its nails are in blister packs. It won't sell me T-nuts or hog rings or timber jacks or a set of trammels.

Are such things necessary? I don't know. I do believe that one of the walls of plastic society is buckling: People are still insisting that they can use their hands. People are finding it (increasingly) necessary to prove their own usefulness and skill in physical statements. Men and women and young people want to make part of their world.

Tool is a noun and a verb, and any human time is caught up in the motion of the verb, never complete but always on the way to mastery. Tools are beautiful. They have scale and direction and economy. Grips invite your hands, edges point at the work, and any unnecessary or decorative part is—for better or worse—instantly recognizable as something outside the skeleton of function.

It is rare now to inherit tools; there are too few craftsman-fathers to go around. We have the catalogues, though—our collective, expensive grandfathers. Catalogue cruising is a pursuit of its own, an exercise in cerebral cabinetry, and many mail-order joiners who couldn't drive a tenpenny nail without blood-letting can identify specialty planes that

would mystify damn good jackleg carpenters.

Perhaps it's just as well that we don't inherit our fathers' tools. Fifteen years ago a garden-variety consumer would have been hard-pressed to buy a plane or cabinet chisel of good quality. It was the off-slope past, the do-it-yourself peak of the late '50s when "home handyman" was a title that had a snappy madras-and-Weejuns sound to it. Whacking up an ironing board holder or a shoeshine kit was good fun and about as cerebral as shuffleboard or canasta. We are a new kind of craftsperson, and it is a time that looks at the inner game of joinery or carpentry with perhaps more interest than at the

finished product. It is also a time when running down the street involves its own rationale, wardrobe, stopwatch and mantra, and with the blessings of availability we must deal with the dangers of mystique. There is an implied obligation in all the catalogues: We view them as tool chests and feel obliged to have the "proper" tools before we can do proper work.

You must puncture the mystique dragon in your own way, but for me the dragon shrinks a little when I think of a Japanese carpenter marching to a job with a small, a very small, chest of tools. I also think of Fred Daley, a small old man and a good house car-

but we can address the simplest question first, that of prices. A survey of identical brand-name tools priced in five or six catalogues will show that prices do vary, inconsistently, and that you must shop for tools among all the suppliers, ordering here for mallets and there for nail sets. One generalization available is this: Some big-volume tool supply houses, like U.S. General and Silvo, carry more abstruse tools than might seem likely, and they may save you a considerable amount over woodworking specialty houses like Woodcraft, Garrett Wade, Leichtung, Princeton and their like. Silvo Hardware Company, for instance, carries the standard Stanley planes but also stocks the Record planes and even one make of wood-bodied planes.

There are times when the tool mystique grows into actual mysticism, times when the shrewdest shopping can't help you and you must go on intuition. This is in the realm of material quality and preference. A 26-inch, 10-point handsaw is not a definite item; it can be a Disston, a Nicholson, a Nonpareil, a Sandvik, a Pax. How can anyone tell you which is best? Nonpareil sawyers look on Pax sawyers with pity, and both look on Disston sawyers with scorn, yet all three may get through the board with the same speed and accuracy. Steel differs, temper varies. No one can tell you which chisels to buy. Barely polite controversy goes on as to which of four or five long-defunct chisel makers were best; chisels pass from hand to hand with large sums of money; counterfeiters appear. Carving gauges present a more confusing situation since handles, shapes and lengths are as unstandard as steel, temper and edges. Japanese tools are, for the most part, handmade; their quality and reputation differ in the same way that samurai swords bore the legends of their makers and their exploits.

This can be said about quality: It takes a master to bring good work out of a poor tool. If you are not a master, buy the best tool you can afford commensurate with its use. We are not the only beneficiaries of the woodworking renaissance. Our children and our grandchildren can inherit tools from us, if we choose and use them wisely.—*Jan Adkins*

Jan Adkins is an art director in Washington, D.C.

penter, walking away from a finished house with one open box of tools, not a large box. Begin with this: With a dozen hand tools of good quality, and with good wood, and with concentration, you can do work of extraordinary beauty. The skill lives in your hands and your will and is extended by the prosthesis of tools only so far. Most specialized tools are conveniences and refinements of simpler devices, and are in all probability superfluous. Shrink the dragon in your own way; the beauty of tools is at odds with the pocketbook, with practicality and even with the learning of simpler skills, but it is an enjoyable narcotic.

With due caution, then, you can order and wade into all the tool catalogues, and what will you find? Which is best? Which offers the best value? Which is most complete? The answer is not as simple as a stack of numbers,

Antique Tools

Buy bargain tools at auction for a happy dose of history.

It has almost become a natural cycle, like the waxing of the moon. Ten times a year, in New Hampshire, a few hundred people gather for an auction of old hand tools. It's the most regular and reliable source of such tools in the country.

"We used to sell them by the apple box full for a buck or two," says auctioneer Richard Crane of Hillsboro, New Hampshire. "But now you see them there individually, and we get 10 and even a hundred times the price we used to." He winks. "Still, there are always bargains." Crane, who offers to auction anything from antiques to animals, has spent 12 years building his reputation as the nation's major source for old hand tools, and he has a clear affection for his work and the people who come to buy. "There's a real fellowship among the tool boys. It's like a fraternity; it's special."

The day starts early. Around seven, in the parking lot, small groups gather at the tailgates of pickups, vans and station wagons. They drink coffee from paper cups and talk tools. This is the warm-up period, as important to the selling as the auction itself.

The doors open at eight, and the tools, numbered and neatly laid out on tables, are now subject to scrutiny. For the next hour and a half, a shuffling procession moves up and down the aisles. Friends greet each other: "Making any syrup, Fred?" And strangers exchange observations on the tools: "That's got some years on it."

Today there are about 200 people, mostly men, dressed in what must be every known variety of flannel work shirt. They're looking, touching, making notes and touching the tools some more. We all received a listing of the 600 lots of tools a few weeks before. It's clear the lists have been studied. Some are dog-eared. Others, like mine, are marked up with bright-colored underlining pens. This is by no means a casual event.

Three kinds of people generally show up here: the dealers, the collectors and the users. But some dealers collect, some collectors deal, and some users collect and deal. And, as at any auction, an air of expectation and competition animates the proceedings.

I'm a user, planning to get some hollow augers for myself and some extras for when I teach workshops in chair making. Three or four lots of augers are scheduled for auction at various times. I'll be here all day, waiting. Some people are better prepared than I am. They come with coolers brimming with sodas and sandwiches. I have some peppermint gum. I casually look over the hollow augers. They're in good, usable condition. I decide I really want them. But I don't look at them too long. I don't want to seem too interested and drive prices up. Besides, I might not get them.

At 9:31 a.m. exactly, the auction starts. Richard Crane wears a black derby. He is short, stout and affable. His partner is Jim Sweet. Tall, lean and young, he wears a suit and a Panama straw hat. A good auction is part vaudeville, and this latter-day Abbott and Costello team promises a good show.

"All right, we start off with lot number one, a box filled with various tools. Who'll open at 25? 25? 25 where? . . . And 30? And

35? And 40? And 45? And 50 . . . 55? 55? Sold, $50."

There will be 600 such lots sold in the next six hours in a never-ending chant of numbers, names and numbers. There are planes, augers, levels, knives, wrenches, squares, tongs, chisels, drills, hammers, saws—anything that ever extended the reach and power of the human hand. It's the power to make things and, in a way, control the future. Owning a tool, even an exotic one, is insurance. You are ready. "It's good to know it's there," said one craftsman, "even if I use it only once or twice in my life."

Crane is up to lot 40, a cow dehorner. Holding it up, he cracks, "The women always seem to be interested in these." It sells seconds later for $40, to a man. Crane takes care to organize and orchestrate his auctions to keep the interest of the collectors, the users and the curious.

Old tools are distinguished by more than age, though that obviously counts. Seventeenth- and eighteenth-century handmade tools are often signed by the individual maker and are highly prized. Then come

struction. They have survived damp cellars, dusty shops and decades of use. Just by being, they are survivors.

Finally, as I mentioned, tools are insurance. It's comforting to know you have the right tool for the right job, if ever the job comes up. In my father's shop there are tools of perpetual mystery. But someday, he claims, he might need them and he will have them. I was always amused by this until I looked carefully around my own shop and saw two large slicks. These are huge overgrown chisels for squaring logs—I've never squared any. There's the bung hole borer for bung holes I have yet to make. And there's the small cooper's froe for the small barrel staves I have never cut.

Malcolm MacGregor runs Piscataqua Architectural Woodwork Company in Durham, New Hampshire, where he makes moldings for houses undergoing restoration. He has just paid $500 for lot number 254, a panel-raising plane made by H. Chapin. "There are times when I might use it," says MacGregor, "but it's really for my collection. A man made this. He made his living making the tools that built America. We value the chairs and cabinets from the seventeenth and eighteenth centuries. But are the tools with which they were made any less special?"

Indeed, tools and tool collecting seem to be coming of age. At the morning parking lot swap, a plane was bought for $2,500. At a recent Crane auction, another plane brought $8,500.

Richard Crane is the first to compare his auctions to the stock market: "You can buy and sell and make some money if you know what you're doing." Crane calls old tools "an almost liquid asset," which—at his regular auctions—can be bought and then sold for a profit in a matter of months.

Tips? Crane says the price of axes is down and it's a good time to buy. Ice saws are now a better bargain, much less than the $800 they once sold for. And levels, rulers and coopers' tools have skyrocketed. It might be a time to sell.

Even though the business and investment side of tools is maturing, there are always new and inexpensive ways into the fascinating world of tools. "Take wrenches," says Crane. "A few years ago, no one wanted them. Then the other tools started going up,

subsequent generations of tools, the "common" tools. These are unauthored, often having been made in small shops or factories that began to produce tools commercially in the mid-1800s. These are sought by users, like me, and by some collectors. But as one upper-crust collector of fine tools put it: "One of those tools would have to be flat-ass new for a real collector to want it."

But whether the old tool is of museum quality linked to one known maker or is a factory-made piece, it still performs the same function for its owner. As Chester Heinzman, cabinetmaker and collector, says, "These tools are what my predecessors used. I have respect for that. I'm in awe of that value."

I now use my grandfather's brace. He was a stationmaster with the New York Central Railroad and may never have used the tool in his life, but now it's mine. I permanently borrowed it from my father. It ties me to both men. It's as much a relic as a tool.

It doesn't have to be family. I sat with two men discussing the construction of the old tool chests they had bought and restored. As they spoke of the joinery of one drawer sys-

tem, they talked as much about a person as an old chest: "He put brass corners on the outside, and on the bottom of the inside he . . ." The chests hooked these men up with an old carpenter, as if an auction were like a seance, calling up the spirits of the workers of a long gone time.

The old tools are visible evidence of a fraternity through time. They bind users together. I use quite a few of them, mostly cutting tools, like knives, chisels, axes and froes. I have many more than I really need, but each one is another chink in the mosaic of my life as a woodworker. In pleasurable reverie I actively imagine the lineage of woodworkers who have used this very same tool; buying it, feeling its weight and balance, using it, sharpening and resharpening it, storing it away, perhaps losing it or giving it away. For a moment, as I hold my pocketknife with the nicked rosewood handle, I forget the estimates, phone calls, invoices and supply lists that clock off my days.

In another way, old tools send me off into the uncertain future with a sense of preparedness. They offer me good steel, sturdy con-

and the boys in the Midwest started getting more interested in the tools that came with the wagons to the plains and even in the tools that repaired the cars out of Detroit. So now we've got a market for wrenches. They're still plentiful and cheap." He winks. "Get 'em now."

The number of people interested in tools is swelling. Malcolm MacGregor says there are only about 200 serious collectors in the whole country. But there are more and more people interested in *using* old hand tools.

"We're seeing more hobbyists asking for the old tools," says Randy Uncapher of M.S. Carter Antiques in Portsmouth, New Hampshire. Twice a year, in April and November, M.S. Carter has a special sale just for users. No collectors. "We want to give the user, the craftsman, the first chance at the collection of tools we've put together."

Well, I bought every lot of hollow augers offered that day. Each time I bid my heart raced, my sinuses cleared and, as I waved my hand, my mind got ready to excuse me if I overbid. The augers are beautiful. All grimy and nicked and broken-in and ready for whatever task I'll put them to.

And, I must confess, I bought two old dull hatchets that I'll never use. But just holding them feels good. Just think of all the people who used them before me; all the chopping, the kindling, the fires on cold nights, the hot apple cider with bourbon. And they're an investment. Richard Crane said so. Well, not in so many words. But now they're mine and they only cost five bucks.—*Daniel Mack*

Daniel Mack is a woodworker in New York City and an avid collector of old tools.

Antique Tool Anthology

There are local, regional and national associations of tool collectors that have regular meetings, featuring tool swaps, demonstrations, newsletters and other information of interest. Here are a few you might contact.

Early American Industries Assoc. (EAIA)
P.O. Box 2128 Empire Plaza Station
Albany, NY 12220

EAIA West
c/o Al Bennett
869 A Ave.
Coronado, CA 92188

Mid West Tool Collectors Assoc.
c/o Morris Olson
2825 Jackson St.
La Crosse, WI 54601

South West Tool Collectors Assoc.
c/o Dr. Ron Baird
3619 W. Mt. Vernon, Rt. 21
Springfield, MO 65802

Three Rivers Tool Collectors Assoc.
c/o Robert Kendra
39 South Rolling Hills
Irwin, PA 15642

Antique Tools and Trades in Connecticut
c/o Dwight Burritt
229 Olde Stage Rd.
Glastonbury, CT 06033

Tools and Trades in Massachusetts
c/o Jean MacRea
193 Harmon Ave.
Cranston, RI 02910

Antique Crafts and Tools in Vermont
c/o Helen Johnstone
8 Rudgate Rd.
Colchester, VT 05446

For information on auctions, the following two sources will be helpful:

Richard Crane
Your Country Auctioneer
Box AC
Hillsboro, NH 03244
A year's worth of listings and catalogues costs $25. His auctions are held in the Hillsboro area 10 times a year. There are two major sales featuring tools for collectors and eight sales of good tools for users. Accepts bids by mail.

William A. Gustafson
Antique Tool Auction
P.O. Box 104
Austerlitz, NY 12017
Offers illustrated catalogues. Accepts bids by mail.

The best place to find dealers is through the publications and meetings of the tool associations. Since most dealers do not publish a catalogue of their tools, send the dealer of your choice a list of the tools you are looking for. He or she will keep your list on file and get back to you when the tools you want are found. You'll be sent a description and price, and it's your option to buy or not. Some dealers will actually send the tools for your examination, and most dealers will refund your money for a tool that isn't quite what you were after. These dealers are the ones I've bought from in the past:

M.S. Carter, Inc.
175 Market St.
Portsmouth, NH 03801
Often has a selection of English tools and has special "Craftsman's Sales" twice a year.

Ludwig's Scattered Treasures
309 Harvard Blvd.
Westlawn, PA 19609

Iron Horse Antiques, Inc.
RD 2
Poultney, VT 05764

Many of the woodworking magazines available on newsstands discuss old tools, and there are many books that do the same. Here are some of the books I'm familiar with:

Country Woodcraft by Drew Langsner, 1978. Rodale Press, Inc. Not in print.
A Museum of Early American Tools by Eric Sloane, 1984. Dodd, Mead and Co. (1985, paperback, Ballantine.)
The Woodwright's Shop: A Practical Guide to Traditional Woodcraft by Roy Underhill, 1981. U. of North Carolina Press.
The Woodwright's Companion: Exploring Traditional Woodcraft by Roy Underhill, 1983. U. of N.C. Press.
The Woodwright's Workbook: Further Explorations in Traditional Woodcraft by Roy Underhill, 1986. U. of N.C. Press.
Hand Tools: Their Ways and Workings by Aldren A. Watson, 1982. W.W. Norton and Co., Inc.

Aged Pages From Times Past

A sampling from old tool catalogues

Nearly as interesting as antique tools themselves are the old-time hardware and dry-goods catalogues from which the tools could be ordered. Throughout the latter phase of westward expansion, toward the end of the nineteenth century, the mail-order business was a booming industry, thanks to the network of rail lines that brought settlers, and goods, to the new territories. Reprinted here are selected items of interest from catalogues printed between 1880 and 1915.

POST-MOUNTED DRILL PRESS
Will drill to center of a 12″ circle. Adjustable crank and table; open yoke for floor drilling. Spindle is bored to take ½″ drill shanks. Wheel-feed model.

CARPENTER'S IRON-BOUND HICKORY MALLET
Round malleable iron rings with hickory head and handle. Head measures 5¾″ X 3″; weight, 3½ pounds.

DISSTON ADJUSTABLE COMPASS SAW
The well-known Henry Disston and Sons brand is your guarantee of the highest quality in hand saws. This adjustable compass saw has a carved and polished apple handle with a thumb lever. Available in 10″, 12″ and 14″ lengths.

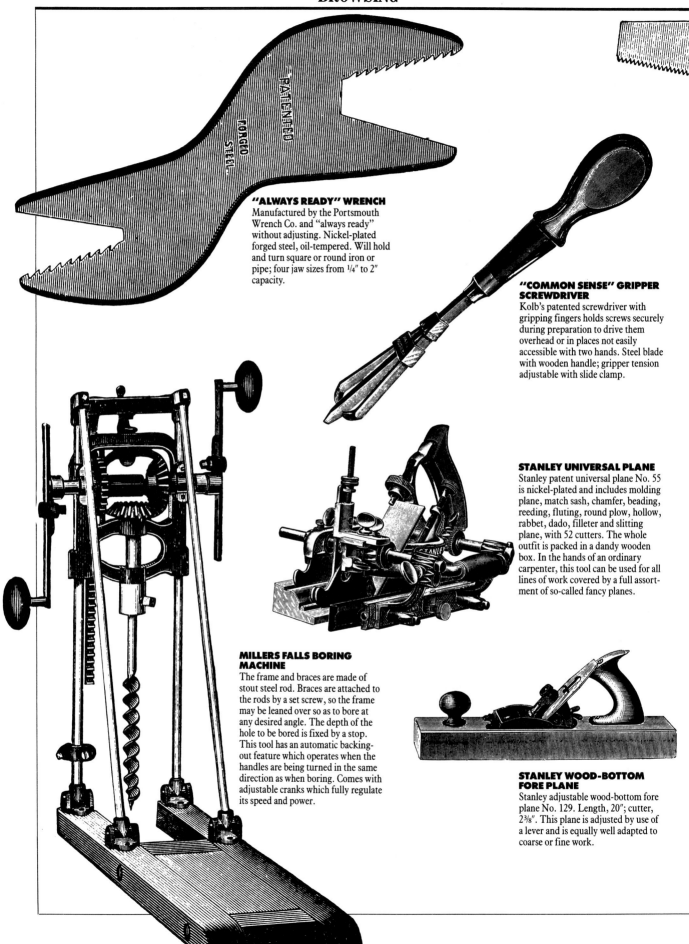

"ALWAYS READY" WRENCH
Manufactured by the Portsmouth Wrench Co. and "always ready" without adjusting. Nickel-plated forged steel, oil-tempered. Will hold and turn square or round iron or pipe; four jaw sizes from 1/4" to 2" capacity.

"COMMON SENSE" GRIPPER SCREWDRIVER
Kolb's patented screwdriver with gripping fingers holds screws securely during preparation to drive them overhead or in places not easily accessible with two hands. Steel blade with wooden handle; gripper tension adjustable with slide clamp.

STANLEY UNIVERSAL PLANE
Stanley patent universal plane No. 55 is nickel-plated and includes molding plane, match sash, chamfer, beading, reeding, fluting, round plow, hollow, rabbet, dado, filleter and slitting plane, with 52 cutters. The whole outfit is packed in a dandy wooden box. In the hands of an ordinary carpenter, this tool can be used for all lines of work covered by a full assortment of so-called fancy planes.

MILLERS FALLS BORING MACHINE
The frame and braces are made of stout steel rod. Braces are attached to the rods by a set screw, so the frame may be leaned over so as to bore at any desired angle. The depth of the hole to be bored is fixed by a stop. This tool has an automatic backing-out feature which operates when the handles are being turned in the same direction as when boring. Comes with adjustable cranks which fully regulate its speed and power.

STANLEY WOOD-BOTTOM FORE PLANE
Stanley adjustable wood-bottom fore plane No. 129. Length, 20"; cutter, 2 3/8". This plane is adjusted by use of a lever and is equally well adapted to coarse or fine work.

COMBINATION HAND SAW, RULE, SQUARE, STRAIGHT EDGE, AWL, PLUMB AND LEVEL

Disston No. 43 is an improved combination saw including a rule, scratch awl, straight edge, square, and plumb and level. Beech handle with brass screws, 26″ in length. Comes filed and set.

SHIP CARPENTER'S ADZE

L. and I.J. White lipped ship adze. Razor-sharp 5½″ bit and spurred head; finest hardwood handle.

IMPROVED KNIFE-HANDLE WRENCH

Genuine L. Coes patented monkey wrench. Easily adjusted with the same hand that holds the handle. Made of the very best materials, case-hardened and fully warranted.

SOCKET CORNER CHISEL

Cast-steel corner or parting chisel comes with a socket-type, iron-ringed wooden handle. V-shaped edges from ¾″ to 1¼″ in width.

HEAVY-DUTY SOCKET SLICK

A stout bevel-back slick with a socket-style handle. Extra-cast polished steel with handle terminating in a comfortable knob. Three-inch or 4″ widths.

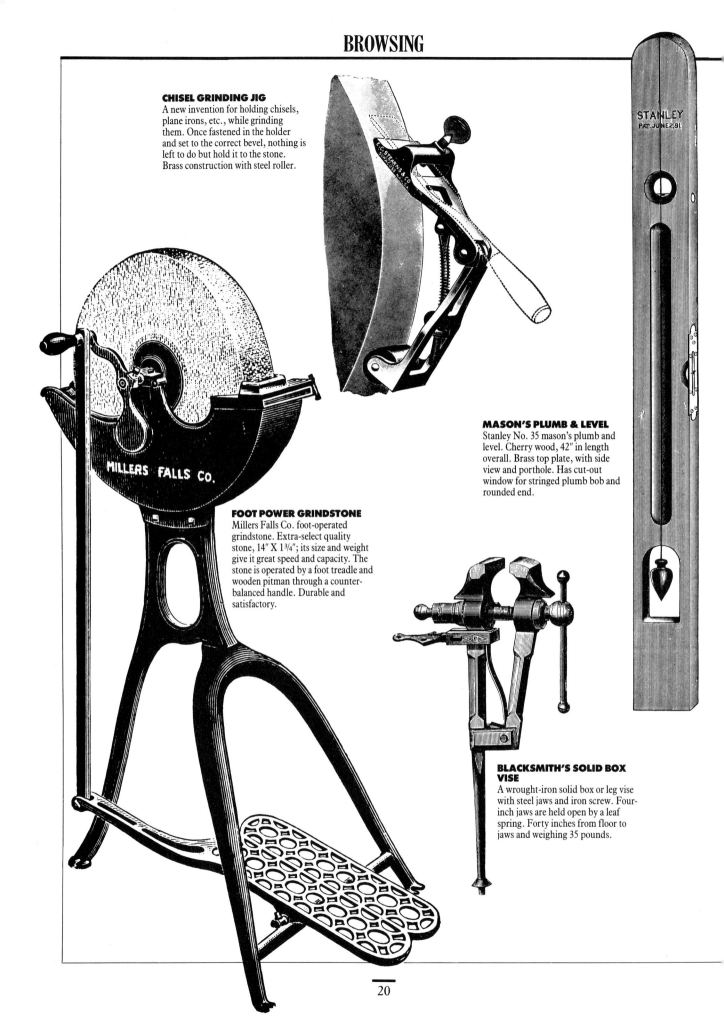

CHISEL GRINDING JIG
A new invention for holding chisels, plane irons, etc., while grinding them. Once fastened in the holder and set to the correct bevel, nothing is left to do but hold it to the stone. Brass construction with steel roller.

MASON'S PLUMB & LEVEL
Stanley No. 35 mason's plumb and level. Cherry wood, 42" in length overall. Brass top plate, with side view and porthole. Has cut-out window for stringed plumb bob and rounded end.

FOOT POWER GRINDSTONE
Millers Falls Co. foot-operated grindstone. Extra-select quality stone, 14" X 1¾"; its size and weight give it great speed and capacity. The stone is operated by a foot treadle and wooden pitman through a counter-balanced handle. Durable and satisfactory.

BLACKSMITH'S SOLID BOX VISE
A wrought-iron solid box or leg vise with steel jaws and iron screw. Four-inch jaws are held open by a leaf spring. Forty inches from floor to jaws and weighing 35 pounds.

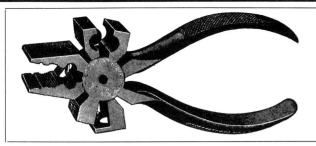

COMBINATION PUNCH, CUTTER AND PLIERS

An unparalleled belt-making and leather-working tool as it combines a variety of functions in one implement. Three separate jaws include standard square-nosed pliers with serrated-tooth nest and small punch, large punch for straps and belt 5/16″ and 3/8″, and hardened cutters. Millface grips on handle.

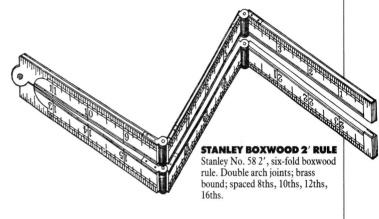

STANLEY BOXWOOD 2′ RULE

Stanley No. 58 2′, six-fold boxwood rule. Double arch joints; brass bound; spaced 8ths, 10ths, 12ths, 16ths.

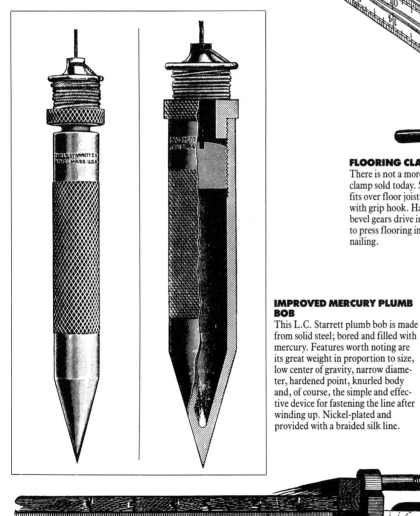

FLOORING CLAMP

There is not a more effective flooring clamp sold today. Sturdy iron frame fits over floor joists and is secured with grip hook. Handle-operated bevel gears drive iron screw and guide to press flooring into position for nailing.

IMPROVED MERCURY PLUMB BOB

This L.C. Starrett plumb bob is made from solid steel; bored and filled with mercury. Features worth noting are its great weight in proportion to size, low center of gravity, narrow diameter, hardened point, knurled body and, of course, the simple and effective device for fastening the line after winding up. Nickel-plated and provided with a braided silk line.

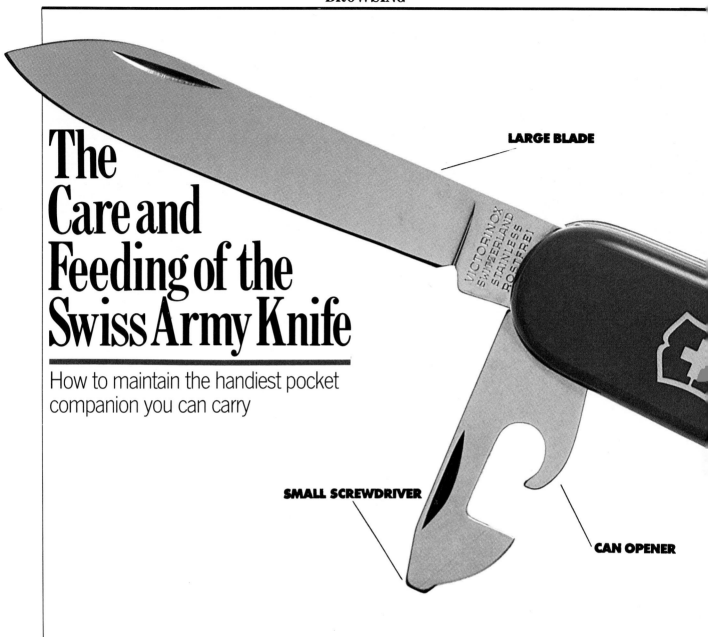

LARGE BLADE

SMALL SCREWDRIVER

CAN OPENER

The Care and Feeding of the Swiss Army Knife

How to maintain the handiest pocket companion you can carry

Many people laugh long and loud the first time they see a Swiss Army knife. The very sight of all those gadgets protruding from a single handle is just too much. Besides which, the blades are made of stainless steel, and "everybody knows" that stainless—because of its inability to take and hold a proper edge—is suitable only for household cutlery. And, besides that, the knife has a chintzy-looking red handle that makes it look like it's been made especially for the "toy-knife" set.

Well, the passage of time has proven us wrong on all counts. Because today, the Swiss Army knife is probably the most popular folding knife in these United States, and deservedly so. It is, after all, more than just a pocketknife: It's a pocket-sized assortment of tools.

Many Models to Choose From

Swiss Army knives come in many models, with various combinations and quantities of attachments. The simplest versions have as few as three accessories and weigh only a couple of ounces, while the grand-deluxe models may sport 11 or more fold-out tools and weigh more than a quarter pound.

A favorite Swiss Army knife is the relatively simple Camper model by Victorinox, which has two blades, a corkscrew, a can opener, a bottle opener and a "punch" (actually a single-blade reamer). It also features a lanyard loop. All-up weight: a smidgen over two ounces.

Another, and very similar, Swiss Army knife comes with a Phillips screwdriver in place of the corkscrew—an undesirable substitution for two reasons. First, unless the

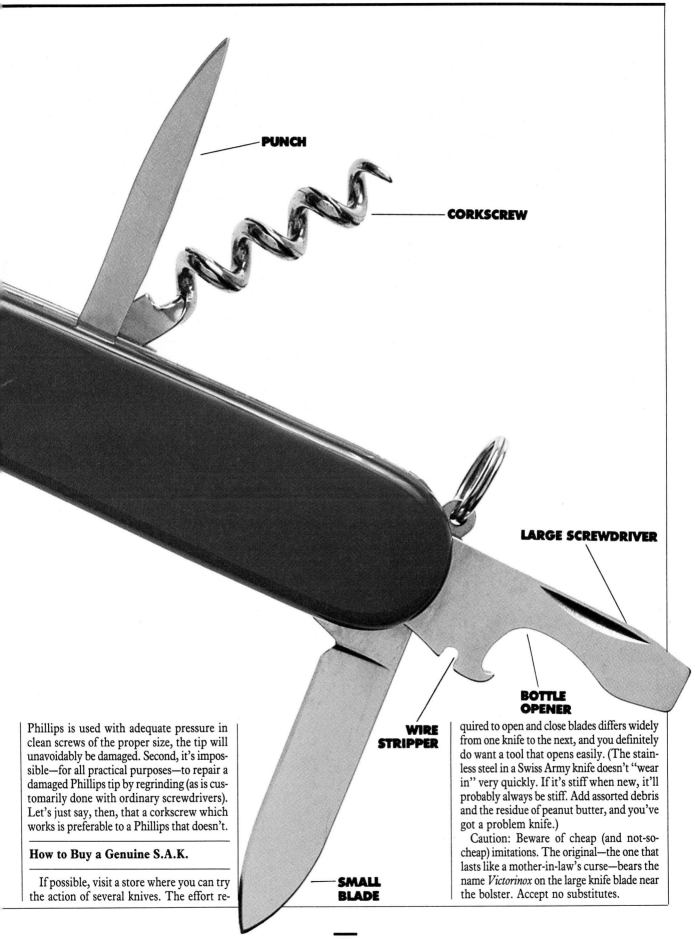

PUNCH

CORKSCREW

LARGE SCREWDRIVER

BOTTLE OPENER

WIRE STRIPPER

SMALL BLADE

Phillips is used with adequate pressure in clean screws of the proper size, the tip will unavoidably be damaged. Second, it's impossible—for all practical purposes—to repair a damaged Phillips tip by regrinding (as is customarily done with ordinary screwdrivers). Let's just say, then, that a corkscrew which works is preferable to a Phillips that doesn't.

How to Buy a Genuine S.A.K.

If possible, visit a store where you can try the action of several knives. The effort re-

quired to open and close blades differs widely from one knife to the next, and you definitely do want a tool that opens easily. (The stainless steel in a Swiss Army knife doesn't "wear in" very quickly. If it's stiff when new, it'll probably always be stiff. Add assorted debris and the residue of peanut butter, and you've got a problem knife.)

Caution: Beware of cheap (and not-so-cheap) imitations. The original—the one that lasts like a mother-in-law's curse—bears the name *Victorinox* on the large knife blade near the bolster. Accept no substitutes.

Keep Those Blades Sharp

Any knife is useless unless it's kept sharp, and the S.A.K. is no exception.

Screwdriver Tips

Many S.A.K. models feature combination screwdriver/can opener attachments. As they come from the factory, however, these accessories are of limited use because the screwdriver tip is too short to reach into the recesses so common with small screws. The solution: Simply grind the shoulders next to the tip to square off the blade and extend its depth. This can be done in a few minutes with a chain-saw file.

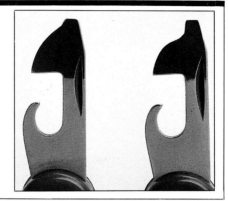

You'll find that the stainless steel blades of a Victorinox—which are quite thin (as knife blades should be)—will take and hold a good edge, but do require more time to sharpen than the softer carbon steel blades of the average pocketknife. If you rely on the old standby—a whetstone—for putting an edge on your Swiss Army knife's blades, use only a natural Arkansas stone; the cheaper synthetic Carborundum stones are dandy for carbon steel, but no match for stainless. When honing, hold the blade of an S.A.K. at a flatter angle to the stone than when sharpening an ordinary penknife.

When a whetstone isn't available (such as on a backpacking trip), you can substitute emery cloth—the sort that comes rolled up like hair ribbon. (A 180-grit cloth is best, though 120-grit will do in a pinch.) All you have to do is lay a short piece of the material on a hard, flat surface and then use it as you would a stone.

To keep your knife in tip-top shape, touch up its blades between regular sharpenings with a few strokes against a butcher's steel.

Knife Know-How

Today's knife buyer is faced with a sometimes overwhelming array of choices. As perplexing as this diversity may seem, though, it is possible to isolate a few points worth considering. These include the type of steel used for blades, handle materials and the method of connecting the handle to the blade.

Knife steels can be divided into two basic categories: carbon and stainless. Briefly, carbon steel is easy to sharpen and holds an edge well under normal use, but tarnishes rapidly—while stainless is harder and therefore more difficult to sharpen properly, but is highly resistant to corrosion and holds its edge longer than carbon.

The hardness of knife steel is usually measured on the Rockwell C (Rc) scale. For general purposes, a knife with a rating of between Rc57 and Rc59 can be considered a good choice. The metal used in cheap knives may drop below Rc50 or even be hard beyond practical sharpening.

By far the most common of the stainless steels used for knife making is 440C. In fact, it's the most popular of all knife metals because it performs relatively well under a wide variety of conditions. Other steels are better in specific applications, but none equals 440C's overall performance.

Traditional knife-handle materials—such as sambar stag, Brazilian rosewood, ivory and the like—still set standards for beauty, but when it comes to utility, synthetics such as Micarta and Du Pont Delrin are hard to beat. Micarta stands up quite well to common use, but for the greatest strength and resistance to chemical deterioration, the newer Delrin—which was developed for the aerospace industry—is probably the best allaround choice.

Common folding knives can accommodate a wide variety of blades and—as in the Swiss Army knives—other useful gadgets, but such implements shouldn't be employed in any situation where a great deal of pressure is applied to the tool: A blade that folds at the wrong time can do serious damage to your hand.

Lockback knives are available in two configurations. Some multibladed variations are equipped with a tab that slips in front of the hilt when the blade is opened. Such an arrangement is helpful, but it doesn't provide a joint as secure as that offered by a true locking knife, which engages a single blade firmly within the pivot mechanism.

Stainless and carbon steel blades, natural and synthetic handles, folding and lockback models—there has never been more for the discerning knife buyer to choose from, and never before have virtually all the choices been so attractive and utilitarian.

To Oil, or Not to Oil?

Because stainless isn't subject to rust, most S.A.K. users never oil their knives and thereby do themselves a disservice. A properly lubricated Victorinox is always easier to open than an unoiled one. (This can make all the difference in the world when your hands are cold or wet.)

Use a premium-quality motor oil (which you can get from "empty" 10W-40 cans at the local service station), but most any kind of oil will do. Just be sure to lubricate all the hinges (my Camper has three).

As for how often you should oil the tool, once a month is plenty (unless, of course, you accidentally run the knife through the washer or drop it in a pail of cleaning solvent).

Expensive, but Worth It

Swiss Army knives are more expensive than the common drugstore-variety penknife—but then, you're not likely to wear out a Victorinox.

A final word of advice: If you buy one of these miniature tool kits, by all means have your name engraved on the handle. (On the handle because the stainless steel blades don't take engraving too well.) There are still a few honest souls left in the world who'll return a tool to its rightful owner, even if that implement happens to be a beautiful, red-handled Swiss Army knife.

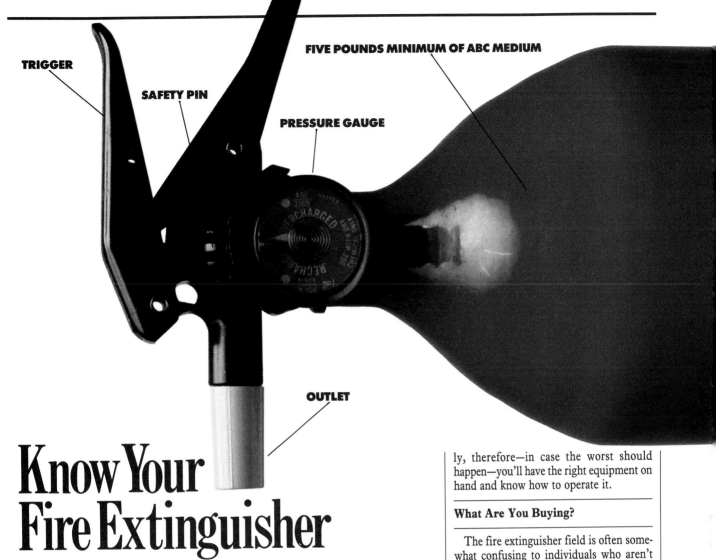

TRIGGER

SAFETY PIN

FIVE POUNDS MINIMUM OF ABC MEDIUM

PRESSURE GAUGE

OUTLET

Know Your Fire Extinguisher

An ABC extinguisher can help you control or put out a fire before it's too late.

Would you be prepared if a fire broke out in your home this evening? Unfortunately, you probably wouldn't, because it's estimated that some 90% of America's households have only the bare-bones minimum (that is, a supply of water and a garden hose) with which to combat a residential conflagration.

Of course, it's never a good idea to try to fight a blaze without calling the fire department. But whatever you can do to extinguish, knock down or even contain a small fire before it gets out of control (and while you're waiting for the pros to arrive) might mean the difference between minor smoke damage and the loss of your home.

And the best way to protect your dwelling (and yourself) is to expect a fire to occur, and to equip your home to a level of defense that's both within your budget and effective

enough to do some actual good should the need arise.

Naturally, having fire protection equipment on hand is no justification for inviting an accident to occur in your dwelling, and taking simple steps—such as not overloading electrical circuits, keeping work areas clean and free of oily rags, storing flammables in approved containers and flipping off circuit breakers before vacating the house—will greatly reduce the chance that an unexpected blaze will ever occur. (As a first line of defense, smoke alarms—either the 110-volt or the battery-operated kind—can alert you and your family to danger before the situation becomes life-threatening.)

However, even if you take every sensible precaution against the common troublemakers, fire could still strike your home. Ideal-

ly, therefore—in case the worst should happen—you'll have the right equipment on hand and know how to operate it.

What Are You Buying?

The fire extinguisher field is often somewhat confusing to individuals who aren't familiar with such devices. To begin with, the units are classed according to the *types* of conflagrations they're designed to handle. There are three kinds of residential fires, each of which depends upon a different material for its fuel source and each of which is designated—for convenience—by a letter. A: *ordinary combustibles*, including wood, cloth, paper, rubbish and plastics. B: *flammable liquids*, such as paint, grease, oil, gasoline or certain solvents. C: *electrical equipment*, a category that includes wiring, motors, control panels and electrical components.

Since most of us are primarily concerned with residential protection, we have pretty much ignored the D category fire (it would require a special extinguisher). The other three classes, however, can all pose threats to your household. Take a look around, both to see how much potential fuel exists and to note where it's concentrated. Chances are you'll find Class A material just about everywhere, and small amounts of B and C fuels concentrated in specific locations (in your garage or workshop, at the electrical service entrance, under the kitchen sink, in the furnace room, etc.).

Then—once you know that extinguisher manufacturers design some equipment to handle certain fire classes specifically (to be installed where only one type of fire is a potential problem), and other units that have the ability to control two or three categories safely and effectively—you can begin the process of selecting the protective devices that best fit your situation.

Making the right choice might be a matter of life and death, too: In the case of an electrical fire, for instance, a *conductive* extinguishing medium (such as water) could transmit a lethal shock to the firefighter (you) in a split second. Furthermore, as a look at the accompanying chart will show, many Class B and C extinguishers are not effective against the most common (Class A) household fires.

There are still other considerations to keep in mind, even after you've determined the proper class of fire extinguisher for the task at hand. For example, the Purple K extinguishers (see the chart), which are actually more effective than the nearly obsolete sodium bicarbonate "quenchers," use a medium that's highly corrosive in a moist environment, and that factor might weigh against their use in certain applications. Probably a better choice than either is the dry-chemical monomonium phosphate type, which is useful for all three fire categories.

By the same token, electronic components can be very sensitive to thermal shock as well as to corrosion, so a "gentle" Halon extinguisher—even though it'll be considerably more expensive to purchase and refill than would equipment using other mediums —would be the obvious choice where thousands of dollars of electronics are at stake.

How Do They Rate?

Besides being designed to deal with specific kinds of fires, an extinguisher is also manufactured to meet or exceed certain efficiency ratings established by Underwriters Laboratories. In fact, test fires are set under controlled laboratory conditions—with specific kinds and measured amounts of fuels— and extinguishers of specific capacities and containing various mediums are then used

to put out those fires. Each piece of equipment's ability to handle the blazes determines its rating, and the operator's capabilities are considered as well (professional firefighters are used for the tests in an effort to standardize the extinguishing process, which could vary in effectiveness with first-time users).

Fire extinguishers' ratings are recorded on a numerical scale, and arranged according to the class (A, B and/or C) of fire in question. For example, a unit that's rated 1A-10BC is capable of knocking out an 8′ X 8′ (64-square-foot) pad of burning furring strips or 25 square feet of ignited petroleum. A larger "gun," rated at 4A-60BC, can handle 196 square feet of strips or 150 square feet of burning liquid. Both, of course, are also rated as suitable for fighting electrical fires. The test fuel samples do, however, change with increased rating levels (starting with the 10A category, for instance, 2 X 2s replace the furring strips), so there's not always a simple method of comparing the effectiveness of two units.

Choose Wisely

How, then—you may well wonder—does one determine what's necessary for his or her household? Well, a multipurpose (ABC) extinguisher will likely be the best choice for most homes, but don't rely on just one unit. Instead, buy several, and make sure they've got enough capacity to offer real protection.

Several 10-pound pressurized extinguishers of the general-purpose type—a size that's easily managed by children or small-statured adults because of an overall 21-pound weight—would be your best main defense if placed at various locations around the house, and a 5-pound canister in the kitchen could serve to round things off. (Quite frankly, if you purchase anything smaller than a 5-pounder, you're being penny-wise and pound-foolish, since chances are it wouldn't have the capacity or discharge time to put out anything but a very minor flare-up. And many of the tiny canisters on the retail market use plastic heads or—worse—are not rechargeable, which, of course, makes them useless after the first firing.)

All in all, it pays to equip your home to an effective level with fire protection equipment. Shelling out the cash for fire extin-

guishers will seem like a terrific investment should you ever have a fire in your home, and it may hurt less in the present if you remember that some insurance companies offer a discount for homeowners who outfit their dwellings with approved fire protection equipment and/or smoke alarms. Be sure to check with your underwriter.

To make a really wise purchase, it's best to check with the people who sell and service the fire protection equipment used in your local commercial and industrial establishments. See what they have to offer, weigh their recommendations, and—if possible— find out how they service what they sell. (Remember, once an extinguisher's been used, it's only as good as the person who recharges it.) Also, be sure you know the refilling costs of each device and its effective life of charge, since both will result in additional expenses and thus might influence your decision.

Practice Makes Perfect

OK, so you've done your research, and you've bought several extinguishers that should be able to tackle the kind of fires most likely to occur in your home. Your next step is to place them in accessible locations and relax, right? Wrong: Now's the time to take one outside, read its label thoroughly, and use it. If your local statutes allow you to do so, start a small trash or brush fire in a safe (this point can't be stressed too strongly) location, and then put it out by sweeping the discharge of the *upright* extinguisher across the *base* of the flames. (One reason an amateur user isn't as effective as a professional is that he or she tends to waste the extinguishing agent by directing it above the fuel that's actually feeding the fire.) Learn to handle your equipment well, because it may someday be the only thing between you and a real disaster.

It's equally important, though, to use common sense in positioning your units. Don't place an extinguisher right above the kitchen stove, or next to the oil furnace: You'd have to reach through flames to get to either one should you need it. Keep the equipment within easy reach, but away from potential sources of fire.

And to be on the safe side, shake your dry-chemical extinguishers every month or two to keep the medium inside from settling and compacting. (Turn them upside down to free the powder, because that material must be loose if the extinguisher is to function properly.) A few minutes spent in such maintenance might save your house.

Finally, visit your local fire department and talk to the people there about fire prevention, family safety and extinguishing techniques. Because they're professionals, they'll be able to give you some excellent advice. They'll also likely remind you that firefighting is not an amateur's job. Keep in mind that because you're right on the premises, you can prevent a minor flame from becoming an inferno; however, should you discover a blaze in its serious stages, the best course of action would probably be to swallow your pride, concentrate on saving yourself and your family, and call the pros in to do what they're trained to do.

FIRE EXTINGUISHER OVERVIEW

Medium	Capacity	Discharge Time	Total Weight	Approximate Dimensions	UL Rating	Classification
Dry Chemical (monomonium phosphate)	A universal dry-chemical powder (usually monomonium phosphate) under pressure. Suitable for Class A, B and C fires, and very effective on Class A overhead fires because the discharge clings to its target. Best for all-around household use. Slightly corrosive and messy but popular and reasonably priced.					
	2½ pounds	10 seconds	6 pounds	5" X 16"	1A-10BC	Classes A, B and C
	5 pounds	10 seconds	10 pounds	7" X 17"	2A-10BC	Classes A, B and C
	10 pounds	18 seconds	21 pounds	8" X 24"	4A-40BC	Classes A, B and C
	20 pounds	22 seconds	40 pounds	10" X 26"	20A-80BC	Classes A, B and C
Halon (bromochlorodi-fluoromethane)	Liquefied Halon gas. Highly effective on Class B and Class C fires. Has low toxicity, is noncorrosive, leaves no residue, doesn't conduct electricity and offers no thermal shock to delicate equipment. Expensive.					
	2½ pounds	9½ seconds	6 pounds	5" X 16"	5BC	Classes B and C
	5 pounds	9½ seconds	10 pounds	6" X 17"	10BC	Classes B and C
	17 pounds	22 seconds	28 pounds	9" X 25"	3A-80BC	Classes A, B and C
Dry Chemical (Purple K)	Treated potassium bicarbonate dry-chemical powder under pressure. About twice as effective as sodium bicarbonate extinguishers, but corrosive under moist conditions. Somewhat messy and more expensive than most BC extinguishers. Largely being replaced by monomonium phosphate types.					
	2½ pounds	9½ seconds	6 pounds	5" X 16"	10BC	Classes B and C
	18 pounds	19 seconds	41 pounds	11" X 20"	60BC	Classes B and C
Dry Chemical (sodium bicarbonate)	Treated sodium bicarbonate dry-chemical powder under pressure. Flows freely. Water-resistant in storage. Very effective for Class B and C fires, but messy and somewhat obsolete.					
	2½ pounds	9½ seconds	6 pounds	5" X 16"	10BC	Classes B and C
	5 pounds	9½ seconds	10 pounds	6" X 17"	20BC	Classes B and C
	10 pounds	11 seconds	22 pounds	9" X 22"	60BC	Classes B and C
	20 pounds	14 seconds	38 pounds	10" X 26"	120BC	Classes B and C
Carbon Dioxide	CO_2 under pressure. Emits contents in a snowlike fog. Limited effectiveness. Can cause thermal shock to delicate equipment.					
	5 pounds	11 seconds	20 pounds	8" X 17"	5BC	Classes B and C
	10 pounds	11 seconds	38 pounds	12" X 24"	10BC	Classes B and C
	15 pounds	11 seconds	50 pounds	12" X 30"	10BC	Classes B and C
	20 pounds	15 seconds	60 pounds	12" X 30"	10BC	Classes B and C
Pressurized Water	Mixture of water and compressed air, usually available with an antifreeze agent. Shoots a thin liquid stream. Limited application, but inexpensive.					
	2½ gallons	45–65 seconds	9 pounds	9" X 25"	2A	Class A only

Note: These specifications are for comparison purposes only and do not necessarily represent any specific fire extinguisher on the market. Different manufacturers may use different extinguishing agents which may not be included on this chart, and all the units listed here are the pressurized canister type. Check with your local dealer for information on external cartridge, wheeled or stationary extinguishers.

PART TWO

Tools, Energy & Room Enough

Whether you drive a tool
yourself or let electricity do it,
the key is control. That and
a work space that is uncluttered
and well lighted.

TOOLS, ENERGY & ROOM ENOUGH

When, as a first-time homeowner, I found I had to borrow things to accomplish even the simplest household jobs, I quickly started assembling a modest collection of tools. Though the half-dozen or so mentioned here were barely a start, I find that they still make up the core of my workshop; over and over I look to these old reliables for quick fixes in and around the house.

There's something to be said for the luxury of being able to carry most of what you need in a small kit bag. For one thing, a fabric gripsack is compact and inexpensive and can be left packed so you're never in doubt as to what's inside. Moreover, a bag is considerably more supple than a toolbox and has no

sharp corners to suffer or lids that refuse to close. Finally, because there's only a handful of items in it, there's little worry that things will get buried at the bottom.

Linemen often use a leather carryall that's just about perfect for this purpose; more realistically, local and mail-order surplus retailers usually have military engineers' bags or tool grips available in canvas for less than $10. I use an oil-stained nylon athletic bag my wife discarded last year. At any rate, it's apparent that there's no need to get fancy. The bag should be at least as long as your largest tool, needn't be wider than 8" or so and no more than that in height. Try to choose a design that has top handles, a

closable opening and a stiff bottom with metal feet.

The three portable power tools covered later in this article have their own carrying cases or at least can be carried separately. For a small job, though, the time taken to fetch a power tool may erase any savings in speed. Around the house, it's sometimes easier, often necessary and almost always more satisfying to do the job by hand.

Setting Out to Buy

I'm by no means an elitist, yet when it comes to tools, I try to buy the best I can afford *within my ability to use them*. If the big-

BASIC

SPIRAL RATCHET DRIVER

COMBINATION
SQUARE

10" CURVED-JAW
LOCKING PLIERS

22-OUNCE,
MILL-FACE,
RIP-CLAW,
STEEL HAMMER

gest mistake is to spend good money on junk tools, the second biggest is to spend even better money on superb tools you don't really need. The dollars you save may allow you a greater variety when you put your package together.

Fortunately, it's not all that difficult to spot quality when it comes to tools. Finish, feel and attention to detail will separate the cosmetic marques from the working brands, even if you're ignorant of reputation. Generally, you'll find that the old name brands remain reliable, though newly imported lines (especially among higher-priced Japanese, German and English products) easily rival our traditional "Yankee" quality. In short,

you get what you pay for, and if you shop carefully, you may get even more.

For general maintenance, it's possible to spend less than $100 and still assemble a good cross section of honest working hardware. For half again as much, you can complement your selection with additional tools chosen to match your specific needs. The listing below certainly isn't carved in stone, but it reflects a choice made from experience, and one that can easily be fine-tuned to your own pleasure.

Hammer: The 16-ounce curved-claw wooden hammer may be an American classic, but it's not the one I'd choose for my one and only. For starters, those pretty wooden han-

dles can break too easily; second, a one-pound head just isn't meaty enough for the heavy-duty framing and whacking jobs that sometimes come up.

My all-time favorite is a 22-ounce rip-claw framing hammer with a solid steel handle and a mill-face head. The extra six ounces of head weight puts some authority into the swing without being unwieldy. The same goes for the 3"- or 4"-longer handle common to the framers. Though many professionals swear by hickory-wood handles, it's more because they tend to absorb shock than because they're particularly bulletproof. A steel slender-shank handle covered with a nylon grip is almost perfectly balanced and nearly

DOZUKI PULL SAW

Your Basic Tool Kit

Tools, like friends, are best when sharp, enduring and well balanced.

1"

3/4"

1/2"

BUTT CHISELS

1/4"

indestructible, and shouldn't wear down your wrist and forearm unless you're beating with it 10 hours a day. Some other handle choices are fiberglass and tubular steel, but you should make your decision based upon how it feels in your hand.

Curved-claw hammers are fine if you pull nails all day, but the straighter rip claw will pull nails *and* sink its fangs into wood, so it works as a pry bar too. And though there's certainly nothing wrong with a smooth-faced head, the mill-face, or "waffle," design grips the nailhead at once and tends to send it home straight. It's also great for dry wall or framing work when you want the head of the nail set slightly below the surface.

Screwdrivers: In my workshop tool cabinet, my mainstream screwdrivers are square-shank plastic-handle models: one $1/4''$ flat blade, a $3/16''$ flat blade, a No. 1 and a No. 2 Phillips head, and a small instrument screwdriver with a $5/64''$ square-ground blade. If you want to carry five screwdrivers around, they certainly won't be a burden, but consider buying one spiral ratchet driver instead.

My choice would be a better quality 10" domestic or imported model; the bargain types aren't a bargain at all. The best thing about spiral ratchet screwdrivers is that they turn clockwise (or counterclockwise) as you pump the handle. A spring feeds the shaft outward automatically once you push it in,

or the shaft can be locked in position if you like. Some brands have a hollow, chambered handle to store the bits, which include $3/16''$ and $1/4''$ slotted blades, a No. 2 Phillips blade, and two or three drill bits from $5/64''$ to $9/64''$. If you plan on driving a lot of screws that require inordinate levels of horsepower, consider buying a bit for your electric drill; if not, the push screwdriver should suit nicely.

Pliers: For some reason, I haven't used a pair of common slip-joint pliers in years, probably because it's been that long since I purchased my 10" curved-jaw locking pliers. For hand-gripping or twisting they work as well as the slip-joints, but for crude wrench

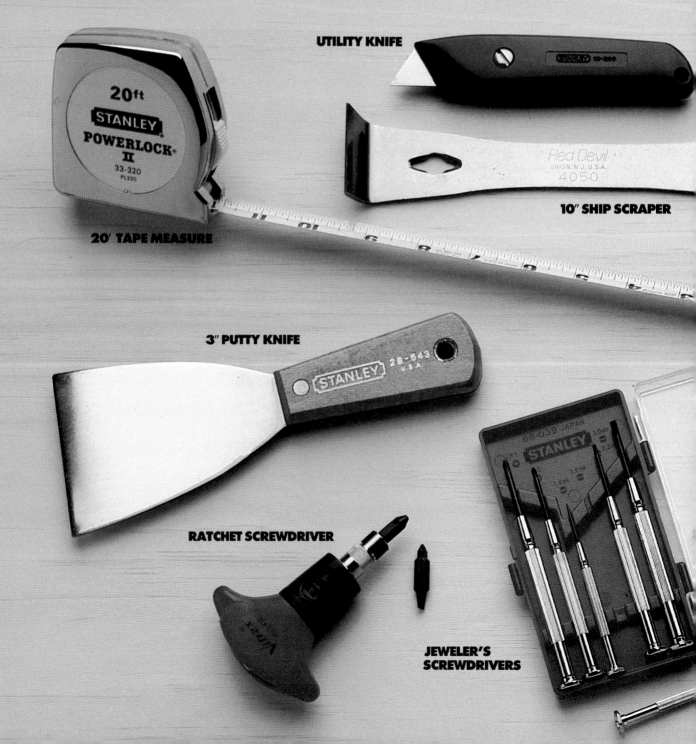

UTILITY KNIFE

10" SHIP SCRAPER

20' TAPE MEASURE

3" PUTTY KNIFE

RATCHET SCREWDRIVER

JEWELER'S SCREWDRIVERS

work their lockjaw bite is far superior. With the curved jaw, they fit pipes as well as square bars and will exert enough pressure to serve as a clamp or small vise if you need one. I like the 10″ ones because they're large enough to do some damage, yet still fit comfortably in one hand for detail work. These are the ones you shouldn't do without.

Square: For some, using a square might seem a bit fussy, but it's a necessity if you do any project building and want the job to turn out right. The handiest one for me has been the combination square, which obviously enough combines several functions. This design has a stock with a perpendicular edge and a 45° miter edge. The stock slides along a 12″ steel blade and can be locked in any position with a drawbolt for use as a marking gauge. There's a spirit (bubble) level built into the stock, and often a removable marking scriber, too.

The great thing about this tool is that it's fairly accurate in all its functions, though that might be optimistic in the case of the level. Look for a 1″-wide blade that incorporates a 12″ graduated ruler, and a milled steel stock (a die-cast head is a good second choice).

Chisels: It's inevitable that someday you'll be forced to mortise a doorjamb or pare down a furniture tenon. When that time comes, a chisel is about the only tool that can do the job right. Paring chisels are too delicate and precise to suit a wide range of home-improvement challenges, so what you most likely want are a small set of butt chisels—comfortable in the hand yet tough enough to beat with a mallet when the need arises. For deeper or heavier work, there are mortise chisels (straight-sided with noticeably stout blades) and their larger cousins, firmers (long and very substantial, with blades 2″ wide or more).

Depending upon what you want to spend, a good starter set would include three or four chisels, ranging in width from ¼″ to 1″ (the smallest size would probably be omitted from a three-piece set). The blades will be bevel-sided and—if this information is available—

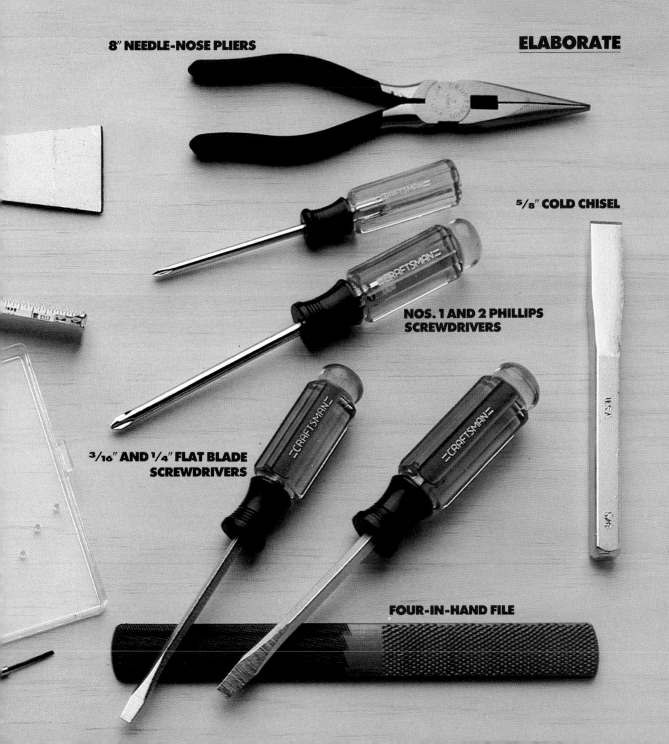

8″ NEEDLE-NOSE PLIERS

ELABORATE

⁵⁄₈″ COLD CHISEL

NOS. 1 AND 2 PHILLIPS SCREWDRIVERS

³⁄₁₆″ AND ¼″ FLAT BLADE SCREWDRIVERS

FOUR-IN-HAND FILE

tempered to a Rockwell hardness of 58 or so to assure a good balance of resiliency and edge-holding characteristics. If you want plastic handles, be sure they're designed to take hammer blows; wood-handled designs should have impact caps for the same reason (some boxwood handles are meant to be struck only with wooden mallets, though). Buy by the set, and you have a good chance of getting a protective pouch in the bargain; you'll need it to keep the edges sharp.

Saw: Even if you use a circular saw for the lion's share of around-the-house projects, you'll want a decent handsaw to take care of close work in tight places. At the bench, a backsaw or trim saw does nicely but you want one that fits comfortably in a 16" bag. Some pruners or folding saws would probably suffice, but my choice is a Japanese Dozuki with a removable blade. I don't know what Dozuki means, but to me it translates as a modified backsaw with an aggressive tooth pattern that somehow makes an exceptionally clean cut. Many Dozukis have a full back frame and a thin blade with 20 to 28 teeth per inch, but for general use, keep your eyes peeled for a thicker, coarser blade with 12 or 14 teeth to the inch. Its added rigidity allows the use of a short back frame so the blade can pass fully through the work, and the teeth are designed to cut on the pull stroke for smooth, bow-free action. Total length is about $20^{1}/_{2}$", but that's reduced by half when the $9^{1}/_{2}$" blade is unscrewed from the handle.

Additional items: The half-dozen core group is a substantial foundation on which to base your portable workshop. But as you tackle a variety of repairs, it'll become painfully apparent that it wouldn't hurt to enhance your collection as different needs arise. A good *steel measuring tape* is worth every bit of the $10 you'll probably pay for it. The 16' size is about the shortest I'd buy, and I prefer the $^{3}/_{4}$" width to the $^{1}/_{2}$" because it stands unsupported for a greater distance. A friction-reducing coated blade and a functional locking mechanism are two musts.

ROSEWOOD SQUARE

SLIDING T-BEVEL

BEVEL-EDGED, SOCKETED CHISELS

TOOLS, ENERGY & ROOM ENOUGH

Sooner or later, a *utility knife* should be part of your pouch. There are several good retractable models made, but the fixed-blade kind with storage built into the split handle is more durable, though you'll need some kind of sheath for it.

Don't be surprised if you discover that a pair of *needle-nose pliers* with a built-in side cutter and wire stripper are pretty convenient for minor electrical work and for setting springs and hooks. Buy only the best quality, preferably with insulated handles and a straight-jaw design. The smaller 5″ size will answer to most jobs, but I prefer the 8″ pliers because they offer good leverage and still allow a firm purchase even on small parts.

A *file* is right handy to have around, but you really need several different types of varied bite. The answer for me is a four-in-hand, sometimes called a horse rasp after one version of the tool. It's an 8″ or 10″ file about 1 1/8″ wide, with one side half-rounded and the other flat. Most designs include a coarse and a medium rasp and a coarse and a medium file to cover most general jobs.

Preparation for painting requires the use of a *scraper*, and the most functional kind I've found looks like a small flat pry bar. It's commonly called a ship scraper, but really doesn't resemble the navy scraper, which was designed to be struck with a hammer. Actually, it's a modified beekeeper's hive tool and

can be used as a pry, nail puller, chisel, scraper and pinch bar. Most are about 10″ long, and all have one straight and one curved end. Quality varies with this tool, so look for a name brand with resilient steel that can be sharpened with a file.

The last item to fill your tool bag ought to be a standard *cold chisel*. If you're buying just one, choose a 1/2″ or 5/8″ tip. But several manufacturers offer attractively priced sets of chisels and punches, which make household metalworking jobs a lot easier.

—*Richard Freudenberger*

Richard Freudenberger is research coordinator for Mother Earth News.

DELUXE

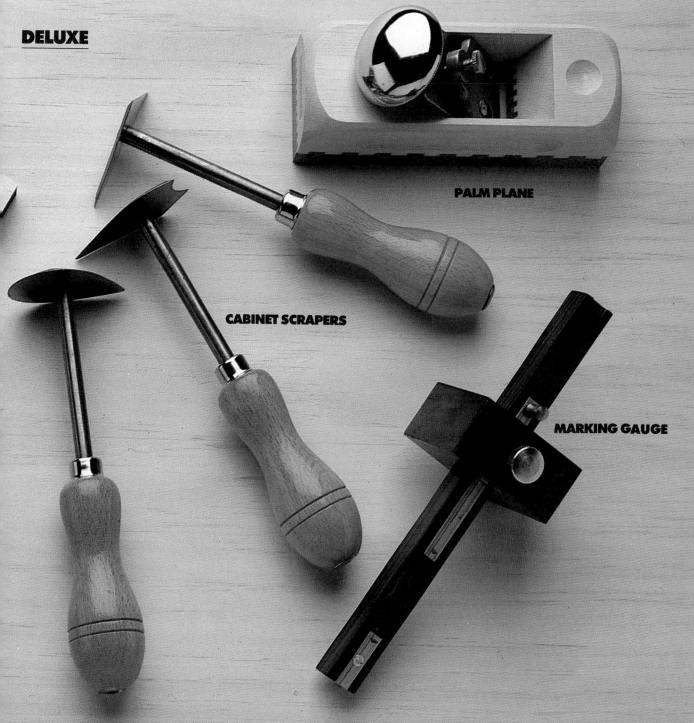

PALM PLANE

CABINET SCRAPERS

MARKING GAUGE

3 Essential Power Tools

Start a collection, but beware the obsession.

One school of thought on carpentry holds that no one should use power tools before mastering hand tools. The logic is hard to dispute: Hand tools demand patience, leaving time to contemplate methods and materials. With a power tool, intimacy is lost; things happen fast, and fine boards can be turned into kindling in no time.

I agree with the hand tool argument—to a point. Anyone who plans to become a professional should probably observe it. But for the occasional carpenter, fitness can be a limitation. An example: Back in my formative days as a wood butcher, I believed strongly in the superiority of hand tools for quality work and would argue beyond the point of absurdity about their efficiency. I often suffered for my pigheadedness.

One summer, my father-in-law—a meticulous craftsman who (horrors) used a circular saw for just about everything—and I were re-siding my turn-of-the-century farmhouse. The requisite 6″ bevel-lap siding wasn't available, so we were faced with ripping 2″ off the proud side of 8″-wide boards. Ever ready to prove my point, I wagered that I could slice a 16′ board with my Pax 5½-point ripsaw quicker than he could do it with his sidewinder.

To make a painful story short, I won the contest (by the barest of margins) but didn't argue when he suggested we resolve the issue by taking the rest of the boards to the shop for a pass through the table saw. That night, my beer-bottle grip was far less tenacious than usual.

Mind you, I still love that handsaw, and I can still cut a straighter line with it, but I've learned (if sometimes begrudgingly) to accept the place of power tools.

Power-Tool Basics

For the person planning to make only occasional use of a power tool, it may be tempting to buy a discount store bargain. Why should an amateur pay the premium for a tool built to last a lifetime in the hands of a professional? Because more than durability separates fine tools from cheap ones. Functional design, power, balance and other details can help the less skilled do a better job with less effort. It certainly isn't necessary to buy the best, but do try to afford tools that will become your allies, not your enemies. And exactly what should you look for?

Start with power. Because manufacturers use different systems for describing the power output of their tools, motor ratings are difficult to compare. As a result, it's best to ignore horsepower output ratings and look at amperage input at full load, as listed on a tool's Underwriters Laboratory–required label. The useful power output of a tool is equal to the amperage it draws minus losses to inefficiency. There are differences in efficiency, but they're seldom larger than 10% and are usually much less. In particular, beware of any claim that a tool "develops" a certain amount of horsepower. This sort of advertising copy is based on amperage draw as the tool bogs down; it's not indicative of sustainable output. The listed amperage is the best, if still imperfect, indicator of power.

Bearings may be the most significant sign of actual tool quality. Less expensive tools have sleeve bearings; better tools have roller or even ball bearings. The type of bearing is particularly important on the motor's output side, since this bearing handles the majority of side loads. An electric drill with sleeve bearings, for example, will work OK as long as you use it only to drill (a thrust load). Chuck a rotary grinder bit into it, though, and the plain bearings won't last long under the side load. Tools with roller or ball bearings are also more pleasant to handle, since they run smoother and quieter.

The latest power-tool technological development is electronic motor control: a digital circuit that maintains constant rpm. This is a significant theoretical advantage on a drill, a circular saw or a router, since it prevents the operator from slowing the tool below a desirable speed by overloading it.

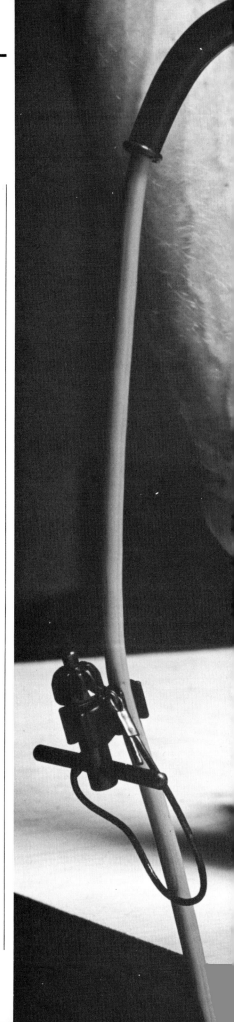

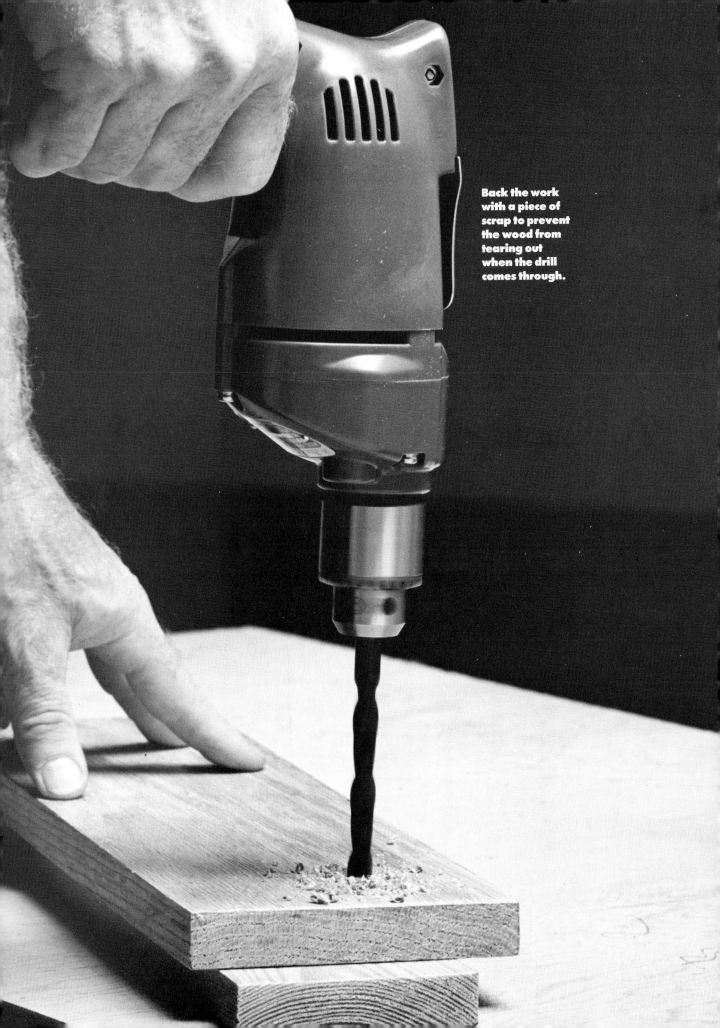

Back the work with a piece of scrap to prevent the wood from tearing out when the drill comes through.

Electronic control is hardly essential, however, and a skilled operator has little need for it. Weigh the added convenience against the increased cost and complication.

Electric Drill

The first tool to consider is an electric drill. This most practical of all power tools comes in a wide range of motor sizes and in three different common chuck sizes: $1/4''$, $3/8''$ and $1/2''$. For general work, choose one with a $3/8''$ chuck. The smallest chuck is suitable only for detail work, and the largest is for heavy work with large bits. A $1/2''$ drill may eventually become a part of your workshop, but it's too clumsy, heavy and expensive to be your all-around drill. Likewise, though a battery-powered drill makes a very useful second drill, it won't take the place of a workhorse $3/8''$ plug-in drill.

Unless you plan to do nothing but drill holes in one kind of material with one size of drill bit, buy a drill with a variable-speed control. The system is more complicated than a simple on-off switch—and therefore slightly less reliable—but makes it possible to perform a variety of drilling tasks and even to drive screws.

Don't buy a drill that isn't reversible. You'll want the ability to remove screws, and reverse is the only way short of pliers to remove a badly stuck drill bit.

For a starting collection of bits, look for a twist drill set made from high-speed steel (HSS) that covers sizes between $1/32''$ and $1/4''$ in $1/32''$ increments. Twist drills are made to punch holes in metal but will do for almost any material. (See "The Secrets of Steel" for an explanation of drill bit steel.) Then pick up spade bits (for drilling wood) between $1/4''$ and $1''$ in $1/8''$ increments. Spade bits are comparatively crude wood borers, but they're cheap and get the job done.

Circular Saw

Variously known as the contractor's saw or by the trade name belonging to the first company to build one, Skilsaw, the circular saw is the mainstay of carpenters. Equipped with the right blade, it will crosscut, rip, saw panels, slice metal or grind away masonry. Placed upside down in a workbench—as shown in "Fitting Out the Workshop"—it will even substitute for a table saw.

There are more than a half-dozen different blade diameters for circular saws, but the most common is $7^{1}/4''$, which gives a cutting depth that's well suited to the lumber commonly found in homes. There are two different types of circular saws: the worm drive and the sidewinder. Worm-drive saws have the blade in front of the motor, instead of to the side, and are uncommon except in the hands of framing carpenters. Though they have some advantages over sidewinders, their extra weight, complexity and cost make them impractical for amateur use.

Look for roller and ball bearings in a saw with a motor rated at least 10 amps for medium duty or 12 to 13 amps for heavy cutting. The larger motor will run another $20 to $30 but may be well worth the cost if you plan to cut wide joists, rafters or the like. Any $7^{1}/4''$ circular saw should have an arbor speed of at least 4,500 rpm to make smooth cuts. You may actually find some of the more powerful saws rated at lower speeds than less powerful ones simply because they slow down less doing their work.

Any quality circular saw should have an ample base plate to make it secure on the work, a lower blade guard that's easy to lift up to start certain difficult cuts, angle and depth adjustments that are secure yet easy to change and an unobstructed line of sight to the point where the blade contacts the work. (To guide the saw on a line, use this reference point, not the notch on the front of the base plate.) A spindle lock makes it easier to change blades. Other extras might include such safety features as a switch lockout, to prevent accidental start-up while you're carrying the tool, and a brake.

When you buy your saw, get a carbide-tipped blade with 24 to 30 teeth. These are usually called general purpose or combination blades because they give a reasonably smooth crosscut and will handle all but the most difficult rips. Expect to pay $20 to $30 for a good one. Later, you can pick up a panel-cutting blade for plywood, a hollow-ground planer for very smooth crosscuts or a specialty blade for steel or masonry.

It may sound a bit odd, but another feature to look for in a circular saw is an adequate cord. Bargain saws typically come with a 6' or 8' wire that makes free movement very

A belt sander—here a 3" X 24" model—is one of the indispensable tools for the home workshop.

difficult if you're plugged into a wall outlet or a multiple outlet box on an extension cord. It's the sort of frustration that leads to cutting one's own cord, something almost every initiate is sure to do—proving dramatically the virtue of double insulation.

Belt Sander

Though the electric drill and circular saw are unarguably the first power tools to buy, the third item on the list is a little harder to choose. If your plans include any furniture making or trim work on an older house, a router is probably the right choice. When you need rounded edges or unavailable molding configurations, there's simply no substitute for this versatile tool.

I, however, bought a belt sander before I got my router. And in pure hours of work—the time the motor has spent spinning—my 3" X 24" sander has seen more use than any other power tool I own. For example, back when I'd yet to realize that the siding on my own house would have to be replaced, I sanded *all* the paint off the exterior woodwork. While the belt sander wasn't indispensable for that job—assuming that I had years of free time to strip by hand—it was an awesome labor saver.

With a hand-held belt sander you can strip finishes from woodwork (as I did), metal, plastics or other materials. You can level the surface of glued-up panels in lieu of a planer. You can bevel or crudely round-over edges. And, with a suitably fine-grit belt and a gentle touch, you can even smooth-sand woodwork before applying finish. Clamped to a bench—with a jig from the manufacturer or a pair of C-clamps—a belt sander will joint edges, round corners and sharpen tools. In short, though mainly for use on flat surfaces, just about any job that involves sanding or grinding can be done more quickly with a belt sander.

Belt sanders are commonly available in three different sizes: 3" X 21", 3" X 24" and 4" X 24". Other sizes are sold, but you'll have trouble finding a ready supply of replacement belts. The dimensions refer to the size of the belt, not to the actual sanding area; in practice there is quite a bit of variation in working area even among sanders that use the same size of belt. On the whole, though, you'll find that the larger belts have more working surface than the smaller ones.

Working area is probably the single most important criterion for choosing a sander. Not only will a sander with a larger pad work more quickly, but, other things being equal, it will also be more stable. The key to getting a smooth finish with a belt sander is keeping the base absolutely parallel to the work—rocking produces gouges. The larger the base, the easier that job will be.

Does this mean you shouldn't consider anything but a 4" X 24"? Not at all. You should balance the size of the working area against the tool's weight. In general, bigger is heavier: 3" X 21" sanders average about $9^1/_2$ pounds; 3" X 24" tools tip at about 13; and 4" X 24" sanders strain the back at an average of $14^1/_2$ pounds. Depending on your physique and fitness, your inability to handle a heavy, powerful tool may be a liability that outweighs greater working area.

Of course, some manufacturers build lighter tools without sacrificing size or performance. Barring carrying a scale to the store with you, a good way to get an idea of what you're up against is to hold the tool straight out in front of you, arms extended. How does it feel after a half-minute or so?

Other things to look for in a belt sander include comfortable handles and good balance. Pick the candidate up and hold it in different positions to see how it feels; compare your subjective impressions to those developed handling other tools. While you're inspecting the tool, check its stamped U.L. label for an amperage rating—the best indicator of power. Look for at least 5 amps on a 3" X 21" sander, a minimum of $7^1/_2$ on a 3" X 24" tool, and no less than $9^1/_2$ on a 4" X 24" model. Finally, amenities such as long cords, easy-to-use belt adjusters and dust collectors are decided pluses.

If, like me, you feel like a kid in a candy store each time you go to the hardware store, you'll actually want to drag these purchases out—revel in the choices, stroke the tools, daydream about what they'll enable you to do. Tools can be a source of pleasure unto themselves—not to mention a financially hazardous obsession—and having the right one is a joyful celebration of power.

—David Schoonmaker

David Schoonmaker is a senior editor for Mother Earth News.

If I Had Some Hammers...

The beat goes on and on.

From its earliest form, a rock in the hand of one of our predecessors 2½ million years ago, to its present ultimate, the Hart Framer (the form of which threatens to transcend function), the hammer has been a fundamental tool—a basic extension of the human anatomy and, therefore, capability. Yet in its very simplicity, the hammer has invited adaptation.

Like a scramble up a family tree, percussive-tool design has climbed from that simple chunk of flint onto dozens of specialized branches. More than any other tool, the hammer has been customized to suit different artisans' needs and, at times, whims.

The typical carpenter, for example, keeps several hammers for different versions of the same job: The comparatively crude task of framing goes quickly with a heavy head swung on a long handle; its milled face bites nailheads tenaciously. Yet when the tasks turn more refined, such a tool has no business marring the face of hardwood trim. A lighter, smooth-faced hammer offers more precision. And for really delicate work, a petite Warrington will set nails without leaving so much as a dimple. To see just how specialized a builder's tool can become, examine the multifunctional yet single-purpose shingling hatchet.

Cognition of rock as hammer was the key to mankind's leap forward in the evolutionary race; today that tool's refinement and diversity exhibit just how many doors have been opened. Heft one and you hold an embodiment of the ingenuity of the people along the path.

FIVE-POUND SLEDGE
Heavy assembly work.

TACK
Setting tacks in upholstery or other fine work.

WARRINGTON CABINET
Hammering and setting small cabinet nails.

TEN-POUND SLEDGE
Moving mountains.

JAPANESE SQUARE HEAD
One side flat, one side rounded for setting nails.

BRICKLAYER
Marking and cutting bricks and other masonry materials, variation used by sedimentologists.

DEAD BLOW
Does not bounce off material on impact.

DRY WALL HATCHET
Lighter than shingling hatchet, rounded head for dry wall nails, edge for cutting.

SHINGLING HATCHET
Serrated head for nails, edge for cutting, positioning pin for row height.

BRASS MACHINIST
Assembling metal objects without marring surfaces.

MALLET
Rubber and plastic heads for assembly without marring surfaces.

BALL PEEN
Assembly of metal projects, indenting, chipping.

CURVED-CLAW FINISH
Nailing for appearance, claw removes nails.

RIP-CLAW FINISH
Indestructible steel handle, claw for prying.

NAILING HAMMER
Holds nails in head or claw for insertion in difficult-to-reach locations.

LIGNOSTONE SHOP MALLET
Assembling wood projects, driving chisels and gouges.

CLAW WITH FIBERGLASS HANDLE
A practically indestructible handle that absorbs some shock.

HART FRAMER
Centralized 21-ounce mass, shock-absorbing hickory handle.

LIGNUM VITAE MALLET
Classic mallet for chisels and gouges.

Laying Out the Workshop

There's more than meets the eye in planning a comfortable work environment.

A proper workshop ought to be a comfortable, comforting, convenient, even contemplative place. Ideally, it should evolve as you establish work habits, so that you move between benches and tools as naturally as you would climb a staircase. In fact, given unlimited space, we'd wholeheartedly endorse the organic approach. In a less than spacious world, however, ambition inevitably overruns area. What constitutes a perfect layout for working with hand tools will become impossible with the addition of a table saw.

You can save yourself a lot of headaches in years to come by setting up your workshop with expansion in mind. Planning is really too rigorous a word for this exercise. Why not think of it as window-shopping?

Basics

After the most fundamental of all workshop layout rules (there's never enough space) come two corollaries: There's never enough storage, and there are never enough scrap and trash receptacles. Install as many cabinets and shelves as you can without compromising the space for workbenches and stationary tools. The anthropometric drawing shows you appropriate heights and reaches for an average (5′9″) individual. Whether you adjust those dimensions to suit your own physique depends on whether you ever expect anyone else to use your shop.

You'll need at least three scrap and trash receptacles in your shop: one for trash, one for wood scraps (which may prove useful later) and one for sawdust and shavings (which have a number of uses). If you plan to recycle metal (i.e., copper and aluminum), you'll want another distinct container.

For the time being, you may be forced to mix metal- and woodworking in the same shop. Even so, separate the work areas to whatever degree possible. You might dedicate one elaborate workbench to woodwork and build a simple bench with a metal vise for greasier tasks. Gasoline from a carburetor just doesn't do much for wood grain, nor does sawdust help clear the tiny orifices in the car part. More important, the two combined only worsen an already significant fire hazard.

Environment

Though it may go without saying, a workshop must be warm. Even if you can stand the chill, most wood glues and finishes won't adhere or dry properly if the temperature is below about 60°F. There are also few sensations less pleasant than grabbing a subfreezing steel pipe with a wet hand. Because there will often be flammable liquids and sawdust in your shop, avoid open combustion heaters such as woodstoves or kerosene heaters. In any event, keep an ABC-type

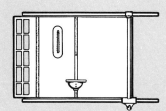

TABLE SAW
Should have good overhead lighting and full access on all four sides.

WORKSHOP ANTHROPOMETRICS

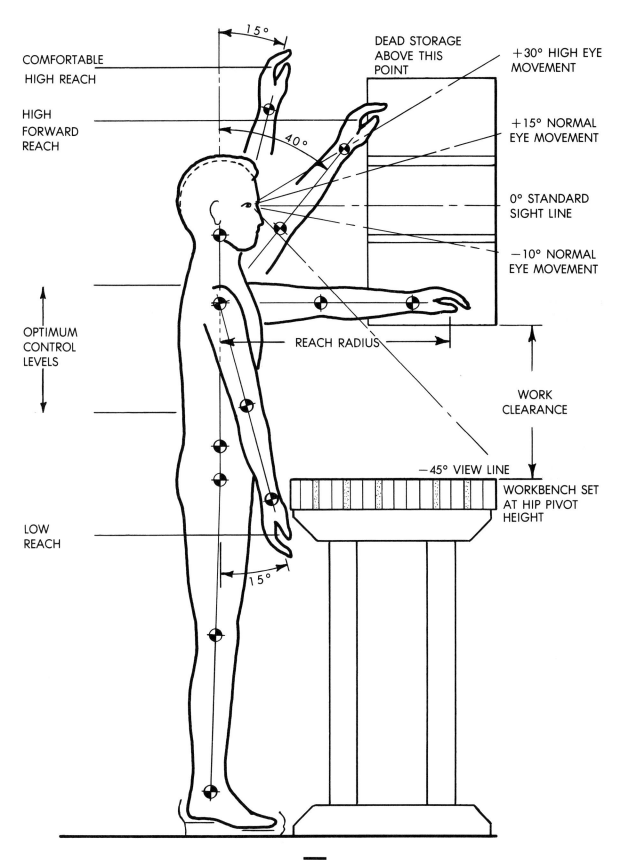

COMFORTABLE HIGH REACH

HIGH FORWARD REACH

15°

40°

DEAD STORAGE ABOVE THIS POINT

+30° HIGH EYE MOVEMENT

+15° NORMAL EYE MOVEMENT

0° STANDARD SIGHT LINE

−10° NORMAL EYE MOVEMENT

REACH RADIUS

OPTIMUM CONTROL LEVELS

WORK CLEARANCE

LOW REACH

−45° VIEW LINE

WORKBENCH SET AT HIP PIVOT HEIGHT

15°

fire extinguisher in a convenient place.

Proper lighting is, of course, a must. When you're studying lighting, don't do it solely from a stool in a corner where you have a panorama of the room. Get up and stand where you'll be working, so you can see how your body's shadow will affect the work area. Make use of as much natural lighting as possible. An ample window on the north wall is a perfect place for a workbench. For supplementary lighting, long fluorescent fixtures with white reflectors give the fewest shadows. Small, movable incandes-cent lights at work spots are very helpful.

You may not have a choice of floors, but if you do, pick wood. Because it's more resilient, wood is more comfortable than con-crete to be on for extended periods. And if you heat your shop only when you're using it, wood will feel much warmer. Though you may be just an amateur woodworker, even three or four hours standing on cold, hard concrete can get after the bunions. If you're stuck with concrete but have at least 8′ of ceiling height, consider adding a wood floor.

Layout

Now it's time for the real fun. Settle into a comfy chair with a selection of catalogues and make a fantasy list of stationary tools. Perhaps a table saw would be at the top of the stack. Most woodworkers consider it to be a more efficient tool than a radial arm saw, but it does require more space: about 9′ X 27′ working room, though windows or doors can serve as in- and outfeeds. A radial arm needs about equal length but can get by with

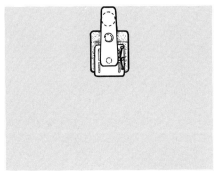

DRILL PRESS
Usually equipped with its own light, so a nearby window isn't necessary. Access from front only.

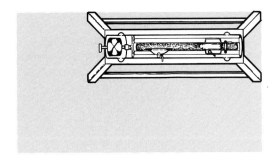

WOOD LATHE
Tends to collect wood chips and turnings. Full front access and room at left side important.

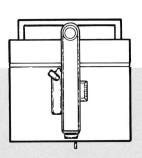

RADIAL ARM SAW
Access from the front, but allow plenty of room on both sides for long work.

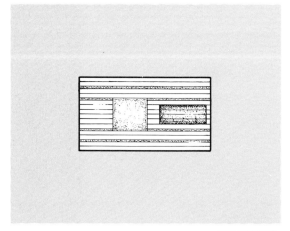

WORKBENCH
Good lighting and open access from all sides.

less than 6′ of depth. These "spheres of influence" are shown on each of the templates. You can photocopy the page, cut out the templates and shift them around on a sheet of four-squares-per-inch graph paper, each square representing 8″ of shop space. Work areas can overlap, since you'll be using only one tool at a time.

After a stationary circular saw, the choices depend largely on what you plan to do. For the mainstream woodworker, the list would probably proceed from a jointer-planer to a band saw to a drill press to a shaper or router table to a grinder and, for someone with a yen for turning, to a lathe. A jointer or planer logically should be as close to the table saw as possible, since stock is often ripped and immediately jointed or planed. Likewise, a shaper would be nearby. A band saw requires about the same space as a radial arm saw, unless you plan to use it only for scrolling; then much less space is needed. Grinders and drill presses are space frugal and work nicely in corners. A lathe fits against a wall and requires only about a 2′-deep working space. One caveat, though. Be sure to fit an incandescent light above the lathe to avoid irritating flickering from the interaction of spinning stock and the frequency of a fluorescent tube.

Play with the layout of your shop, trying different configurations for different imaginary tasks. Even if your wish list of tools will be a long time in fulfillment, you'll improve your existing workshop's layout by mentally exercising the possibilities. Working with your hands is equal parts dexterity and creativity, and the place you work should reflect that balance.

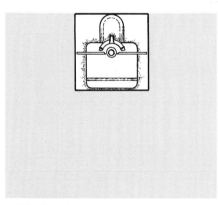

WOOD SHAPER
Main access from front of tool, with clearance at the sides helpful.

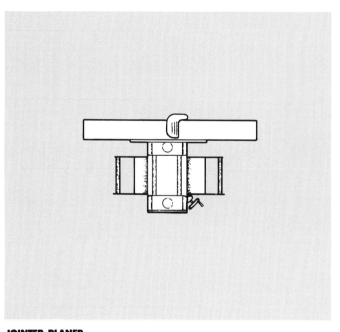

JOINTER-PLANER
The loudest machine in the woodshop. Working access from two sides for long boards.

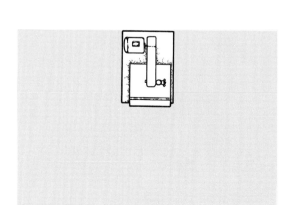

BAND SAW
Takes up limited space, but requires decent lighting and access on three sides.

BENCH GRINDER
Best to keep separate from other machines. Access needed from the front.

Fitting Out the Workshop

Planning your work area for maximum utilization and comfort

In his day, Noah took on the world's biggest contract job without so much as a sawhorse to his name. At the opposite pole, some—lacking the "right" workbench or the newest equipment—would sooner chuck it all than make do with something less than perfect.

Balderdash. Generations of industrious folk have accomplished wonders using tools and equipment made by their own hands. Lest we forget, the medieval system of trade education—from apprentice to journeyman to master, still very much alive in Europe today—demands that the student work with self-crafted implements, if only to foster patience and a genuine rapport with the chosen medium. If master craftsmen can create works of art with homemade tools, the rest of us should feel perfectly comfortable making household repairs with them.

The Tool Chest

"A place for everything and everything in its place." Samuel Smiles penned these familiar words in *Thrift*, and even those stoically indifferent to such venerable bromides would have to acknowledge the aptness of this one for the home workshop.

For what is more frustrating than anticipating an orderly roll call of trusty regulars, only to confront a motley scramble of confusion? Even assuming a more practical tack, tools—tough as they are—shouldn't be insulted by casual treatment or assaulted by

NO. 6 X ³⁄₄" WOOD SCREW

SPRING

¹⁄₄"

³⁄₄"

³⁄₄"

5"

PEN SPRING

⁵⁄₃₂" PIN HOLES

¹⁄₈" X 1³⁄₄" LOCK PIN (ROUND ENDS)

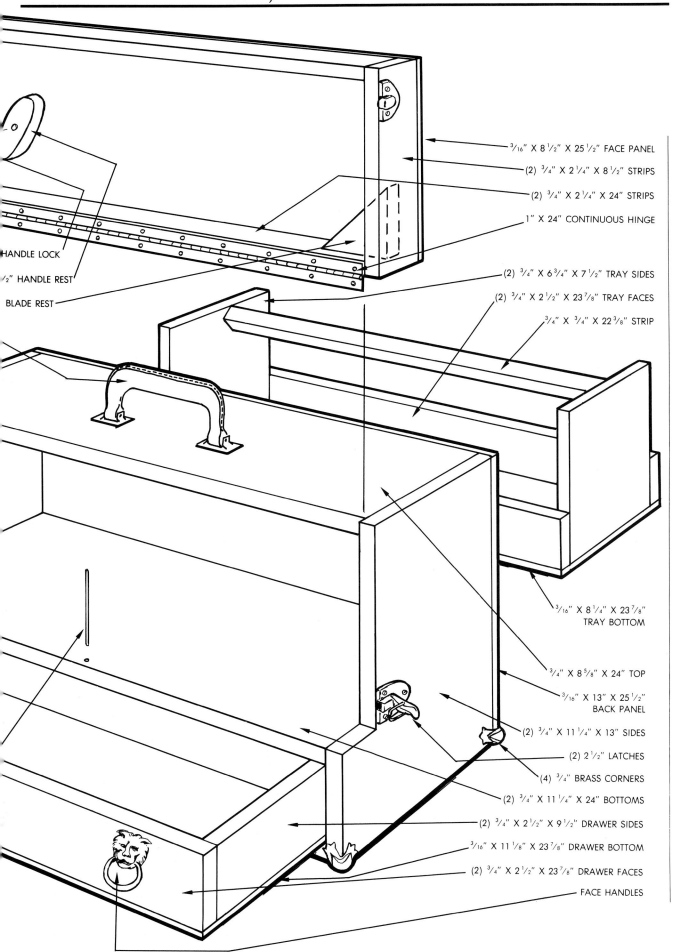

HANDLE LOCK

1/2" HANDLE REST

BLADE REST

3/16" X 8 1/2" X 25 1/2" FACE PANEL

(2) 3/4" X 2 1/4" X 8 1/2" STRIPS

(2) 3/4" X 2 1/4" X 24" STRIPS

1" X 24" CONTINUOUS HINGE

(2) 3/4" X 6 3/4" X 7 1/2" TRAY SIDES

(2) 3/4" X 2 1/2" X 23 7/8" TRAY FACES

3/4" X 3/4" X 22 3/8" STRIP

3/16" X 8 1/4" X 23 7/8"
TRAY BOTTOM

3/4" X 8 5/8" X 24" TOP

3/16" X 13" X 25 1/2"
BACK PANEL

(2) 3/4" X 11 1/4" X 13" SIDES

(2) 2 1/2" LATCHES

(4) 3/4" BRASS CORNERS

(2) 3/4" X 11 1/4" X 24" BOTTOMS

(2) 3/4" X 2 1/2" X 9 1/2" DRAWER SIDES

3/16" X 11 1/8" X 23 7/8" DRAWER BOTTOM

(2) 3/4" X 2 1/2" X 23 7/8" DRAWER FACES

FACE HANDLES

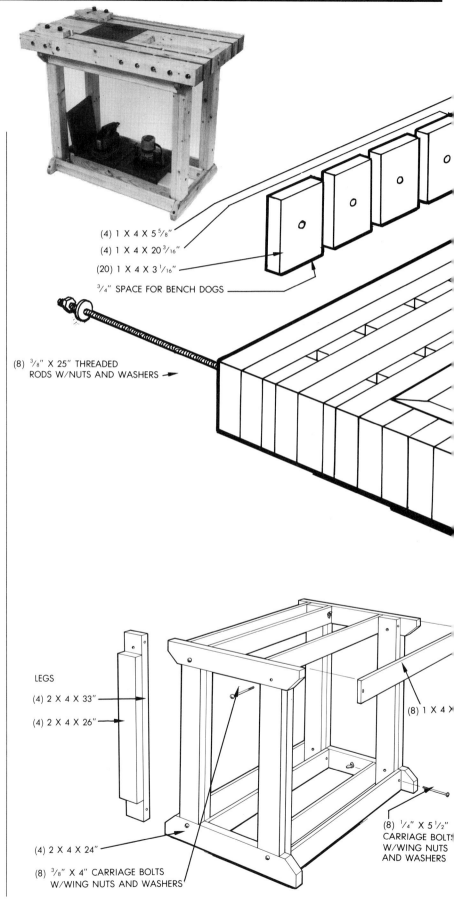

(4) 1 X 4 X 5⅝"

(4) 1 X 4 X 20³⁄₁₆"

(20) 1 X 4 X 3¹⁄₁₆"

¾" SPACE FOR BENCH DOGS

(8) ³⁄₈" X 25" THREADED
RODS W/NUTS AND WASHERS

LEGS

(4) 2 X 4 X 33"

(4) 2 X 4 X 26"

(8) 1 X 4 X

(4) 2 X 4 X 24"

(8) ³⁄₈" X 4" CARRIAGE BOLTS
W/WING NUTS AND WASHERS

(8) ¼" X 5½"
CARRIAGE BOLTS
W/WING NUTS
AND WASHERS

deliberate contempt. So it's only fitting that we offer this design for a classic American tool chest: simple, functional and able to rise from the teeth and temper of the very tools it will house.

The material needn't be a concern. About 12' of 1 X 12 shelving board and a 26" X 42" slab of paneling or hardboard will frame the box; a handful of 1½" and ¾" wire brads, some yellow wood glue (aliphatic resin) and a small assortment of hardware will finish it off. For the sake of appearance, you might wish to choose a nobler wood than pine, but you can pare some expense and still present a proud face by selecting a species similar to our South American banak. It has the properties of yellow poplar but the look of Honduras mahogany; to match it, choose a lauan plywood for the chest's paneled parts.

The Versatile Workbench

A woodworker with a chisel but no bench is like a typist with a typewriter but no desk. A solid, stable surface of the right height, with provisions to secure the work, is simply indispensable.

Dennis Burkholder had the small shop—where tools should perform as many services as possible—in mind when he designed this many-faceted bench. The solid top of laminated 2 X 4s holds ¾" steel dogs in a dozen different pairs of holes to facilitate stopping material or securing it in triangular vise blocks. A tray keeps tools out of the way and from rolling away. A circular saw, router or saber saw can be set upside down in the 12"-square tool opening to allow the bench to be used as a table saw, router table or stationary jigsaw. And because the legs are assembled and attached with removable fasteners, the workbench can be broken down into a package not much larger than a fold-up card table.

The Decorous Work Aid

Once you've become accustomed to a real shop workbench, sawhorses seem to come up a bit short for outdoor jobs. No vise, no work surface, no storage. Nails end up in your mouth; tools sprout from your pockets. Holding a board still for sawing borders on yoga. There's really no need to go without

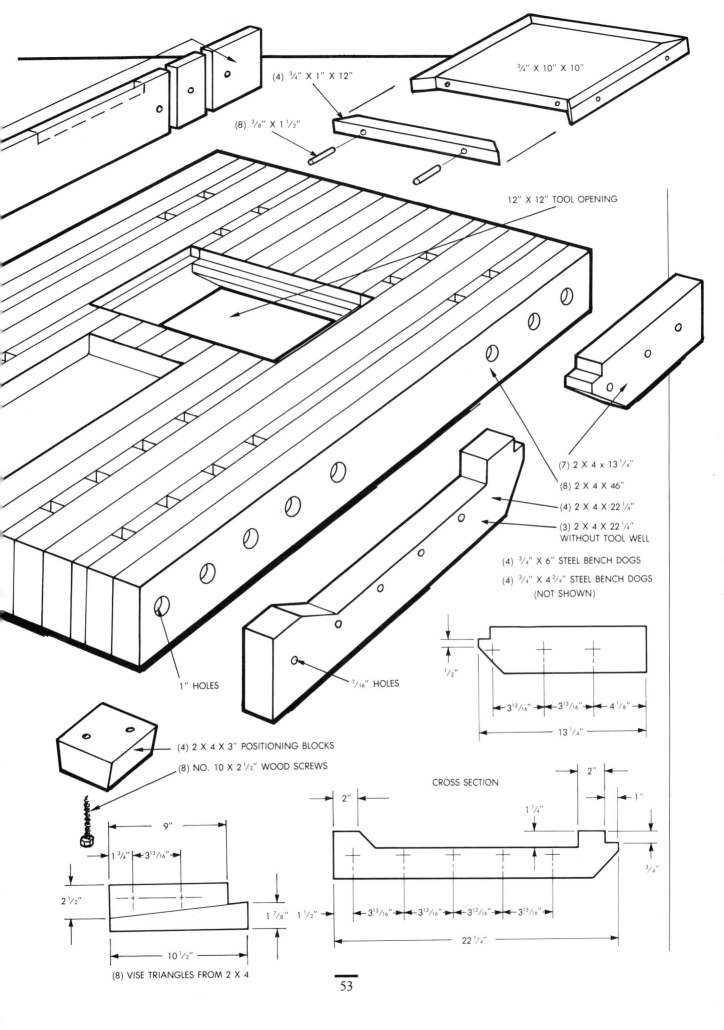

(4) ¾" X 1" X 12"

(8) ⅜" X 1½"

¾" X 10" X 10"

12" X 12" TOOL OPENING

(7) 2 X 4 x 13¼"

(8) 2 X 4 X 46"

(4) 2 X 4 X 22¼"

(3) 2 X 4 X 22¼"
WITHOUT TOOL WELL

(4) ¾" X 6" STEEL BENCH DOGS

(4) ¾" X 4¾" STEEL BENCH DOGS
(NOT SHOWN)

1" HOLES

7/16" HOLES

½"

3¹³/₁₆" 3¹³/₁₆" 4⅛"

13¼"

(4) 2 X 4 X 3" POSITIONING BLOCKS

(8) NO. 10 X 2½" WOOD SCREWS

CROSS SECTION

2"

1"

2"

1¼"

¾"

9"

1¾" 3¹³/₁₆"

2½"

1⅞" 1½"

3¹³/₁₆" 3¹³/₁₆" 3¹³/₁₆" 3¹³/₁₆"

10½"

22¼"

(8) VISE TRIANGLES FROM 2 X 4

when you go out, however. Instead, carry our ingenious ''work aid.''

Like a double-jointed pair of scissors, the two halves of the bench's top close tighter as you bear down, making a very effective vise. There's room for tools and a selection of fasteners in the two compartments below the top. A couple of C-clamps will hold down a miter box for comfortable trim work. And when you're done, the carpenter's third arm folds up like a TV table.

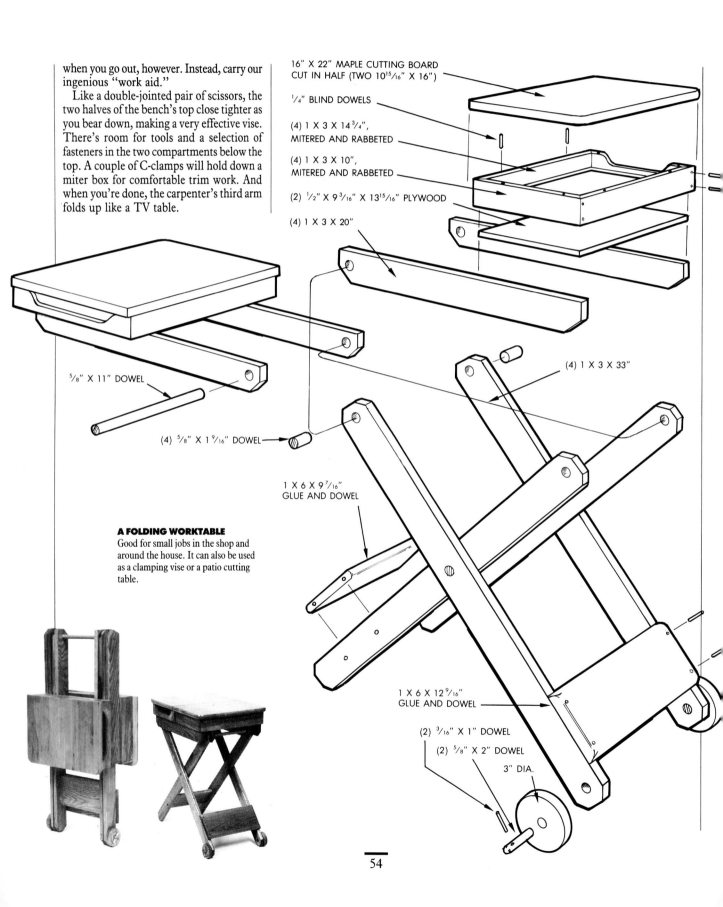

16" X 22" MAPLE CUTTING BOARD CUT IN HALF (TWO 10¹⁵/₁₆" X 16")

¼" BLIND DOWELS

(4) 1 X 3 X 14¾",
MITERED AND RABBETED

(4) 1 X 3 X 10",
MITERED AND RABBETED

(2) ½" X 9³/₁₆" X 13¹⁵/₁₆" PLYWOOD

(4) 1 X 3 X 20"

(4) 1 X 3 X 33"

⁵/₈" X 11" DOWEL

(4) ⁵/₈" X 1⁹/₁₆" DOWEL

1 X 6 X 9⁷/₁₆"
GLUE AND DOWEL

1 X 6 X 12⁹/₁₆"
GLUE AND DOWEL

(2) ³/₁₆" X 1" DOWEL

(2) ⁵/₈" X 2" DOWEL

3" DIA.

A FOLDING WORKTABLE
Good for small jobs in the shop and around the house. It can also be used as a clamping vise or a patio cutting table.

Picking the Right Table Saw

Choosing the flagship of the home workshop is a compromise between needs and wants.

It's probably safe to say that the table saw is the flagship of any home workshop. It's the first stationary tool most people purchase and, by and large, the one that sees the most use. But not all saws are cut from the same cloth; price aside, saw construction and design can vary considerably among different manufacturers, and even pieces of equipment of the same marque may differ depending upon their intended uses.

So, understandably enough, choosing the right saw can be a confounding and intimidating task. Consequently, we've done some homework and have come up with a number of parameters that will help you evaluate your prospective purchase in view of your needs.

You Can't Always Get What You Want

All too often, the difference between what you'd like to have and what you need could double the cost of your purchase. The first question to ask yourself is what kind of work the saw will be doing. If your chores are minor fix-up or hobby jobs that won't involve large pieces of stock, consider the bench-top models. Though they have smaller blades (usually under 10"-diameter) and tables, are designed for light service and generally aren't precision-machined, they might retail for less than half the price of a basic stationary saw. (Then again, smaller saws are not necessarily small in quality.)

If your needs are more substantial, set your sights higher, but consider the sheer size of the machine and its table. Will the saw fit in the shop space you have available for it? A good rule of thumb is to allow a working space that's 8' wide by 16' long for the tool. Less will do, but there's no point in buying a machine whose usefulness is going to be limited by its environment.

Try to match blade diameter to your work as well. Naturally, larger blades allow a deeper cut, but a 10" model will handle most home woodworking tasks. Keep in mind, though, that you'll be able to do small work on a large saw, but the opposite isn't always possible. Also, remember that table dimensions vary even among saws with the same size blade, and that the length of the rails upon which the rip fence travels determines the effective width of the table and thus the maximum rip-cutting width of the saw.

Furthermore, think about the distance from the front of the table to the cutting edge of the blade when it's at full height. The greater this distance, the better you'll be able to control your work, because the table, rather than your hands, will be supporting the load.

Look Before You Leap

There are at least a half-dozen construction or mechanical considerations you ought to investigate before you lay down your hard-earned cash. Starting at the top, examine the quality of the table itself. Generally, it'll be made of either cast iron, cast aluminum, stamped steel or some kind of composite. All things considered, a cast-iron platform is likely the best, because it's probably machined accurately, it's less prone to damage or warpage and it has enough mass to minimize vibration. On the other hand, aluminum—especially if it's been anodized—will resist rust better, and composites are both strong and inexpensive.

Next, look at the rip fence guides. Better saws have two tubular rails—one in front and one in back—that the fence locks to simultaneously. Some have a single front rail of angle or flat iron that's also accurate, while others rely upon an edge built into the tabletop. The whole idea is to keep the fence parallel with the blade. A fine-adjustment knob and a positive lock are very convenient, as is a scale built right into the rail so you don't have to measure distances from the blade itself.

Check out the miter gauge as well; it should move smoothly, without looseness. A movable control surface is a nice feature, since it can be adjusted for work of various sizes; a stop block on the gauge helps support the stock, too.

The blade carriage assembly just might be the most critical part of the saw, since it holds the blade to the table and governs its angle and height. Again, a cast-iron unit would be the first choice, though it comes at a price. Cast aluminum runs a close second, and stamped steel third (though the latter does have a significant cost advantage).

While we're on the subject, it'd be worth your while to double-check the method used to adjust for angle cuts. A tilting-arbor setup

(in which the blade axle moves and the table stays stationary) is used almost exclusively. If you run across a saw on which the table tilts, remember that the work tilts with it and might be difficult to handle as a result.

Closely related to the carriage assembly is the power-drive mechanism. On a *motorized* saw, the blade is fastened directly to the motor shaft. A better alternative is the more expensive *motor-driven* design, in which one or more belts are used to drive the blade, which is mounted on a separate arbor.

Finally, pay attention to the motor type and specifications. The figure most bandied about is horsepower, which can be misleading if you don't understand how it's measured. Sometimes, manufacturers will quote peak, or developed, horsepower values, which aren't a true yardstick because they indicate power under no-load conditions. Instead, look for a *rated*, or *continuous*, horsepower figure, which is an in-use, real-world standard. As a double check, ascertain the machine's amperage rating; a 110-volt mo-

tor must draw at least 10 amps to develop one continuous horsepower. (On a 10″ saw, a 1-hp motor might be too small. In general use, a 1¹/₂-hp motor would be better.)

In addition to power ratings, there are a few other things to look for in a motor. If you have or can easily arrange for a 220-volt line, the additional power may be helpful in ripping thick stock and in other heavy-duty applications. Also, determine whether the motor's housing is drip-proof or totally enclosed; the latter costs more, but

Able to rip and crosscut various materials, the table saw is the fundamental stationary power tool.

provides the windings with protection against sawdust and moisture. While you're at it, check to see if the motor has a reset button (and hence is overload-protected) and whether it's an induction type or a brush-equipped, series-wound (universal) model. The brushless AC-induction type maintains a fairly constant speed under load and requires minimal maintenance. Finally, compare shaft bearing construction. Bushing or sleeve bearings are inexpensive and quiet, but ball bearings function better under load.

These buyers' guidelines are not all-in-clusive by any means, so your best bet is to study—and even try out—the product before you buy. Most table saws come with a blade guard, a miter gauge, a fence and a throat plate, but dozens of accessories are also available for specific applications. If you're unsure as to the reputation of a product, cast a critical eye over its finish quality and check the trueness of the table with a straightedge. Also, make sure you can get replacement parts when you need them. Lack of an odd

component can turn a "great buy" into a motorized mastodon.

The following is a list of manufacturers or distributors whose products are oriented toward home shop, professional or light commercial use. Most are available through retail markets.

Andreou Industries
22-69 23rd St.
Astoria, NY 11105

Black & Decker Corp.
701 Joppa Rd.
Towson, MD 21204

Buffalo Tool Corp.
1111 N. Broadway
St. Louis, MO 63102

Delta International Machinery Corp.
246 Alpha Dr.
Pittsburgh, PA 15238

Elektra Beckum U.S.A. Corp.
401-403 Kennedy Blvd.
Somerdale, NJ 08083

Garrett Wade Co. (INCA)
161 Ave. of the Americas
New York, NY 10013

Grizzly Imports, Inc.
P.O. Box 2069
Bellingham, WA 98227

Jet Equipment & Tools
P.O. Box 1477
Tacoma, WA 98401-1477

Makita U.S.A., Inc.
12950 E. Alondra Blvd.
Cerritos, CA 90701

Sears, Roebuck & Co.
Sears Tower
Chicago, IL 60684

Skil Corp.
4300 W. Peterson Ave.
Chicago, IL 60646

Wilke Machinery Co.
120 Derry Ct.
York, PA 17402

The following is a list of manufacturers whose products are oriented more toward production than home shop or commercial use and are thus priced accordingly. We've also included the address of Gilliom Manufacturing, Inc., which supplies plans, parts and castings for a line of kit-built woodworking tools.

Boice Crane
P.O. Box 429
Gothenburg, NE 69138

Gilliom Manufacturing, Inc.
P.O. Box 1018
St. Charles, MO 63302

Hitachi Power Tools U.S.A., Ltd.
4487-E Park Dr.
Norcross, GA 30093

Griggio
Holz Machinery Corp.
45 Halladay St.
Jersey City, NJ 07304

Oliver Machinery Co.
1025 Clancy Ave. N.E.
Grand Rapids, MI 49503

Powermatic-Stanwich Industries, Inc.
Morrison Rd.
McMinnville, TN 37110

Tannewitz
O-794 Chicago Dr.
Jenison, MI 49428

Ulmia
Mahogany Masterpieces
RFD 1, Wing Rd.
Suncook, NH 03275

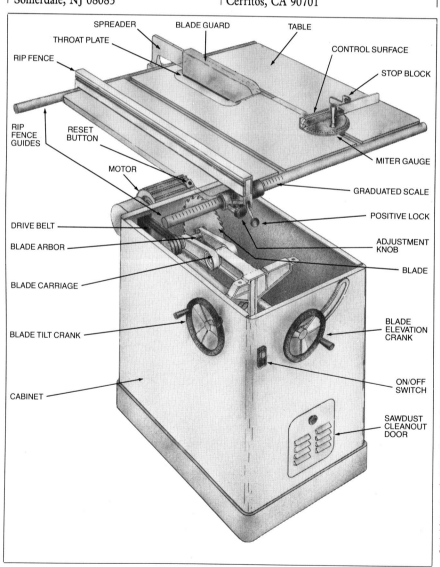

A Band Saw to Suit Your Needs

A band saw is the serious woodworker's tool-of-choice for resawing lumber.

Versatility is the band saw's strong suit. For the cost of a single tool, the home woodworker actually has the use of 1) a precision machine that's capable of cutting curves, circles and intricate shapes in wood up to 6" thick; 2) a hard-working ripsaw that can accurately slice a hefty piece of lumber into thinner boards; and 3) with the addition of a special platen and an abrasive belt, a convenient edge sander for flat or contoured stock.

All band saws share the same basic design. A loop of steel blade, centered on two (or sometimes three) large wheels mounted in the same vertical plane, does the cutting; adjustable guides fastened near the center of the blade's straight span keep the toothed edge in line, both laterally and against rearward pressure; and a motor, connected by belt (or, less often, directly) to the lower wheel, moves the blade. The upper wheel(s) is merely an idler and can be adjusted to keep the blade tracking a straight path.

So if there's not a whole lot of difference between one design and the next, what explains the wide variations in price among tools of similar capacities? Read on, and you'll find out.

Match the Tool to the Task

Before you purchase this major tool, you might first ask yourself what kind of work you'll be doing with your band saw. If you plan on tackling a considerable amount of resawing, especially of oak and other furniture-grade hardwoods, be certain the tool has sufficient power and cutting capacity to slice board after board without overheating. (A 3/4- or 1-hp motor—at least—and a cutting depth of 6" or more are desirable under these circumstances.)

On the other hand, if the majority of your work will involve small pieces of stock and precision cuts, you may do just as well with a bench-top model—or even a scroll saw, which is another tool entirely.

Then again, you might be in the market for a general-purpose band saw that'll handle a little bit of everything you throw at it. If this is the case, be sure to choose one that can accommodate a good variety of blade widths and configurations, and for your own benefit, assure yourself that the manufacturer has given some thought to the convenience of the necessary blade-changing operations.

While we're on the subject of multipurpose applications, you should be aware that many of the larger saws are designed as—or can easily be adapted to become—combination wood-, plastic- and metal-cutting machines. Since a wood blade cuts at a relatively high speed (usually in excess of 2,000 surface feet per minute), a multistep pulley drive or a jackshaft is commonly used to reduce that rate, by one-quarter to one-tenth, to avoid heat buildup when the wider metal-cutting blades are being used. Look for one of these features, plus at least a 1/2" blade-width capacity and a 3/4-hp or larger motor if you plan on cutting mild steel or any other ferrous metals.

And think about the tool's other capacities. The 6" cutting depth mentioned earlier is common and should be more than sufficient for most tasks. But the throat depth (the distance between the blade and the column that supports the upper wheel) is important too, especially if you'll be working with plywood or other sheet stock. In conventional band saw designs, this dimension is dictated by the diameter of the two band wheels (usually 10", 12" or 14"), but a three-wheel configuration relies on triangulation to keep the column and the unused part of the blade as far as 2' from the cutting edge.

The table size—typically in the neighborhood of 14" square—isn't all that critical, though extensions are usually available as options if you need them. Many band saw manufacturers also offer or include rip fences and miter gauges to aid in precision cutting, and incorporate a tilting trunnion into the table mount to allow that surface to be set at up to a 45° angle.

You Get What You Pay For

Quality comes at a price, and with a band saw, quality is synonymous with utility and ease of operation. Before you buy, make an effort to examine, and even use, the tool you've got your sights on. Keep in mind that unless you're planning on moving it from site to site, the machine's weight is an asset, since sheer mass helps to dampen vibration. For this reason, cast-iron frame construction is a plus, as is a heavy, machine-ground table with sufficient integral ribbing. Look, too,

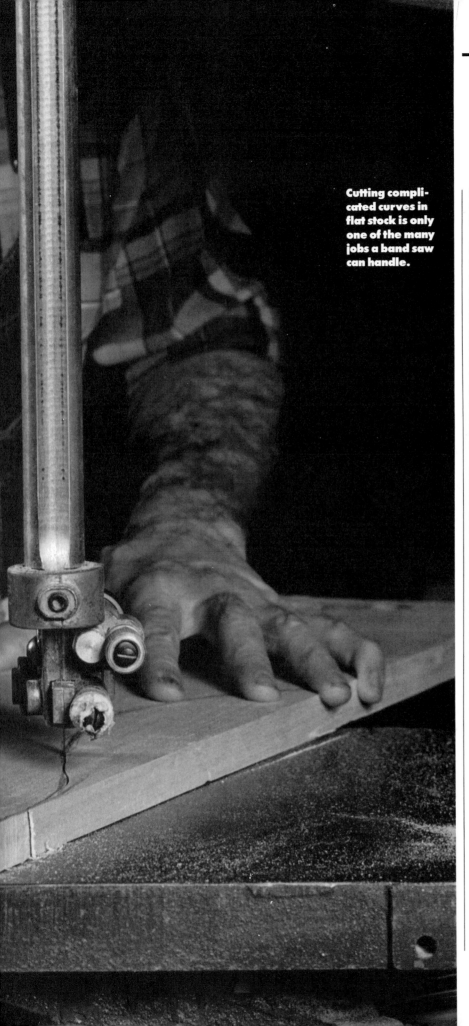

Cutting complicated curves in flat stock is only one of the many jobs a band saw can handle.

for signs of surface drilling on the band wheels, as this will indicate that they've been balanced.

Critical to the saw's precision—or lack of it—is blade guide construction. In a perfectly tuned band saw, the blade will run freely without touching the sides of the guides and will make contact at the rear only when stock is actually being cut. Most guides have a ball bearing stop at the back and steel, brass or phenolic blocks—or a set of ball bearings—to the sides. Regardless of the method used to keep the blade true, it's important that the working components have a range of adjustment. By the same token, the idler wheel(s) should be adjustable as well: laterally, to keep the blade tracking correctly, and vertically, to allow convenient tensioning of that steel band.

The blade's accuracy means little if the table is not square, however. Check to see that its supporting trunnion is sturdy and can lock the table firmly in place at any desired angle. Make sure, too, that it returns perpendicular to the blade; many saws have a threaded stop so the platform can be set correctly.

On some of the larger saws, you can choose the motor according to your needs. For general use, a 3/4- or 1-hp unit would be perfectly adequate for a 14″ machine, but assure yourself that the figure quoted is a continuous, or rated, horsepower and therefore appropriate for long periods of use. (Remember that a 110-volt motor should draw between 10 and 13 amps to develop one continuous horsepower.) Other points of concern are that the power plant be overload-protected, have sealed bearings and preferably have a totally enclosed, rather than just a drip-proof, housing.

The drive mechanism also deserves a brief mention. All but the smallest saws should use a V-belt drive to the lower wheel. Direct-drive setups are inexpensive, but they increase stress on the wearing parts and have a tendency to bog down under load.

Last, but certainly not least, check out your potential purchase from a user-safety standpoint. Does it have a substantial rear blade guard? Does the front guard slide down the guidepost with the upper guide and cover all but the actual cutting edge of the blade? Are all moving parts fully shrouded or enclosed? Both bench and stationary models should be stable and vibration-free, with a throat plate around the blade, an easily accessible shutoff switch and provision for a work light.

The saw you purchase will affect the quality of your work for a long time to come. By taking the time now to examine the products in your price range and relying on investigation rather than impulse, you should get your hard-earned money's worth.

If your needs exceed the capability of even a top-of-the-line home-shop tool, you might investigate the following manufacturers, which supply the production and large commercial markets. (As another alternative,

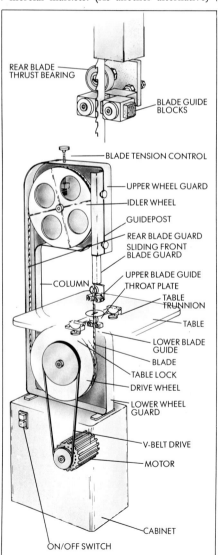

REAR BLADE
THRUST BEARING

BLADE GUIDE
BLOCKS

BLADE TENSION CONTROL

UPPER WHEEL GUARD

IDLER WHEEL

GUIDEPOST

REAR BLADE GUARD
SLIDING FRONT
BLADE GUARD

UPPER BLADE GUIDE

COLUMN

THROAT PLATE

TABLE
TRUNNION

TABLE

LOWER BLADE
GUIDE

BLADE

TABLE LOCK

DRIVE WHEEL

LOWER WHEEL
GUARD

V-BELT DRIVE

MOTOR

CABINET

ON/OFF SWITCH

we've included the address of Gilliom Manufacturing, Inc., a Missouri-based company which offers plans, parts and castings for a broad selection of kit-built woodworking tools.)

Gilliom Manufacturing, Inc.
P.O. Box 1018
St. Charles, MO 63302

Hitachi Power Tools U.S.A., Ltd.
4487-E Park Dr.
Norcross, GA 30093

Holz Machinery Corp.
45 Halladay St.
Jersey City, NJ 07304

Oliver Machinery Co.
1025 Clancy Ave. N.E.
Grand Rapids, MI 49503

Parks Woodworking Machine Co.
1501 Knowlton St.
Cincinnati, OH 45223

Powermatic-Stanwich Industries, Inc.
Morrison Rd.
McMinnville, TN 37110

Tannewitz
O-794 Chicago Dr.
Jenison, MI 49428

The following is a list of manufacturers or distributors whose products are oriented toward home shop, professional or light commercial use. Most are available through retail markets.

Andreou Industries
22–69 23rd St.
Astoria, NY 11105

Black & Decker (U.S.), Inc.
2721 Millbrook Rd.
Raleigh, NC 27658

Delta International Machinery Corp.
246 Alpha Dr.
Pittsburgh, PA 15238

Elektra Beckum U.S.A. Corp.
401–403 Kennedy Blvd.
Somerdale, NJ 08083

Garrett Wade Co. (INCA)
161 Ave. of the Americas
New York, NY 10013

Grizzly Imports, Inc.
P.O. Box 2069
Bellingham, WA 98227

J. Philip Humfrey, Ltd. (General)
3241 Kennedy Rd., Unit 7
Scarborough, Ont.
Canada M1V 2J9

Jet Equipment & Tools
1901 Jefferson Ave.
Tacoma, WA 98402

Laskowski Enterprises
8180 W. 10th St.
Indianapolis, IN 46224

Mini Max U.S.A.
3642 N.W. 37th Ave.
Miami, FL 33142

Ryobi America Corp.
1158 Tower Ln.
Bensenville, IL 60106

Sears, Roebuck & Co.
Sears Tower
Chicago, IL 60684

Skil Corporation
4801 W. Peterson Ave.
Chicago, IL 60646

Tab Merchandise Corp.
(Buffalo)
1111 N. Broadway
St. Louis, MO 63102

Wilke Machinery Co.
120 Derry Ct., RD 22
York, PA 17402

The Worthy Drill Press

Don't underestimate this amazingly versatile workshop workhorse.

If you thought a drill press was strictly a production metalworking machine, it's time to reconsider: These one-time behemoths have been slimmed down, lightened up and priced in a range comparable with other home shop tools. What's more, with the addition of a number of accessories, a drill press can do far more than bore right-on-the-money holes in wood or metal: It can be used as a router, drum sander, circle cutter, rotary planer, buffer, shaper and mortising chisel, as well.

Though drill presses are available in both standing and bench-top models, the floor units are nearly always the better buys unless you're specifically looking for a more compact tool. (If that's the case, you'll still find valuable information in this article; some of the bench units are available as shortened versions of the heavy-duty stationary models, while others are clearly meant for lighter, less severe service.)

Let's take a look at the machine itself. With the exception of the industrial-type radial drill presses (which incorporate a horizontal arm to allow a range of lateral adjustment), most of the tools on the market share a similar design. Starting at the bottom, the *base* serves as a pedestal, a column support and—in some circumstances—a secondary work surface. The *column* is a stanchion that carries an adjustable *worktable* and supports the machine's main element, the *head*.

This all-important component consists of the motor, a step-pulley drive system and a spindle that rotates within a housing known as the quill. The quill's vertical movement is controlled by the feed lever, and its stroke can be limited with the depth stop. A splined-shaft arrangement allows the spindle—and the chuck fastened to the end of it—to move up and down with the quill.

Know Your Options

One of the most attractive features of a drill press is its versatility, so keep that in mind when window-shopping. If your sole purpose in buying the tool is to precision-bore holes in small pieces of stock, a bench-top model may suit you fine. On the other hand, if you wish to take full advantage of the machine's total capabilities, the standing version is probably a better choice, since with its longer column, it can accommodate small, large and oddly shaped workpieces.

Consider, too, the availability of multiple spindle speeds. If you'll be working with metal as well as wood, the drill bit must be capable of turning at a relatively low rate, normally in the hundreds of revolutions per minute (rpm). Wood boring requires a medium range, while dressing operations, such as shaping, demand the highest speeds.

Practically speaking, a selection of four or five speeds that span a wide range of rpm may be more valuable than a lot of settings within a narrow scope. Look for a machine that can operate at between 500 and at least 4,000 rpm if you want maximum versatility; if you plan to use it only for drilling, a 2,000-rpm ceiling should be fine.

The tool's worktable warrants some attention, also. All tables slide up and down on the column, and pivot around it as well, but many manufacturers mount the work surface on an adjustable horizontal axis or offer a tilting and turning table as an accessory. This feature is well worth some additional expense, since it simplifies bevel drilling considerably.

Finally, satisfy yourself that the machine's capacities are sufficient to handle your intended work. Typically, a drill press is sized by its swing, or twice the distance from the column to the center of the chuck. Almost as often, manufacturers will simply state that their product will drill to the center of a given size workpiece.

The quill travel, or stroke, determines the single-pass depth of the bore; a range between 3" and 5" is satisfactory for full-size machines. Likewise, the capacity of the chuck dictates the size of the bit, though some manufacturers indicate that reduced-shank drills can be used to bore oversize holes in certain metals.

And Know Your Machine

Like most any stationary shop tool, a drill press's weight is an advantage, especially in dampening internal vibration. A large, solid base—complete with floor-mounting holes and clamping slots—is always a bonus, as is a machine-ground cast-iron worktable. Check for heavy support ribbing in both platforms, and be sure the table has built-in cross slots and perhaps even a substantial clamping ledge at its perimeter.

Look, too, at the column. A floor-standing model, particularly, has to support a lot of weight on that post, so it should be at least 3″ in diameter and firmly attached to the base. When clamped, the table mount should not wiggle or shift, either.

Moving to the head, check the alignment of the motor and drive pulleys, and determine if there's excessive play in the shafts. Does the belt tension mechanism function smoothly and effectively? Try to ascertain, as well, the motor's amperage draw. A 110-volt motor will use between 10 and 13 amps to develop one continuous horsepower; some manufacturers quote "peak" horsepower because it's slightly higher, but that measurement will have little relevance in the workshop.

Significant, both for accuracy and safety, is the amount of lateral play

When boring on the drill press, always back the work to prevent damage to the metal table.

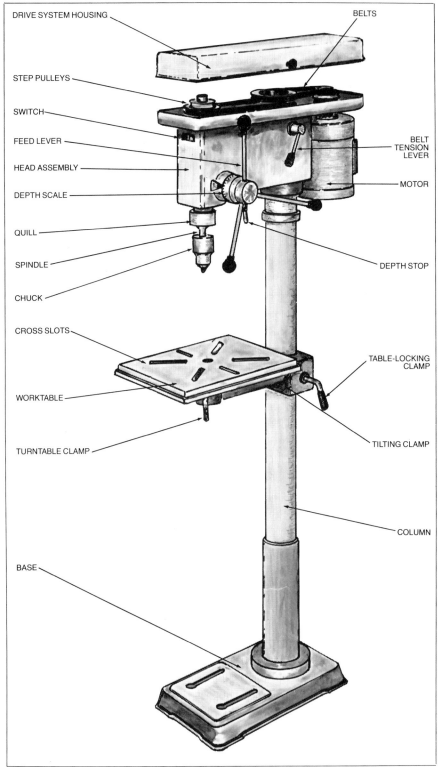

DRIVE SYSTEM HOUSING

STEP PULLEYS

SWITCH

FEED LEVER

HEAD ASSEMBLY

DEPTH SCALE

QUILL

SPINDLE

CHUCK

CROSS SLOTS

WORKTABLE

TURNTABLE CLAMP

BASE

BELTS

BELT TENSION LEVER

MOTOR

DEPTH STOP

TABLE-LOCKING CLAMP

TILTING CLAMP

COLUMN

in the spindle and quill. Simply put, there should be none when the spindle is lowered to its maximum extent, because any such movement is exaggerated at high rpm.

Before you buy a drill press, try to get your hands on a display model and make the various adjustments as you would in your own shop. Operate the feed lever and the depth stop, and vary the height and pitch of the table. See how difficult it is to change speeds, and check to see that basic instructions for switching pulleys are clearly marked on the tool's housing.

Finally, remember that no major tool is a good buy unless it can be serviced and upgraded. Can the manufacturer or distributor guarantee availability of repair parts? What about work-saving accessories and attachments that make full use of the machine's capabilities? Once you've gotten satisfactory answers to these questions and the important ones involving the tool's construction, you'll know that you'll be getting real value for your money.

The following is a list of manufacturers or distributors whose products are oriented toward home shop, professional or light commercial use. Most are available through retail markets.

American Machine & Tool Co.
Fourth Ave. & Spring St.
Royersford, PA 19468

Buffalo Tool Corp.
(Guardian Power Products)
1111 N. Broadway
St. Louis, MO 63102

Delta International Machinery Corp.
246 Alpha Dr.
Pittsburgh, PA 15238

Grizzly Imports, Inc.
P.O. Box 2069
Bellingham, WA 98227

Jet Equipment & Tools
P.O. Box 1477
Tacoma, WA 98401-1477

Sears, Roebuck & Co.
Sears Tower
Chicago, IL 60684

Plan On a Planer

A thickness planer gives you the power to prepare wood of any size.

Though it never hurts to have a working knowledge of hand tools, the thought of dimensioning a large board with jack planes is enough to make most home woodworkers cringe. It's a fact of life that nearly all shop projects will go more smoothly with straight stock of consistent thickness, and, fortunately, there's a power tool that offers the serious woodworker looking for a complete home shop the capability to custom-size boards to any dimension: the thickness planer.

There was a time when such a tool would have been found only in a large production shop and would have had the capacity to accommodate full-size door frames. But manufacturers with their ears to the ground have developed down-scaled machines that retain the important features of the production jobs, yet cost a fraction as much. These home-shop planers range in price from somewhere under $1,000 (complete and ready to roll) to just over $2,500, and are typically sized to accommodate foot-wide boards, give or take several inches.

The Plane Truth

Though even a low-cost model represents quite an investment, home thickness planers do have clear-cut limitations that can only be understood by looking into the designs of the machines. Characteristically, the tool is comprised of a frame-mounted *table*, or *bed*, that's equipped with steel rollers and has the capability of being raised or lowered in fractional increments. An *infeed* and an *outfeed roller* are fixed above the table; both are power driven. A drumlike *cutterhead*, set between the rollers, is geared to spin at a much higher rate of speed, perhaps 4,000 or 5,000 rpm. The cutterhead is equipped with two or three adjustable knives that run the length of the drum, and a *chipbreaker*—usually spring-loaded—is fastened just forward of the cutterhead, both to press the stock flat against the table and to break the slivers cut by the rotating knives.

This arrangement is, of course, ideal for shaving wood, layer by layer, from pieces of stock, but it's not designed to remove a board's warp or cup. The reason is that as a warped board passes into the feed roller, it gets flattened against the table in preparation for the cutterhead. After the pass is made, the stock exits from the outfeed roller, where, no longer under pressure, it's likely to spring back to its original shape—a bit thinner, but probably no less distorted.

Put another way, a thickness planer will make both sides of a slab of wood smooth and parallel to each other, but it won't necessarily make them straight. That task must be left to a jointer, which prepares face sides and edges by removing high spots without first flattening the board; ideally, a jointer would be used prior to planing to guarantee one square side, though often at the cost of a considerable amount of stock on a badly warped board.

Know What to Look For

Surprisingly enough, all planers function in essentially the same manner. But the differences that do exist among the manufacturers' dozen or so offerings are significant enough to warrant a close inspection prior to making a purchase. Too, some machines are marketed under more than one brand name, and some distributors make their own modifications to a manufacturer's product; so be aware of these factors while comparative shopping.

One feature that's a traditional mainstay of commercial shop planers is sheer mass, and plenty of it. Though it'd be difficult to argue against this, more than one manufacturer leans toward portability, and thus relies upon angle steel framing or aluminum castings to reduce weight and expense. Suffice it to say that cast iron is strong, resistant to warpage and unmatched for dampening vibration; on the other hand, liberal use of it relegates a tool to in-shop, stationary service—period.

It's worth noting that some manufacturers offer optional stands, while others incorporate cabinets right into the design. Again, which you choose depends upon how you plan to use your machine. Perhaps the ideal setup in terms of flexibility is one in which a substantial base is used to support a self-contained tool. That way, the business part of the machine can be separated from the stand and carried to another location, where it can be mounted or rejoined to its legs.

If you anticipate planing a large amount of long stock, you'll want to consider support beyond the boundaries of the planer table.

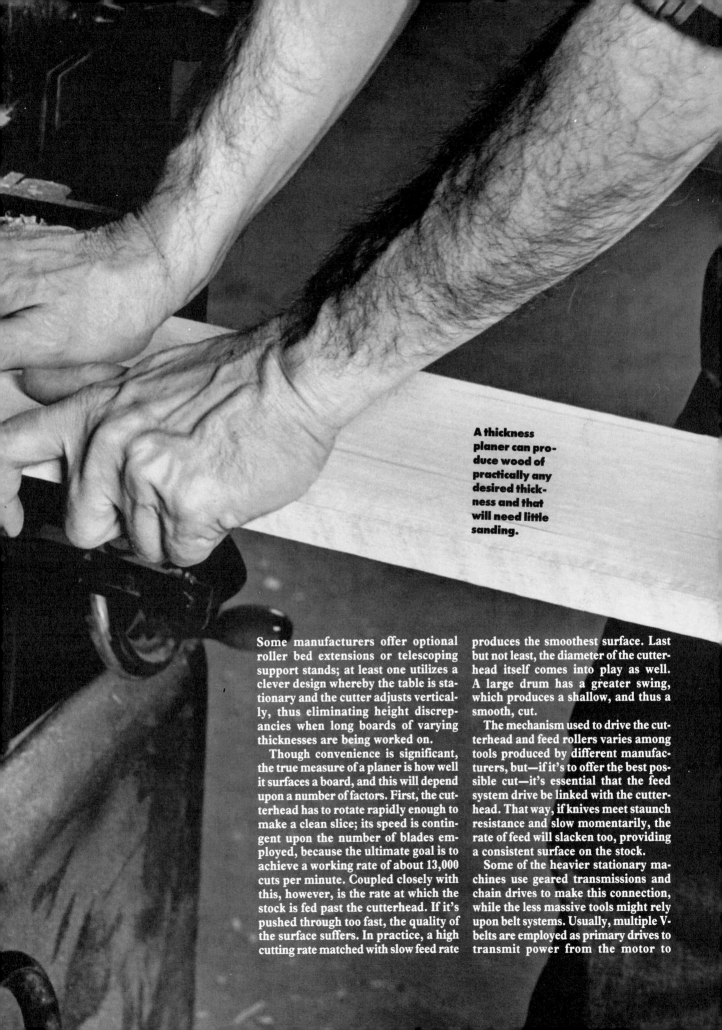

A thickness planer can produce wood of practically any desired thickness and that will need little sanding.

Some manufacturers offer optional roller bed extensions or telescoping support stands; at least one utilizes a clever design whereby the table is stationary and the cutter adjusts vertically, thus eliminating height discrepancies when long boards of varying thicknesses are being worked on.

Though convenience is significant, the true measure of a planer is how well it surfaces a board, and this will depend upon a number of factors. First, the cutterhead has to rotate rapidly enough to make a clean slice; its speed is contingent upon the number of blades employed, because the ultimate goal is to achieve a working rate of about 13,000 cuts per minute. Coupled closely with this, however, is the rate at which the stock is fed past the cutterhead. If it's pushed through too fast, the quality of the surface suffers. In practice, a high cutting rate matched with slow feed rate

produces the smoothest surface. Last but not least, the diameter of the cutterhead itself comes into play as well. A large drum has a greater swing, which produces a shallow, and thus a smooth, cut.

The mechanism used to drive the cutterhead and feed rollers varies among tools produced by different manufacturers, but—if it's to offer the best possible cut—it's essential that the feed system drive be linked with the cutterhead. That way, if knives meet staunch resistance and slow momentarily, the rate of feed will slacken too, providing a consistent surface on the stock.

Some of the heavier stationary machines use geared transmissions and chain drives to make this connection, while the less massive tools might rely upon belt systems. Usually, multiple V-belts are employed as primary drives to transmit power from the motor to the cutterhead assembly. Naturally, belts require more frequent maintenance than do gears or chains, but they're also less expensive to replace.

When you're choosing a machine, it's important to consider how you'll use it. If your work involves surfacing large pieces of rough-sawn hardwood, a stationary model with a 3- or 5-hp, 220-volt motor and a higher (or variable) feed rate will probably serve you best. On the other hand, if you're more of a hobbyist and tend to work with smaller pieces of mixed-species stock, perhaps a $1\frac{1}{2}$- or 2-hp tool set up with a slow feed would be more to your liking. At any rate, don't judge a machine's capability by the horsepower claims alone. Some manufacturers quote peak, rather than continuous, power; so it's best to use the motor's amperage rating as a yardstick.

It's also critical that you establish the capacities of the machine you intend to buy before you put your cash down. Determine how wide and thick a piece of stock it will accept, and how thin a board it's able to produce. Too, give some thought to the maximum depth of cut it can make in one pass without stalling (in hardwood), and to how short a section it'll feed without jamming.

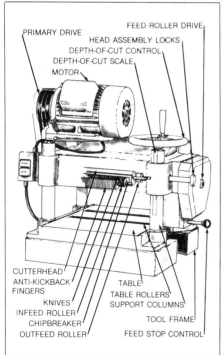

PRIMARY DRIVE
FEED ROLLER DRIVE
HEAD ASSEMBLY LOCKS
DEPTH-OF-CUT CONTROL
DEPTH-OF-CUT SCALE
MOTOR

CUTTERHEAD
ANTI-KICKBACK
FINGERS
KNIVES
INFEED ROLLER
CHIPBREAKER
OUTFEED ROLLER
TABLE
TABLE ROLLERS
SUPPORT COLUMNS
TOOL FRAME
FEED STOP CONTROL

Some Finer Points

In addition to these essentials, there are other details you'll want to keep an eye out for as you shop around. For the sake of convenience, make certain that the knives on the cutterhead are accessible and reasonably simple to replace and adjust. At least one manufacturer utilizes a built-in shaft lock that makes this process safer and easier. Likewise, consider the adjustment of the feed rollers and the chipbreaker; if these don't work correctly, neither will the tool. Finally, check out the depth-of-cut mechanism, including the scale. It should travel smoothly and consistently, without requiring an excessive amount of hand effort.

Other points to be aware of include features such as an emergency stop control for the feed mechanism; an effective anti-kickback system for stubborn stock; steel rollers, preferably with a fluted pattern included on the infeed rolls; and a balanced cutterhead assembly.

In general, the machine should be substantial enough to take the kind of abuse that normal use would give it. If possible, check for play in the drive mechanism, the rollers and the table mount. Also, be aware that power planers are extremely loud in operation—some enough so that ear protection is mandatory. Additionally, they create incredible amounts of dust and shavings; so you might want to consider purchasing a dust-collection hood if the model you're interested in is not equipped with one.

Besides optional feed rate reduction kits, there are often molder, jointer and sander attachments available. Whether or not you purchase these extras is up to you, but do take the time to get a clear understanding of the warranty, and especially the post-sale availability of parts and service. Remember, even a bargain-priced tool is far too expensive if it can't function for simple lack of parts availability.

The following manufacturers or distributors offer products oriented toward home shop, professional or light commercial use.

Delta International Machinery Corp.
246 Alpha Dr.
Pittsburgh, PA 15238

Foley-Belsaw
6301 Equitable Rd.
Kansas City, MO 64120

Grizzly Imports, Inc.
P.O. Box 2069
Bellingham, WA 98227

Hitachi Power Tools U.S.A., Ltd.
4487-E Park Dr.
Norcross, GA 30093

J. Philip Humfrey, Ltd. (General)
3241 Kennedy Rd., Unit 7
Scarborough, Ont.
Canada M1V 2J9

Jet Equipment & Tools
P.O. Box 1477
Tacoma, WA 98401-1477

Makita U.S.A., Inc.
12930 E. Alonda Blvd.
Cerritos, CA 90701

Parks Woodworking Machine Co.
1501 Knowlton St.
Cincinnati, OH 45223

Ryobi America Corp.
1158 Tower Lane
Bensenville, IL 60106

Sears, Roebuck & Co.
Sears Tower
Chicago, IL 60684

Total Shop Woodworking Tools
P.O. Box 25429
Greenville, SC 29616

Wilke Machinery Co. (Bridgewood)
120 Derry Ct.
York, PA 17402

Williams & Hussey Machine Co.
Elm St.
Milford, NH 03055

Woodmaster Tools, Inc.
2908 Oak St.
Kansas City, MO 64108

Turn to a Wood Lathe

No other single power tool can render a tree into a finished product.

When compared with other tools in the home workshop, the woodturning lathe is unique by virtue of its singular purpose: It's designed to allow rapid and symmetrical shaping or carving by rotating the workpiece on a driven center. Don't, however, assume that the lathe is too limited in function to be useful. Tackling even a moderately intricate project without one would be a major chore, and a well-equipped machine is flexible enough to handle a wide variety of turning tasks, as well as shaping, sanding and finishing jobs.

A cursory look at any wood lathe will reveal the major components that all lathes share. Probably most important is the *bed*, which determines the center-length capacity of the tool and establishes how true it will be. This foundation supports the *headstock*, which contains the spindle drive mechanism, and the *tailstock*, which secures the workpiece opposite the driven spindle and adjusts laterally to suit the length of the work involved. A tool rest, also fastened to the bed, supports the hand-held gouges and chisels used in turning and can be slid along the bedways to face the work at any point. Though some lathes are designed as bench-top models, most manufacturers offer stands or cabinet bases to make their machines freestanding.

A Look at the Lathe

Lathes are sized by the maximum diameter of work they're able to turn. This dimension, which is known as the swing, is determined by the height of the drive spindle above the bed, or the radius of the swing. The tool's center-length capacity—or distance between headstock and tailstock centers—is limited by the length of the bed, and necessarily must be a foot or more shorter, since the headstock and tailstock occupy some of the bedways' space.

If your work is going to be limited to hobby turning or simple crafts, you probably won't need anything more than a moderate-sized, light-duty bench lathe. As you set your sights on more intricate projects, such as furniture components, large bowls and turned containers, you'll appreciate the features and convenience of the larger, base-mounted, stationary machines.

As with any major purchase, there are a number of things to be aware of if you're doing some serious shopping. One nice feature offered by about half the manufacturers is an outboard turning capability, which allows the user to mount a faceplate on the outer end of the headstock to accommodate a larger-diameter workpiece than would normally fit over the bed. This is usually achieved by extending the drive spindle through that end and machining it with a left-handed thread, though several firms do save that extra tooling step and the cost of a separate faceplate by designing their headstocks to swivel, or slide to the opposite end of the bed.

Too, most cast-iron bed lathes are available with a gap-bed feature—a recess built into the bed beneath the drive spindle which allows inboard faceplate turning of a larger-diameter piece than would fit over the bedways.

Because the various stages involved in taking a piece of stock from its raw state to a finished product require specific turning rates, virtually all lathes are equipped to operate at three or more different spindle speeds. Generally, these range from 800 to 2,500 revolutions per minute, but the costlier, more versatile machines span a wider range. Some offer variable-speed options that allow rpm changes while the machine is in operation. Knowing how your potential purchase is set up is important, because if you're inclined toward working with larger pieces of stock, the machine's spindle speeds should be considerably slower.

Another worthwhile feature included in some models is an indexing mechanism, usually built into the headstock. It's nothing more than a lock that allows the spindle to be fixed at any number of equally spaced positions within a complete revolution. Not only does it provide a convenient method of holding the spindle in place while adding or removing faceplates and other accessories, but it's indispensable when you're routing flutes or drilling holes that must be symmetrically arranged.

Look, too, for through-drilling capability if you plan on turning lamp bases or other hollow pieces. Most often, the tailstock spindle will have a center hole to allow right-on-the-button end-drilling; at least one manufacturer includes a larger headstock bore-through as well.

Finally, don't be put off if you find a lathe

with all the desirable features, but with a limited center-length capacity. Some machines can be equipped with optional bed extensions that increase the distance between centers. (The Conover lathe is unique in that you can determine the length according to your needs; the metal components are furnished, then it's assembled around buyer-supplied hardwood bed planks.)

Take a Closer Look

The lathe, like any other shop tool, is only as good as the parts that go into it. If one ax-

iom applies to this machine, it's that balance is all-important. Unfortunately, because of knots, wood is seldom uniform in density, and workpieces that have been glued together from different species of wood will be decidedly imbalanced. In either case, the disparity puts a great deal of strain on the headstock and drive mechanism, so it's imperative that both these components are sturdy and well designed to limit wobbling and vibration.

If you're in the market for a heavy-duty machine, look for a substantial cast-iron headstock frame; if it's the type that swivels

or moves for outboard turning, be certain it locks *solidly* to the bed in both positions. Also, check out the spindle shaft and bearings. A 12″ lathe should have at least a 1″-diameter axle and sealed ball or roller bearings to survive substantial rotational and radial loads.

Only to a slightly lesser extent is the durability of the tailstock important. Though it contains considerably fewer moving parts, it too must fasten firmly to the bed and maintain a straight line to the driven center, regardless of where it's positioned on the ways. Consider, as well, the stroke of the tail-

A wood lathe is the best tool for complex turnings, such as chair legs and lamp bases.

stock spindle. That shaft should have a travel of at least 2″, not only to allow you to secure the work properly, but to facilitate the use of a chuck and drill bit. The spindle should also lock securely in any position.

And just as critical as the headstock and tailstock is the bed upon which they rest. Though some of the tube rail and box beam designs are quite substantial, quality cast iron has the advantage of sheer mass. It absorbs shock and vibration, boosts rigidity and is built for the ages.

The question of how much power you need can only be answered when you know the size of the work to be turned. Quite naturally, the larger the diameter and mass of the stock, the greater the need for horsepower. In general, the lighter-duty machines can get by comfortably with a motor built to deliver $^1/_2$ continuous horsepower. With a heavier machine, a $^3/_4$-hp unit is common, though 1-hp and greater motors are often fitted too.

Speed control is also related to power requirements. When you're roughing large-diameter pieces, you may need turning speeds as low as 200 or 300 rpm, but you'll also need torque at the spindle. A conventional stepped-pulley design is fine, because it offers simplicity as well as the necessary "low gear" ratio. For added convenience, manufacturers have developed a mechanically controlled, continuously variable belt drive system that allows speed changes in motion while still maintaining torque; but some smaller machines use variable voltage controls to govern speed, which reduce motor power when it's needed most and thus sacrifice function for ease of operation.

Don't forget to also investigate a manufacturer's accessory offerings before making your purchase. In addition to a spur drive center, a faceplate and a standard tool rest, most suppliers have a full line of optional extras that will enhance the tool's capabilities considerably. These would include a ball-bearing live center for the tailstock spindle, a jawed scroll chuck, a drill chuck, crotch and cup centers, outboard tool rests and larger faceplates. Be aware, too, that many machines are (or can be) equipped with Morse taper spindles, which offer a positive grip on the centers and convenient changing as well. And if you're interested in duplicating pieces, check out the copier attachments that some firms make available; their high initial cost may be warranted if you need to make a number of similar parts.

It could probably go without saying that the best way to decide upon a machine is to try it out first; but even if that's not possible, you can at least assure yourself of its value as an investment if you're guaranteed that the tool is manufactured by a reputable firm and that there will always be repair parts

and service available. With that understood, your purchase can't help but make your workshop ventures take a "turn" for the better.

The following is a list of manufacturers or distributors whose products are oriented toward home shop, professional or light commercial use. Most are available through retail markets.

Advanced Machinery Imports, Ltd.
(Hegner)
P.O. Box 312
New Castle, DE 19720

American Machine & Tool Co.
Fourth Ave. & Spring St.
Royersford, PA 19468

Buffalo Tool Corp.
1111 N. Broadway
St. Louis, MO 63102

Conover Woodcraft Specialties, Inc.
18125 Madison Rd.
Parkman, OH 44080

Delta International Machinery Corp.
246 Alpha Dr.
Pittsburgh, PA 15238

Elektra Beckum U.S.A. Corp.
401-403 Kennedy Blvd.
Somerdale, NJ 08083

Emco Maier Corp.
2757 Scioto Pkwy.
Columbus, OH 43026-2334

Garrett Wade Co.
(Konig-Drechselbank)
161 Ave. of the Americas
New York, NY 10013

Grizzly Imports, Inc.
P.O. Box 2069
Bellingham, WA 98227

Highland Hardware (Tyme)
1045 N. Highland Ave. N.E.
Atlanta, GA 30306

Jet Equipment & Tools
P.O. Box 1477
Tacoma, WA 98401-1477

Powermatic-Stanwich Industries, Inc.
Morrison Rd.
McMinnville, TN 37110

Sears, Roebuck & Co. (Craftsman)
Sears Tower
Chicago, IL 60684

Williams & Hussey Machine Co.
Elm St.
Milford, NH 03055

Wilke Machinery Co.
120 Derry Court
York, PA 17402

Russ Zimmerman (Myford)
RFD 3, Box 242
Putney, VT 05346

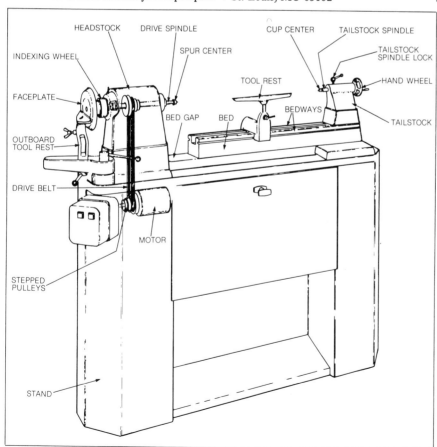

Choosing the Right Jointer

An essential tool for any carpenter who plans to graduate to cabinetmaker

A good jointer can save untold time and expense in any woodshop. As its name implies, this tool is used to prepare stock for smooth, matching joints, essentially by removing a board's high spots to create a straight slab of wood with face sides and edges.

Its mate, the thickness planer, can make a highly accurate cut once it has a true side to reference, so many manufacturers offer combination jointer-planers to satisfy the need for both tools in one compact unit.

The Jointer Jungle

Despite the differences in appearance among jointers of various manufacture, the tools function in essentially the same manner. A cylindrical cutterhead equipped with two or three full-length knives is mounted on a frame and driven at speeds of up to 10,000 revolutions per minute (rpm), either by belt or directly by the motor shaft. Separate tables, mounted before and after the cutterhead on inclined ramps, or ways, can be individually raised or lowered in increments to expose the knife edges by degrees. A pivoting safety guard uncovers the blades as the work passes over the cutterhead.

To accommodate bevel and rabbet cuts, a fence is fastened to one side of the tables. It's usually made to tilt 45° to the right and left and can also be moved laterally across the feeding surface. Generally, the entire unit is mounted on a stand or cabinet at a comfortable working height, but some manufacturers offer bench-top models as well.

In most stationary tools—and the jointer is no exception—substantial mass is desirable to dampen vibration and maintain accuracy. A cast-iron frame and cast-iron components certainly have the benefits of strength and warp resistance, but if portability is a concern, cast alloy offers similar characteristics with a reduction in weight.

The tables, too, affect the precision of the work. It stands to reason that the longer the infeed and outfeed surfaces, the greater the consistency of the cut. Unfortunately, many woodworkers simply don't have room to accommodate a $5^1/_2'$ bed, but some might find a happy medium in designs with folding table extensions which can be dropped for storage. Ideally, the tables should be fastened to the jointer frame in a manner that allows as little play as possible throughout the platforms' range of adjustment. Ramps equipped with dovetailed or slotted-channel ways afford a minimum of unwanted movement.

Since the cutterhead is the heart of the jointer, its design is critical to the machine's performance. Naturally, the drum spindles should be equipped with ball bearings, and the entire unit balanced for high-speed operation. This is especially important in cutterheads with two blades, since they must spin faster to maintain the rate of 12,000 or more cuts per minute. Too, the diameter of the cutterhead has a direct effect on the quality of the finished stock: A larger drum has a shallower arc, which in turn produces a smoother, less rippled cut.

A well-designed fence can make the difference between an ordinary tool and a truly versatile one. It should go without saying that the fence should be firmly mounted and at least half the length of the overall table. At least one manufacturer offers a fence that, in addition to tilting and sliding, can be skewed, or angled, on a pivot to facilitate cutting certain species without damaging the stock. For safety, all models with a laterally adjustable fence should have a provision for guarding the exposed part of the cutterhead behind the fence face.

The size of the drive motor will depend upon the capacity of the jointer and the type of work you plan on doing with it. A 6″ machine with $^3/_4$ horsepower would more than likely be adequate for a hobbyist dressing odd pieces of mixed stock. On the other hand, someone working with larger hardwood boards on a regular basis would probably be better off with a 10″ or 12″ jointer coupled to a motor with $1^1/_2$ or more horsepower. Be careful not to interpret horsepower claims as the sole measure of a machine's cutting ability. Some manufacturers state peak, rather than continuous, power, so it's best to use the motor's amperage rating as a standard. A minimum of 10 amps of power is required to generate about one horsepower at 110 volts, or two horsepower at 220 volts.

The Two-in-One Tools

The jointer and the thickness planer are subordinate only to the table saw in the hierarchy of woodshop stationary tools. That's because once a board has been rough-cut to

size, it must be faced and edged to make it smooth and square in preparation for working.

Since the jointer has the ability to remove high spots, warp and other inconsistencies which keep a board from being perfectly straight, that tool should be used first to dress one side of the rough stock. Once that is done, with that face flat, the thickness planer can be put to immediate use surfac-ing the board's opposite side to make both faces parallel.

In view of the fact that the jointer and planer work hand in hand, at least nine manufacturers have combined both tools into one compact machine that performs both functions. Domestic and European firms favor an over-and-under design in which the same cutterhead does both the jointing and planing. The Japanese are partial to a side-by-side setup in which two separate cutter-heads share a long shaft.

Each version has its pros and cons, but the major points to remember are that 1) the over-and-under models can joint and plane stock of equal width, but at the cost of reset-ting the machine for each function; 2) the side-by-sides, though readily accessible for either operation, have jointer widths only half those of their planers; and 3) over-and-

Jointers yield square edges for—you guessed it—jointing and also square up warped stock.

unders lack the extra-long jointer tables featured in their Oriental counterparts.

Don't Forget the Details

Once you've established the capacities and capabilities you'll need, begin looking for the finer points separating the cream of the crop from the run of the mill. Try to ascertain the effectiveness of the cutterhead guard throughout its full pivoting range, but be certain it's unobtrusive enough that you'll never be tempted to circumvent or remove it. Check to see that the tables move up and down freely and consistently, with a minimum of effort. It helps when one turn of the adjustment wheel represents a stated measure of movement. And look for accurate, easy-to-read scales in a convenient place.

Since the adjustment of the knives on the cutterhead is of major importance, pay particular attention to the blades' accessibility and the ease with which they can be replaced or adjusted. Some manufacturers have had the foresight to include knife gauges or other implements to assure correct settings.

Be sure that you investigate the warranty and the availability of parts and service. In the end, the amount of time you put into researching your purchase will show up in the quality of work you get out of it.

The following is a list of manufacturers or distributors whose products are oriented toward home shop, professional or light commercial use. Most are available through retail markets.

American Machine & Tool Co.
Fourth Ave. & Spring St.
Royersford, PA 19468

Andreou Industries
22-69 23rd St.
Astoria, NY 11105

Black & Decker Corp. (De Walt)
701 Joppa Rd.
Towson, MD 21204

Delta International Machinery Corp.
246 Alpha Dr.
Pittsburgh, PA 15238

Elektra Beckum U.S.A. Corp.
401-403 Kennedy Blvd.
Somerdale, NJ 08083

Emco Maier U.S.A.
2757 Scioto Pky.
Columbus, OH 43026-2334

Foley-Belsaw
6301 Equitable Rd.
Kansas City, MO 64120

Garrett Wade Co. (INCA)
161 Ave. of the Americas
New York, NY 10013

Grizzly Imports, Inc.
P.O. Box 2069
Bellingham, WA 98227

Hitachi Power Tools U.S.A., Ltd.
4487-E Park Dr.
Norcross, GA 30093

Jet Equipment & Tools
P.O. Box 1477
Tacoma, WA 98401-1477

Makita U.S.A., Inc.
12950 Alondra Blvd.
Cerritos, CA 90701

Parks Woodworking Machine Co.
1501 Knowlton St.
Cincinnati, OH 45223

Powermatic-Stanwich Industries, Inc.
Morrison Rd.
McMinnville, TN 37110

Sears, Roebuck & Co. (Craftsman)
Sears Tower
Chicago, IL 60684

Wilke Machinery Co. (Bridgewood)
120 Derry Ct.
York, PA 17402

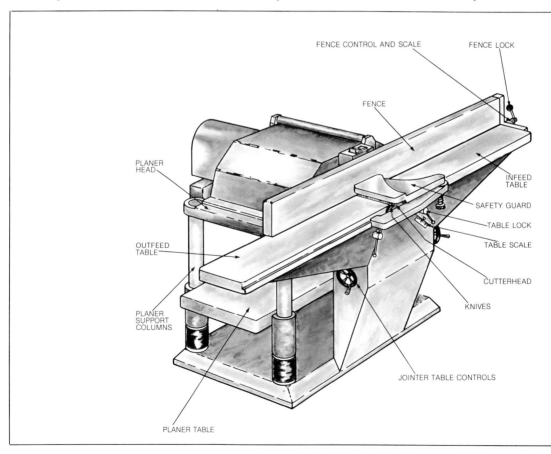

Multiple-Purpose Tools

Combination tools may incorporate as many as five conventional stationary power tools.

True to their names, multipurpose, or combination, shop tools each combine the function of five or more popular woodshop tools into a single unit—one that takes up far less floor space than even a carefully chosen assortment.

European woodworkers, who put a premium on space, provide a good market for combination tools. Here in the States, we tend more toward single-function machines, but lathe-based multipurpose designs are still popular in home shops.

The lathe-style machines use a variable-speed headstock equipped with a quill feed. With the tool positioned horizontally, the addition of a table converts the lathe into a table saw, a horizontal borer or a disc sander. In a vertical mode, the lathe becomes a drill press. Accessories may include a jointer, band saw, jigsaw and belt sander.

European manufacturers generally build their combination machines around table saws, which also drive jointers and thickness planers. A spindle shaft extended horizontally works together with a three-axis table for slot mortising or side-boring, and a vertical shaft is included for spindle shaping. Options include sanders, tenoners and jointer-planer blade sharpeners. One exception is the Emcostar 2000, which is a combination table saw and band saw. A spindle shaper and disc sander are included in the basic machine, and lathe and mortiser attachments are optional.

Convenience Is the Key

Although the point of buying a combination tool is to save work space, that goal shouldn't be achieved at the expense of performance. Make sure, when choosing a machine, that each function—and especially the ones you'll be using often, like the table saw, the band saw and the jointer—has somewhat the same characteristics you'd look for in a solo tool. Naturally, the more expensive machines boast the biggest work surfaces and the largest capacities, but in addition to measurements, you should also be discerning about such features as fence and miter accuracy, ease of adjustment and safety factors.

Equally important is the convenience of switching from one mode to another. In fact, that adaptability is the key to a successful combination tool. Even though some man-ufacturers state that you can change operations almost instantly, it's not so obvious that the machine settings themselves take considerably longer to adjust.

On the plus side, it is possible with some designs to carry the machine settings from one tool mode to the next, thus saving setup time between sequential woodworking operations. And several of the higher-priced imports use multiple motors so the machines can be split, or so two people can tackle separate undertakings simultaneously.

Shop to Suit Your Needs

For the cost of one of the bigger machines, you could fill a large shop with individual tools. But if your budget and work space are small, a moderately priced combination machine might be the answer. Just make sure that each component has the same characteristics you'd look for in a solo tool.

The following manufacturers or distributors offer products oriented toward home shop, professional or light commercial use.

AMI, Ltd.
P.O. Box 312
New Castle, DE 19720

Emco Maier U.S.A.
2757 Scioto Parkway
Columbus, OH 43026-2334

Henry Wiegand Corp.
P.O. Box 831
Claremont, NH 03743

International Woodworking
Equipment Corp.
3816 IH-35 South
San Marcos, TX 78666

Shopsmith, Inc.
3931 Image Dr.
Dayton, OH 45414

Total Shop Woodworking Tools
P.O. Box 25429
Greenville, SC 29616

Wilke Machinery Company
120 Derry Court
York, PA 17402

The Secrets of Steel

In this guide to basic metallurgy, you'll learn which steels go into which tools, and why.

Steel. Just the mention of the word stirs the blood of old soldiers, defensive line coordinators and antique tool aficionados. These last are particularly passionate. They are likely to take one peek into Grandpa's tool chest and grow weak with nostalgia. "They simply don't make steel like that anymore," they are sure to tell you, shaking their heads to convey a sense of corruption and lost innocence. Perusing mail-order catalogues for old tools only reinforces this form of ancestor worship. In them we read, for example, that it is mandatory that any steel tool worth bothering about achieve a certain hardness (60 points on the Rockwell C scale, a measure of such things). Clearly, we are dealing here with a bias toward the past. The question is whether or not (or when) that bias is justified.

It turns out that the average perspective on steel is a blend of fact and fiction, with considerable emotion thrown in. In fact, even experienced tool users are generally hard put to give an accurate, objective definition of the stuff. Yet more confusion results when brand names enter the picture, for the history of metallurgy, and of advertising, is strewn with such buzz words as Sheffield steel, cast steel, nickel steel, chrome-vanadium steel and Damascus steel, among others. Headed for the local hardware store to buy a wrench or a good pair of pliers, what is one to think? What, indeed, *is* steel?

In its simplest guise, steel is just iron that contains less than 1.7% carbon and is malleable under certain conditions. Pure metallic iron doesn't occur in nature, but must instead be extracted from one of several ores. Ores contain iron bound in iron oxides, the most common of which is rust. The iron-making process combines the ore with a flux such as limestone and heats the mixture. The oxygen bound in the oxide burns off, releasing carbon monoxide and carbon dioxide and liberating the iron as commercial cast iron with a carbon content of 4% or above. In steelmaking, the carbon content is further decreased to below 1.7%, and other impurities are removed.

From Damascus to Miki City

Steel was made by the ancients, but without predictable results and only in small amounts. In fact, one of the first steels to be

It's a long way from stacked billets to polished knives.

formed was the so-called Damascus steel, named after the town in modern Syria where the process evolved. The same method, however, was practiced simultaneously in Japan and yielded the renowned samurai swords. After the Meiji Restoration of 1868, the samurai class was abolished, and the unemployed sword makers turned their talents to making some of the finest woodworking tools in the world.

The tradition continues to this day in Japan but is largely lost in the Fertile Crescent. Rural America, of all places, nurtures the honorable history of Damascus steel; many competent practitioners of the art can be found among custom knifemakers.

The Damascus process is akin to blacksmithing. An iron billet is heated in a forge in the presence of a flux, which removes

1.6%, hardness doesn't increase, but the ability to hold an edge improves markedly. A high-carbon steel is often called a water-hardened steel, because this is the only quench that can be used during heat-treating.

For tools that aren't subjected to high temperature or to wet or corrosive environments, a water-hardened steel is quite adequate. Woodworking tools meet such criteria, and Grandpa's fabled instruments are probably made from such a high-carbon steel.

Alloys

Long ago, steelmakers developed the process of alloying: adding other ingredients to steel to gain useful properties. The addition of tungsten, for instance, makes high-speed steel (HSS), which has the property of hot hardness. This means that the steel maintains its temper at high working temperatures. Modern manufacturing depends on cutting tools made from such steels.

Alloying steel with nickel and large amounts of chrome makes stainless steel, which no modern kitchen could do without. A few other common alloying elements and what they do to improve steel follow:

Manganese reduces brittleness and improves forgeability. Large amounts (above 0.6%) permit oil- rather than water-quenching. The oil quench is less severe and results in less warping and distortion.

Silicon isn't really an alloying element in itself but rather acts as a deoxidizer. In concert with other elements, it improves the hot-forming ability of the steel.

Vanadium improves the forgeability of the steel and tends to be a strong carbide former. In large amounts, grindability suffers, and there's a characteristic white spark.

Molybdenum in small amounts improves hardening and toughness. In large amounts, it is an economic alternative to tungsten.

Cobalt increases the hot hardness of a steel but reduces toughness.

Chromium improves hardenability and together with carbon increases wear resistance and toughness. A chromium tool steel shouldn't be confused with a stainless steel, which has a very high percentage of chromium.

Nickel is usually used with other alloying elements, particularly chromium, to improve toughness.

some of the carbon from the metal's surface. Then the hot billet is folded in half and hammered out flat again. More flux is added and the procedure is repeated. In Japan, this method of steelmaking is ritualistic; the billet is folded a minimum of 10 times, which yields 1,024 layers of steel. The result is a stratified piece of material with layers ranging in make-up from iron to structural steel to high-carbon tool steel. Correctly done, the technique produces a superlative piece of steel that holds a keen edge and is very tough. (To a metallurgist, *toughness* is the ability to withstand shock.)

The down side of the Damascus process is that it is slow, unpredictable and demanding. Each piece must be individually tested, and the customer pays for the rejects. Fortunately, modern steelmaking has removed much of the guesswork. With no disrespect to Grandpa, we enjoy much higher-quality steel than he ever did. For the most part,

we're probably lucky that they don't make steel like that anymore.

Hardness, Meet Heat-Treating

Tool hardness is generally measured on the Rockwell C scale, a test that measures the penetration of a diamond-pointed tool into the work under a specific load. Diamond rates Rc100, and structural, or mild, steel measures around Rc30. A file generally Rockwells out to about 65.

Hardness and carbon content are intrinsically but indirectly related. To be tool-quality, a steel should have a carbon content between 0.6% and 1.7%—an amount that allows heat-treating for extra hardness. Below 0.5% carbon, we have structural steel that cannot be heat-treated. With heat-treating, hardness rises as carbon content rises, to a limit of about Rc65 at about 1% carbon. As the carbon content rises above 1% toward

Two factors influence what steel will be used to make a tool: the ultimate demands on the tool, and how it will be manufactured. Common manufacturing methods include cutting, grinding, machining and forging. Nowadays forging usually means drop forging, a process in which a molten steel blank is placed between male and female dies in a press. The press is repeatedly closed on the blank to forge it to the desired shape. Drop-forged tools, such as wrenches and hammers, are known for their toughness.

A high-speed steel wouldn't be a good choice for a tool which was to be forged. HSS doesn't forge well and has to be machined and ground to shape. Likewise, a steel with large amounts of vanadium isn't good for a tool that requires a lot of grinding.

In today's competitive marketplace, we must realize that every manufacturer is under cost restraints. Picking the right steel is a careful balance between quality and economy.

The How of Heat-Treating

The composition of the steel is only half the battle in producing a fine tool; heat-treatment is equally important. Steel is usually delivered from the mill in a soft (called fully annealed) state because it is much easier to cut, shape and work. The steel is usually kept soft throughout the manufacturing process, leaving heat-treatment as one of the last steps.

Today, more tool failures can be traced to heat-treating problems than to the steel itself. Modern steelmakers make highly consistent steel; it's heat-treating that imparts the specific qualities desirable for particular tools—the balance of hardness and toughness.

Simple water-hardened steels were traditionally heat-treated by the local blacksmith as part of fashioning tools for local use. Today this method is practiced mostly as a marriage of artistry and nostalgia, but it does offer a down-to-earth way to understand the process.

When the blacksmith has the tool forged to its final shape, he places it back in the forge and brings it to a bright cherry red color. Then he quenches the tool by plunging it into water. Although the quenching process seems rather casual, it *must* be done in such a way that steam pockets don't build up

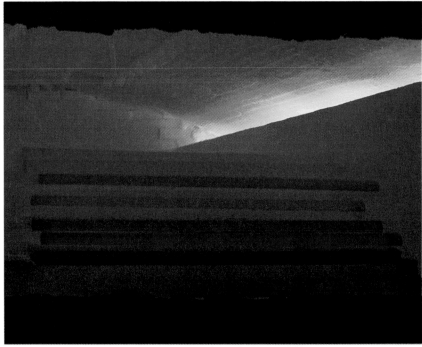

around the work. Steam insulates, preventing heat transfer and creating soft spots. After quenching, the blacksmith's steel is as hard as it can get—limited only by the carbon content. With 1% or more carbon, this is Rc60 to Rc65.

The problem with a water quench is that it's very severe, and warpage, distortion and even cracking can occur. It's not uncommon for a knife blank to come out of the forge nice and straight but emerge from the quench badly bowed. Sharp inside corners are avoided with tools made from water-quenched steels because cracks often form at such places.

Metallurgists working in the first half of this century therefore came up with oil- and air-quenched steels to avoid such problems. For the steel structure to change from soft to hard, the rate of cooling during quench is crucial. By alloying manganese into the steel, the rate of cooling is slowed and oil rather than water quenching can be used. Today we even have steels that can be air-quenched by simply placing them in front of a fan. Such steels have made possible the high-precision parts of the space age.

Proper quenching isn't enough to produce a useful tool, however. A steel that's merely quenched is so hard that it lacks toughness

and would be like a frozen turkey when dropped. Therefore, our blacksmith next *tempers* the tool by drawing back some of the hardness to a good compromise between hardness and toughness. To temper, he first polishes the tool to a bright finish. Then he slowly and evenly heats it over the forge, watching carefully.

Carbon steels turn specific colors at specific temperatures. As a rule of thumb, edge tools such as knives and chisels are drawn to pale yellow or straw, which is around Rc60 or better. Other tools—such as axes, auger bits and cabinet scrapers—need more toughness, so they're drawn back to bright blue to achieve Rc45.

This same blue made Colt percussion pistols beautiful to behold and gives clock springs their characteristic color. In fact, a blue temper was often called spring temper. Today we don't necessarily blue guns; we sometimes black oxide them. Black oxide suffers cosmetically but wins on corrosion resistance and cheapness of application.

One advantage of tempering by eye is that on a tool with a thin edge, such as a chisel, the heat can be applied to the shank in back of the edge. The heat then travels up to the edge. If the edge is pale yellow or straw, the shank is generally bright or even light blue.

Tool Steels by Letter Classification

Type of Steel	Letter	Main Alloying Element
High-speed tool steels	M	Molybdenum types
	T	Tungsten types
Hot-work tool steels	H1–H19	Chromium types
	H20–H39	Tungsten types
	H40–H59	Molybdenum types
Cold-work tool steels	D	High-carbon—high-chromium
	A	Medium-alloy—air-hardened
	O	Oil-hardened
Shock-resisting steels	S	. . . .
Water-hardened steels	W	Carbon

For example, an M2 steel is an HSS in which large amounts of molybdenum replace some of the tungsten as the principal alloying element. M2 is an excellent HSS used extensively for cutting tools in the metal-working industry. O1 is an oil-quenched tool steel used in machine shops to fashion small tools, drill bushings and the like.

Thus the tool has hardness at the edge and toughness in the shank—a good combination.

Most modern toolmakers temper by placing the work in an accurately controlled oven and heating to the desired temperature. The work doesn't have to be polished, and the skill, art and guesswork are eliminated.

Shopping

Let's look at some common hardware store items and analyze what steels should be used, starting with screwdrivers: They come in all grades and are used for just about any conceivable purpose. A good screwdriver should be made from a high-carbon steel. It's not generally subjected to high temperature or a corrosive environment, so an HSS or stainless steel is unnecessary. What's needed most in a screwdriver is toughness, and a properly heat-treated, water-hardened steel does the job in style. Heat-treating is the key: The tool should be drawn to about Rc40.

Very cheap screwdrivers are made from low-carbon steel, often called 1018 or cold-rolled steel. As anyone who has used such an imitation knows, the tip mushrooms and slips when any real torque is applied. A 1018 screwdriver is useless as a pry bar, because it bends easily. (You aren't supposed to use a screwdriver as a crowbar. But let's face it, we all do.)

On the other end of the spectrum, there are very expensive screwdrivers claiming exotic steel and special grinding methods. However, a middle-of-the-road screwdriver is probably the way to go. You get high-carbon steel and good heat-treatment. You might have to regrind the tips of new screwdrivers anyway, and it's a procedure you might as well get used to doing. Just avoid burning the steel with the grinder, and relegate older (progressively smaller) screwdrivers to smaller and smaller screws.

Next, let's look at drills. Traditional woodworking auger bits are made from high-carbon steel and are heat-treated to about Rc45. Such tools have stood the test of centuries, and there's little need to change today's manufacturing techniques. Perhaps because they're not a part of the average homeowner's tool collection, there's not been too much impetus to build cheap versions for the mass market.

The ubiquitous twist drill is another matter. Twist bits are used for drilling both wood and metal, making them universal in many people's minds, and there's a wide variance in quality and steel. Cheap twist drills are usually made from high-carbon steel.

They're fine for woodworking but fail miserably when applied to metal. The least heat build-up and they lose their temper and edge.

HSS is a far superior material for twist drills. It offers hot hardness along with increased toughness and edge-holding ability. Most good twist drills have HSS marked on either the box or the shank of the drill itself. Cheap drills say either carbon steel or nothing at all. You'll find that the quality of a twist drill is commensurate with its price.

Then there are chisels. The traditional material is a water-hardened steel, and in this case what was good for Grandpa is good for us. A chisel isn't subjected to high temperature or great shock, so carbon steel does nicely. The exceptions are chisels used for wood turning. Most experienced wood turners turned in their chisels some years ago. HSS is far superior, because turners grind constantly and you have to worry about overheating. This is really a special case, however, and for plain old wood chisels, stick with carbon steel.

Finally, let's look at knives. Steel for a knife should meet about the same criteria as that for a chisel, save one—corrosion resistance. Even pocketknives are subjected to corrosive environments. Be that as it may, years ago no self-respecting tool maniac would be caught dead with a stainless-steel knife. Stainless just wouldn't hold an edge the way high-carbon steel would, and even chefs wouldn't touch it. Back then, stainless meant cheap knives in the public mind.

Then, in the early '60s, a new 440 family of stainless steels burst upon the scene, and the public accepted it quickly. The grade used in cutlery is 440C, and it combines the rust resistance of stainless steel with the toughness and edge-holding quality of tool steel. Most good knives even advertise the use of 440C stainless. It's great steel and highly recommended for the pocket and the kitchen.

The intricacies of metallurgy have barely been touched on here. And as a buyer's guide, the information is limited to the products of manufacturers who show the good grace (or confidence) to tell you what the tool is made of. But knowledge is empowering in itself. The result of your awareness may be to encourage toolmakers who take pride in their work, and from that we'll all benefit.

A Handsaw Selection Handbook

When you master this basic hand tool, you gain the versatility of the traditional cutting edge.

In centuries past, carpenters and other workers in wood constructed the finest buildings and furnishings the world has ever known—items that today are considered classics—and they did it all without ever once pulling the trigger on a portable circular saw or flipping the switch on a radial arm. They used handsaws, plain and simple.

Few carpenters or cabinetmakers these days, professional or avocational, would give up their power tools, and for good reason. But even today, for some jobs, *only* a handsaw will do. Let's review some of the more common, though not necessarily commonly known, types of handsaws and their uses in modern carpentry and cabinetmaking.

Saw Talk

When discussing and shopping for handsaws, it's helpful to have a handle on the ap-

plicable terminology. Aside from the straightforward names for the parts of a handsaw (see the illustration), the term you're most likely to encounter is *PPI*, or points per inch. Look for it on the cardboard wrappers of new saws, as well as on the blades of some models, where it's stamped into the metal near the handle. PPI refers to the number of teeth, or points, a particular saw carries per inch of blade. (Since the count often ends in the middle of a tooth, most manufacturers round up to the next highest number. Thus, a saw with a PPI of 8 might actually have 7½ teeth per inch.) In general, the higher its PPI, the slower a saw will cut and the smoother it will leave the sawn edges.

A second term that indicates something about how a particular saw will cut is *set*. If teeth were simply cut into the edge of a piece of metal to form a saw blade, the *kerf*, or

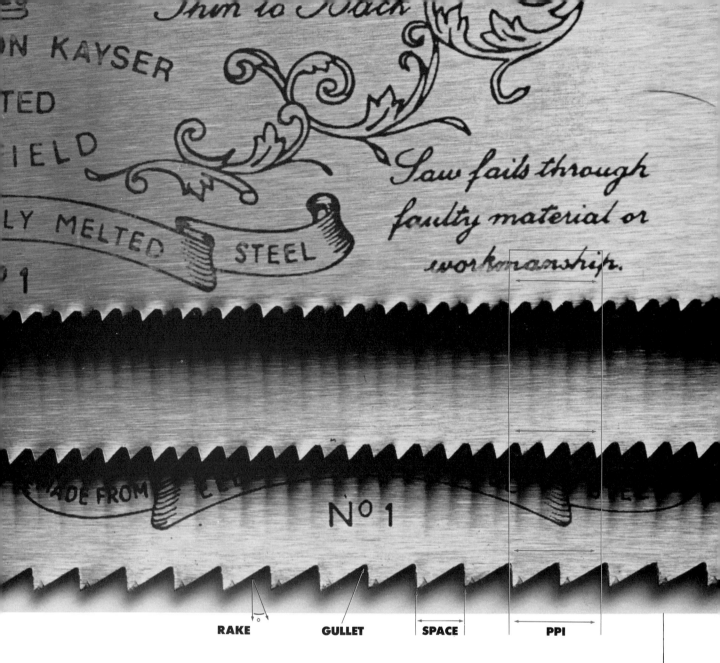

RAKE   **GULLET**   **SPACE**   **PPI**

channel cut by that blade, would be exactly the same width as the blade itself. Inevitably, as the friction of cutting warmed the blade, pinching would result. To help alleviate pinching, some clever Roman saw maker invented set.

To set a saw is to bend the teeth slightly outward, away from the blade, in an alternating pattern—one tooth right, the next tooth left and so on—along the full length of the blade. A saw with set teeth cuts a channel somewhat wider than the thickness of the blade. Generally, the larger the teeth (and, consequently, the lower the PPI), the greater will be the set, the faster the saw will cut, the wider will be the kerf and the rougher will be the resultant sawn surfaces. The hand tool used to perform the setting operation looks something like a convoluted pair of pliers and is called, quite logically, a saw set.

Other handsaw jargon you might someday encounter includes *space*, the tip-to-tip distance between two teeth; *gullet*, the slot, or valley, between two teeth; *pad*, a British term for handle that sailed with handsaws to America and has, to some extent, held on; and *rake*, the angle, or slant, at which a saw's teeth incline forward or backward. A saw having forward-raked teeth (as most have) will cut on the forward stroke, while a saw having teeth with reverse rake (as with some Japanese models) will cut on the pull stroke; a saw with neutral (no) rake will cut (though not always efficiently) in both directions.

General-Purpose Handsaws

While some cabinetmaking cuts are curved or made at angles with the stock's grain (mitered), the overwhelming majority of carpentry cuts are made in one of two directions—either with the grain (ripping) or across the grain (crosscutting). There's a special handsaw design for each of these operations, though at first glance they look almost identical.

Both *crosscut saws* and *ripsaws* have backs that are skewed—that is, angled down from the handle to the point. (In fact, the technically proper name for this style of handsaw is *skew-backed*.) Standard lengths for both designs are 26″ for full-sized tools and 16″ for compact models intended to fit in a carpenter's toolbox. The difference between crosscuts and ripsaws lies not in their overall forms but in the configuration of their teeth.

Ripsaws have relatively large, wide-set teeth measuring 3 to 7 points per inch ($5\frac{1}{2}$ is common). The faces of ripsaw teeth are chisel-sharpened (filed flat, or perpendicular to the plane of the blade). When ripping, or sawing with the grain, chiseling is the

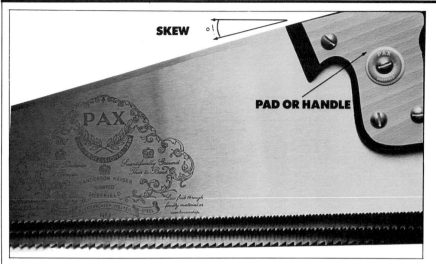

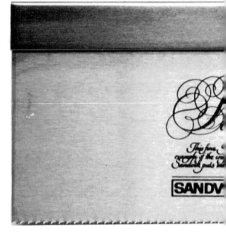

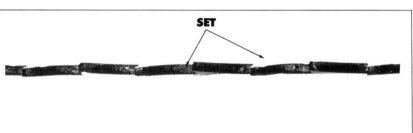

most efficient form of cutting—rather like planing on a miniature scale.

Crosscut saws have smaller, more close-set teeth than do ripsaws; they come in PPIs from 7 to 12, with 10 points per inch considered standard and suitable for both rough carpentry and cabinetwork. The faces of crosscut teeth are sharpened on a bevel to the plane of the blade, like a knife. This allows the teeth to slice (as opposed to chiseling their way) through the grain of the wood.

Do you really need both a crosscut and a ripsaw? Well, yes and no. Certainly every serious woodworker needs a good crosscut handsaw; its uses, both for rough-in construction and in the project shop, are numerous. There's always a board in need of being cut to length, and frequently it's more time- and energy-efficient simply to have at it with a handsaw than to mess with unchaining an electrical extension cord and searching for

an outlet while setting up a power tool.

But ripping—now that's a cut of a different breed. For serious handsaw ripping, such as sawing an 8′ 2 X 4 its full length to make two 2 X 2s, and for most other ripping, even of thin stock, it's far more efficient to use a portable circular saw or, better yet, a table unit. It's understandable, then, why most folks who own ripping handsaws simply don't use them all that much.

Special-Purpose Handsaws

If your only or primary use of a handsaw will be for household repairs and crafting the occasional doghouse, bookcase or other simple carpentry or cabinetry project, a crosscut or combination crosscut-ripsaw will probably be all the handsaw you'll ever need. But should your projects someday become more demanding, so will your need for

special-purpose tools. Fortunately, one of the handsaw's greatest attributes is its low price; you can purchase a whole assortment of good handsaws for less than the price of a single portable power saw of comparable quality. Let's look at a few of the most useful special-purpose designs.

Backsaws and dovetails. A *backsaw* is a crosscut handsaw with a standard (fingers-through) handle and a thin but rigid rectangular blade that's 10″ to 30″ long (12″ and 14″ are common and useful sizes). To assure absolute rigidity, the backsaw's blade is reinforced with a steel or brass rib running the full length of its back—thus the name. To provide smooth cuts, the backsaw's teeth are fine, numbering from 10 to 16 PPI, with 12 or 14 being a good choice.

A backsaw is handy any time you need to make smooth, dead-straight cuts, as when fabricating precision joints. Used in conjunc-

BACKSAW

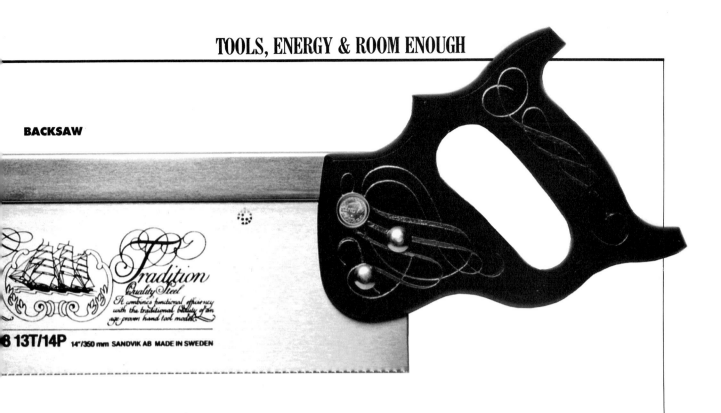

DOZUKI

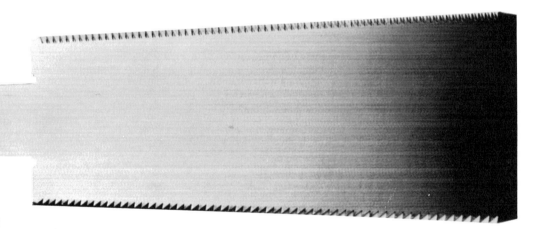

tion with a *miter box*, the backsaw becomes the perfect hand tool for cutting the corner joints of molding and picture frames. (A miter box is a portable jig that provides a stable sawing platform and clamps a backsaw at any of several adjustable angles while allowing it to slide smoothly back and forth for sawing. Once you set a miter box up for, say, 45° cuts, all you have to do is position the stock on the box's cutting shelf and start sawing—no need to lay out a guideline on the stock or to recheck the angle on subsequent cuts, and no chance of making slanted or off-angle cuts.)

The *dovetail saw* is a small backsaw. It, too, has a thin rectangular blade stiffened with a rib along its back, but the dovetail is only about half the size of the backsaw, with a cutting depth (teeth to back) rarely exceeding 2″. It ranges in length from 8″ to 10″ and in PPI from 15 to 21. Another significant difference between the backsaw and the dovetail is that the latter's handle is of the type used on files and chisels, jutting straight out or angling slightly up from the top back of the saw, rather than being a standard fingers-through grip.

As suggested by its name, the dovetail (also sometimes called a *cabinet*, or *tenon, saw*), with its small size and fine teeth, is designed for cutting joints and other precision work required in cabinetmaking and furniture building. It is not, however, used with a miter box.

Compass and keyhole saws. The saws we've discussed thus far all have one thing in common: They're designed for making straight cuts and straight cuts only. The blades of all of them, even the little dovetail, are far too wide to follow the radius of even a slow curve. For that, we need a saw with a narrow, tapered blade—a *compass saw*.

With a 12″ to 14″ tempered steel blade that comes almost to a point at the front and is only an inch or two wide where it fits into a pistol-grip handle, the compass saw can be inserted into a starter hole made with a drill, then manipulated to saw out either an arcing or a rectangular shape entirely within the interior of the stock.

The teeth of a compass saw are of the crosscut (bevel-sharpened) type, set lightly if at all, and, at 8 to 10 PPI, are fairly large considering the saw's delicate size. A compass saw's blade is most often clamped in its handle with studs and wing nuts, allowing for ease of blade replacement. (In fact, some manufacturers now offer "saw nests" consisting of one handle and several interchangeable blades of various sizes and tooth patterns.)

An even more petite (10″ to 12″ long) and fine-toothed mate of the compass saw is the

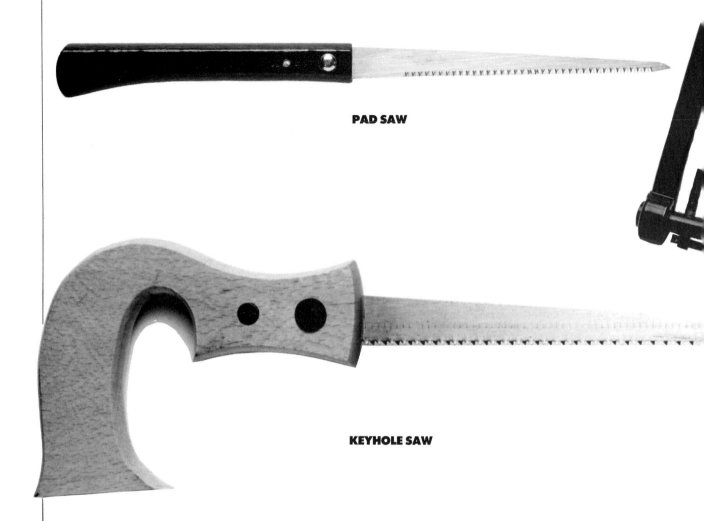

PAD SAW

KEYHOLE SAW

keyhole saw. The keyhole may have either a pistol-grip or a file-type handle, the latter sometimes being called a *pad saw* or a *minihacksaw*.

Suitable for sawing plasterboard and composition paneling as well as wood, compass and keyhole saws are favorites of electricians and plumbers, who frequently must cut small openings in ceilings, floors and walls through which to run wires and pipes.

Coping saws and their kin. A *coping saw* (sometimes called a *scroll saw* or *jigsaw*) looks something like a blocky hacksaw and consists of a U-shaped spring-steel frame with a file-type handle. The coping saw mounts a thin, flexible, band-type blade under tension across the open end of the U (generally employing a mounting pin at the front and a wing-nut screw adjustment at the rear). The PPI of a coping saw blade may be so high as to defy counting with the naked eye.

For making interior cuts, one end of the blade may be detached, slipped through a drilled starter hole in the stock, then reattached to the frame for sawing. Similarly, the blade can be reversed for cutting on either the push or pull stroke.

The coping saw is, in effect, the hand-powered equivalent of the electric band saw and is used for the same purposes: cutting tight curves and the most intricate scrolls.

Coping saws average about 12″ long (blade length) with 5″ to 7″ of clearance between blade and frame. This blade-to-frame clearance is known as "throat"—which explains why one variety of coping saw having exaggerated clearance is known as a "deep-throat." An extra-small coping saw is called a *fret saw*, and though designed for shaping the intricate fretwork of wooden stringed instruments, it also has numerous uses in cabinetwork.

Handsaw Shopping

What to look for in a handsaw?

The blade of a top-quality saw will be of fine tempered steel: Thump it a good one with your knuckles and listen for a ring rather than a thud, then flex it and look for it to spring back straight, promptly upon release. A good blade will also be highly polished to help reduce friction in sawing. (Some models are available with Teflon-coated blades, which are wonderfully smooth—for as long as the coating lasts. For an odd-job saw, Teflon is great; but for a saw that will receive regular and rugged use, no.)

The blades of the best crosscuts and ripsaws are double-taper-ground, making them slightly thicker at the toothed edge than at the back and slightly thicker at the heel than at the toe. This aids the set of the teeth in

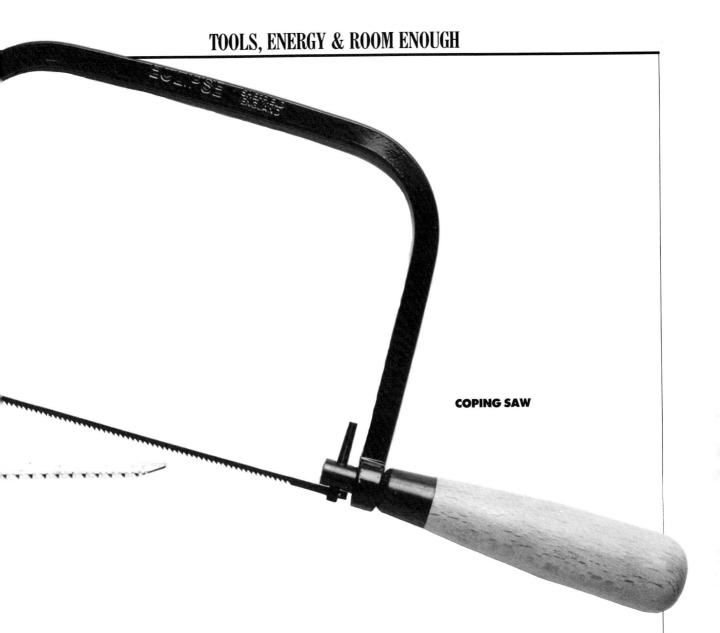

COPING SAW

preventing kerf pinching. Professional-quality handsaw blades also are often ever-so-slightly crowned, or arched, along the toothed edge, so that the center of the cutting edge is a bit higher than either the toe or heel.

Hold the saw up to good light and inspect the faces of the teeth. Are they sharpened evenly and smoothly? Looking down the row of teeth, is the set consistent?

Look for sturdy and well-finished handles of hardwood or good tough plastic. Check the fit in your palm. Is the angle at which the handle is mounted to the blade comfortable for your build and sawing style? Now, holding the blade in one hand and the handle in the other, check for looseness; there should be none.

Want an easier way to determine quality in handsaws? In four words—shop for brand names. Handsaws are such inexpensive tools

to begin with that it just doesn't pay to "save" a few more dollars or cents by purchasing discount quality.

Storage and Maintenance of Handsaws

A good handsaw deserves the same respect and care due any fine tool. Never force a saw into a cut: Go gently, allowing the tool to penetrate the wood at its own set pace. When working, be careful where you place your handsaws between uses—never on the ground or floor where they might get tromped on, and never tossed carelessly in a tooth-dulling heap with other metal tools. Many sawhorses have shelves beneath the top crosspiece; these shelves are excellent places to store your handsaws between cuts.

For longer-term storage, either hang your handsaws vertically on a wall or in a tool cabinet (many saws come with a hole near the toe

of the blade for just this purpose) or store them in a specially designed cabinet that allows the saws to rest on their backs, teeth up, with a lid to protect the teeth from being dulled or accidentally injuring someone. Shorter, toolbox-model saws should be placed on special trays to keep them away from other tools.

It's a good idea to wipe the blades of your handsaws occasionally with a lightly oiled cloth. If a blade should become corroded (as after being exposed to salt water or left out in the rain), restore its smooth finish by polishing with fine-grade steel wool, then oil lightly.

Occasionally, at intervals determined by use and care, your handsaws will need to be resharpened and reset. Our forebears in the woodworking trades, of course, took care of these little chores themselves. Today, most of us take our saws to a sharpening shop.

Build a Superior Sawhorse

With ingenuity, even something as fundamental as a sawhorse can be improved upon.

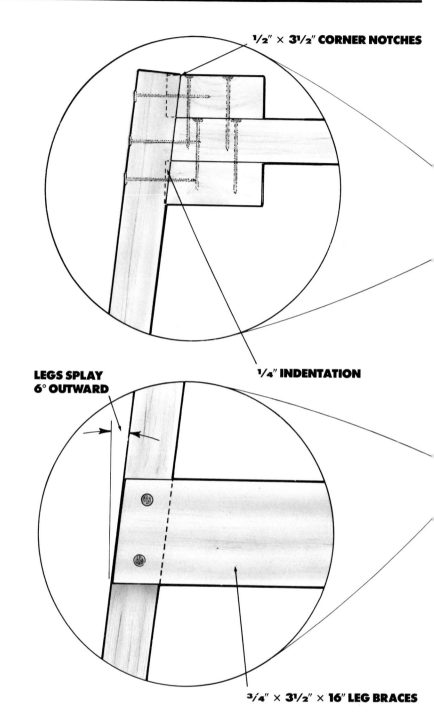

1/2" × 31/2" CORNER NOTCHES

1/4" INDENTATION

LEGS SPLAY 6° OUTWARD

3/4" × 31/2" × 16" LEG BRACES

Though the traditional sawhorse is a staple of every construction site, there's always room for improvement; and if a wobbly workstand and an unwieldly 2 X 4 ever combined to give you an unkind cut, you might be interested in knocking together our "foolproof" framing horse.

Take a look at the design. The longitudinal trough at the top is sized to accommodate a 2 X 4 of any length, and prevents it from skewing under pressure from the saw. The crosswise channel near the center of the horse lets the blade pass through the work freely, and the flush, 1' X 3' surface serves as a compact bench for hammering or measuring.

Perhaps best of all is the fact that the whole project can be put together from three 8' 2 X 4s and a scrap of 1 X 4, at a cost roughly equivalent to that of just one pair of conventional sawhorse brackets. Nearly as tempting, it'll require only a handsaw, a hammer and a tape measure to build.

The first step is to cut the 2 X 4s, using the illustration as a guide. Pay particular at-

tention to the 101/4" crosspieces at the top, as they must be trimmed at a slight angle to butt squarely against the splayed legs. Likewise, when cutting the 1/2" X 31/2" corner notches in the 14" and 19" platform boards, use that same angle to assure a good fit. The 36" brace rails should also be notched slightly at their upper corners for the same reason; a 1/4" indentation measured at the surface will suffice.

Next, using 8d common nails, fasten the legs to the sides of the brace rails at the

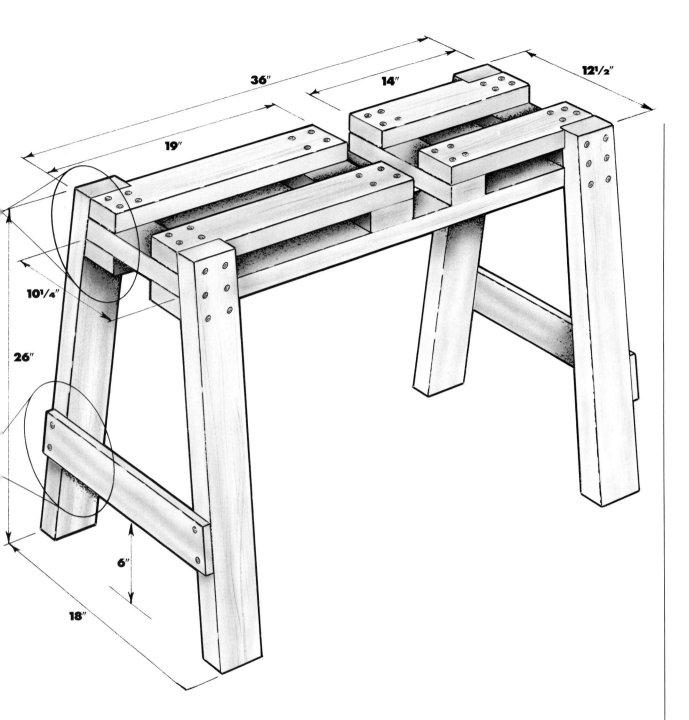

36"

14"

12½"

19"

10¼"

26"

6"

18"

notches. There should be 3" of 2 X 4 protruding beyond the upper surface of the rails, and the legs ought to join those bars perpendicularly. Once that's done, you can connect the two halves of the horse by nailing the two 10¼" cross braces between the ends, and the 10¾" struts near the center—one 14" from one end, and the other 19" from the other, leaving a 3" space between.

Finish up by laying the platform boards over the cross braces and nailing them down (make sure a sample 2 X 4 slips between

them). Drive a few more fasteners through the sides of the legs and into the ends of the short braces and the edges of the corner notches, then lock the whole shebang up tight by cutting your scrap of 1 X 4 into two 16" lengths and tacking each one between the outer edges of each leg set, about 6" up from the bottom. Finally, check the joints and trim any protruding corners with the handsaw to make sure they're flush.

At first, you'll probably be taken with the fact that this cutting bench makes stud trim-

ming a breeze, because the lumber stays where you put it and the blade doesn't tend to bind. But after a while, you'll begin to realize that it works with shorter boards as well, and gives you the option of using a circular saw in the center or a handsaw at the ends. Then too, it could be lengthened if necessary to provide additional support for even longer pieces.

Any way you cut it, it'd be hard to beat this pony for the price, especially when you consider that one does the work of two.

Three-Way Sharpener

Knife and tool blade maintenance made easy

To a person accustomed to working with cutting tools, a sharp edge is one of life's little pleasures. And few whetstone wielders would deny that the triple-face sharpener shown here is a great new twist on an old grind.

To begin with, the tool is sturdy yet compact, which is a welcome combination in a work area where space is at a premium. In addition, its multiple-stone arbor provides coarse, medium or fine honing surfaces at the turn of a handle and secures each one in position with a simple horseshoe pin clamp. Furthermore, the arbor rests in an oil- or water-filled pan that continually bathes the two unused stones in their appropriate lubricating medium. If you wish, you can also make a protective cover that doubles as a ramp for use with roller-type chisel- and plane-blade sharpening guides.

If you think you might like to give this inexpensive multiple-stone hone a try, you'll need to gather up a 32" length of 1 X 4; a piece of $^3/_4$" plywood or one-by that's at least $4^1/_4$" wide and about 14" long; a block of hardwood measuring 2" X 2" X 3"; a $^1/_2$" X 12" steel shaft; a $^3/_{32}$" X $1^1/_2$" expansion pin; a $^1/_2$"-bore, 3"-diameter pulley; a $^3/_{16}$" X 13" steel rod; a $^1/_2$" X $9^1/_2$" rubber hose with a $^3/_{16}$" orifice; a $^1/_8$" X $^3/_4$" X $20^1/_4$" piece of aluminum flat stock; a $2^1/_2$"-deep, $5^1/_4$" X $9^1/_4$" bread pan; three $^3/_4$" X 2" X 7" sharpening stones in your choice of composition and grade; and the assorted fastening hardware called for in our illustration.

The box is easily made by first ripping the 1 X 4 down to $2^3/_4$" in width, then cutting it into two $5^1/_4$" and two $10^3/_4$" pieces. Drill a $^1/_2$" hole—centered and $^3/_8$" below one edge of each of the shorter boards—then fasten the box sides to the ends using eight

No. 6 X $1^1/_4$" flathead wood screws. (Take the time to countersink the heads and fill the holes, too.)

Next, push the pan firmly into the frame and mark the positions for the holes that will receive the arbor shaft, using the $^1/_2$" bores in the ends as guides. Remove the pan to drill the openings, then set it back in place and secure it to the box with four No. 6 X $^1/_2$" wood screws fastened through the rim lip.

To make the arbor, you'll first need to cut the hardwood block into an equilateral triangle with $^1/_2$"-wide flats instead of corners. Then, by carefully dividing lines struck between the centers of each opposite flat surface, you can determine the exact center of the block and bore it longitudinally with a $^1/_2$" Forstner or auger bit. With this done, cut the piece into three 1"-wide sections to

make a set of triangular stone supports.

Before you install the blocks, slide one of them onto the shaft until it's at a point that will correspond with the center of the bread pan when the arbor's in place. Then drill a $^3/_{32}$" hole through a wide flat, the middle of the rod and part of the block behind it. Remove the wood, and slip the shaft into the holes in the frame and pan, sliding the blocks on as you go and making certain the drilled piece is in the center.

Once the shaft is positioned in the frame, cut your aluminum stock into three equal pieces; arrange the blocks so the middle one is lined up with the hole in the axle and the end sections are centered about 6" apart. Tap the expansion pin into the cross-bored socket, then turn the other two blocks so the flats are in line. Set an aluminum strip on one row

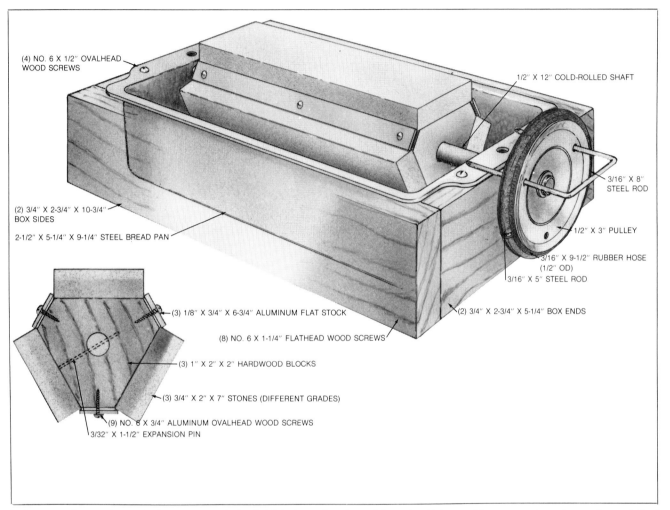

(4) NO. 6 X 1/2" OVALHEAD WOOD SCREWS

1/2" X 12" COLD-ROLLED SHAFT

3/16" X 8" STEEL ROD

(2) 3/4" X 2-3/4" X 10-3/4" BOX SIDES

2-1/2" X 5-1/4" X 9-1/4" STEEL BREAD PAN

1/2" X 3" PULLEY

3/16" X 9-1/2" RUBBER HOSE (1/2" OD)

3/16" X 5" STEEL ROD

(3) 1/8" X 3/4" X 6-3/4" ALUMINUM FLAT STOCK

(8) NO. 6 X 1-1/4" FLATHEAD WOOD SCREWS

(2) 3/4" X 2-3/4" X 5-1/4" BOX ENDS

(3) 1" X 2" X 2" HARDWOOD BLOCKS

(3) 3/4" X 2" X 7" STONES (DIFFERENT GRADES)

(9) NO. 8 X 3/4" ALUMINUM OVALHEAD WOOD SCREWS

3/32" X 1-1/2" EXPANSION PIN

of narrow flats and drill $^3/_{32}$" pilot holes through the metal and into the wood. Enlarge the openings in the strip, insert the aluminum screws, then repeat this procedure on the other two rows.

To fasten the stones in place, simply lay them on the broad flats and tighten the strips so their edges catch the lower shoulders of each stone. (You may need another pair of hands to accomplish this.) If you plan on using stones larger or smaller than the ones we chose, you'll have to adjust the size of your hardwood triangles accordingly—and perhaps that of the strips as well—but the method of securing the abrasives will remain the same.

At this point, you can attach the pulley to the exposed end of the arbor shaft and mark the location of the three $^7/_{32}$" holes

that hold the horseshoe clamp. These should be drilled equidistant from one another so that any pair will be even with the top of the pan as the pulley is rotated into position. Cut an 8" piece from the $^3/_{16}$" X 13" steel rod and bend it into a U shape with a spread to match the holes; taper the rod's tips, then reorient the pulley on the shaft so the clamp and one of the stones are on the same plane. You can make a simple grip by bending the leftover section of rod into an arc and using it to join the ends of the rubber hose to form a loop around the pulley groove.

The sharpening guide ramp is assembled with basic butt joints. First cut your $4^1/_4$"-wide, $^3/_4$" board into $1^5/_8$", $3^1/_4$" and $8^1/_2$" lengths, then use a coping saw to make $^1/_2$"-wide slots in the center of the legs—1" deep in the shorter piece and 3" deep in the longer

one. (You can terminate the cuts by predrilling a $^1/_2$" hole at the top of each slot.) Attach the platform to the legs with No. 6 X $1^1/_4$" flathead wood screws, fill the holes, and check to make sure the surface is flush and even with the stones when the ramp is in place. With that assured, coat the tool's wooden parts with varnish or polyurethane to provide a working finish.

Perhaps one of the nicest features of this bench tool is that when it's filled with an inch or so of oil or water lubricant, it's heavy enough to stay put without being clamped; and its reservoir keeps the stones moist for instant use when needed. But its primary value is that it provides a convenient method of maintaining a variety of cutting edges, a workshop chore that's all too often neglected.

True Grit

Build a surface sander to prepare perfect boards.

Chances are, if you're only an occasional woodworker, you'll never really need a surface sander. But if you do a fair amount of woodcrafting, this 12″ homebuilt tool will make a nice addition to your shop.

The framework is made of 16-gauge (about .070″), 1″-square tubular steel stock, which can be replaced with a heavier-walled material if necessary. The table is a 3′-long section of ³/₄″ plywood cut from a cabinet door; that seven-ply birch panel was an excellent choice because it's resistant to warp and has an extremely smooth finish. The sanding drum and feed rollers were fabricated from hardwood disks and dowels, respectively. The drum is spiral-wrapped with 1″ aluminum oxide machinist's cloth held with adhesive, and the rollers are covered with 1¹/₂″ reinforced rubber hose sections.

To keep the design uncomplicated, the drum is powered, but the feed rollers oper-ate manually with a hand crank. The infeed and outfeed rollers turn in unison, since they're connected with a V-belt. As you might imagine, drum sanding requires appreciable horsepower, even for a benchtop unit like this. The sander performed satisfactorily coupled to a 1-hp, 1,750-rpm capacitor-start motor, though a split-phase type would work just as well because starting torque requirements aren't that critical. A 5″ drive pulley should achieve about 3,000 rpm at the sanding drum—the equivalent of 3,450 surface feet of sanding per minute.

The sander's depth of cut is adjusted by raising or lowering the table, which is mounted on a bed hinged to the base to form a parallelogram. A length of threaded rod fastened between two clevis shafts on the base and table bed sets the table height. Any irregularities in the surface of the workpiece are taken up by spring-loaded pinion guides, which allow the rollers' axle shafts to rise up slightly under pressure from below.

An exploded illustration identifying the machine's parts and dimensioned plan views are provided to aid you in putting together your own sander. Furthermore, there are a few tips that should help.

Probably the most intimidating component is the drum, which must be assembled carefully, since it'll be exposed to a good deal of stress when the tool's in operation. The 12″-long wooden cylinder is composed of a dozen 1″ X 4³/₈″ disks glued together and pinned to a ¹/₂″ steel axle. Though the pieces—or the whole drum—could be turned on a lathe, we used a 4¹/₂″ fly cutter bit in a drill press to cut the hardwood circles.

With the disks cut and ¹/₂″ holes drilled in their centers, an aliphatic carpenter's glue or a plastic resin can be applied to cement the pieces together on the shaft. For extra insurance, you should pin the last disk (opposite the pulley) through the axle; this disk will then serve as a locator for positioning the entire drum. To be certain, trial-fit the axle and mark the hole before actually gluing the disks in place. Once the drum's fully cured, true it on a lathe or mount it in the pillow blocks and drive it with the pulley so you'll be able to cut it to a true 4³/₈″ diameter with a chisel and temporary tool rest.

The feed rollers also require some attention, though their precision isn't as critical because they don't turn at high speed. Each is made from an 11⁷/₈″ section of 1¹/₂″ banister dowel (or hardwood turned to that dimension), but instead of having straight-through axles, they use pinion shafts made from ¹/₂″ lag screws. These pinions must be centered in the rollers, so mark your starter holes very carefully before drilling the ¹¹/₃₂″ pilot holes, especially when setting up the longer 6″ lag bores at the pulley ends. Once the pinions are secured, you can cut off the heads and true the rollers as you did the drum. Don't remove too much stock, though, because the rubber hose sleeves must fit snugly over the rollers, even though each gets pinned at the pulley end.

When setting up the table frame, remember that it must remain level as it's raised and lowered. The best way to guarantee this is to be sure the holes in the hinge posts are exactly the same distance apart in each piece, and that the hinge pins in the bed and base are spaced equidistant as well.

The control mechanism simply uses the threads on the rod to hold the table at the desired height. The shorter, base-mounted clevis shaft is cross-bored and tapped for ⁵/₁₆-18 thread, while the bed-mounted piece gets a full ⁵/₁₆″ hole to allow the rod to rotate freely (it's captured with locking nuts on both sides of the shaft). Both clevis shafts are end-drilled and tapped to accept the ¹/₄-20

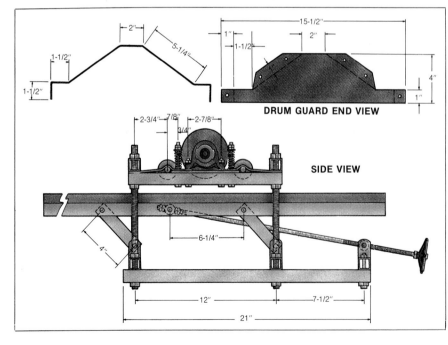

DRUM GUARD END VIEW

SIDE VIEW

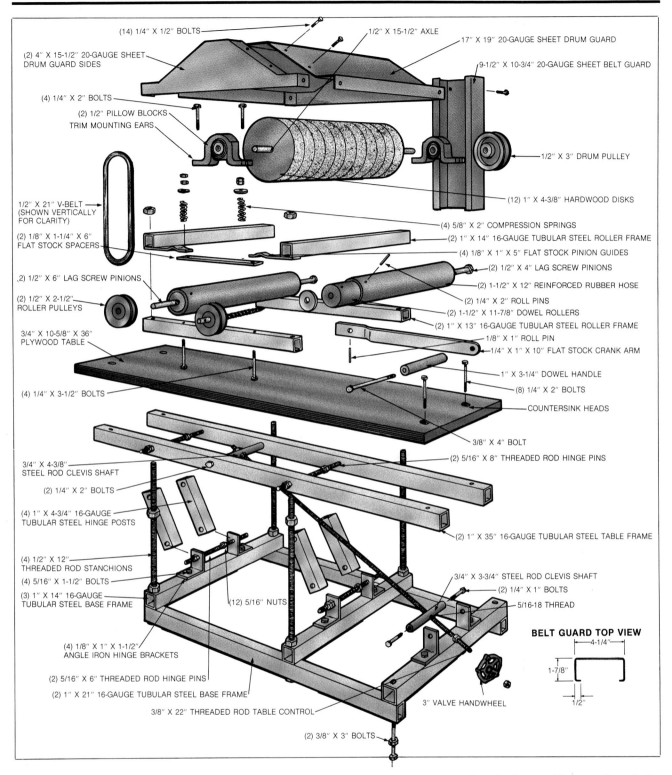

(14) 1/4" X 1/2" BOLTS

1/2" X 15-1/2" AXLE

17" X 19" 20-GAUGE SHEET DRUM GUARD

(2) 4" X 15-1/2" 20-GAUGE SHEET
DRUM GUARD SIDES

9-1/2" X 10-3/4" 20-GAUGE SHEET BELT GUARD

(4) 1/4" X 2" BOLTS

(2) 1/2" PILLOW BLOCKS
TRIM MOUNTING EARS

1/2" X 3" DRUM PULLEY

1/2" X 21" V-BELT
(SHOWN VERTICALLY
FOR CLARITY)

(12) 1" X 4-3/8" HARDWOOD DISKS

(2) 1/8" X 1-1/4" X 6"
FLAT STOCK SPACERS

(4) 5/8" X 2" COMPRESSION SPRINGS

(2) 1" X 14" 16-GAUGE TUBULAR STEEL ROLLER FRAME

(4) 1/8" X 1" X 5" FLAT STOCK PINION GUIDES

(2) 1/2" X 4" LAG SCREW PINIONS

,2) 1/2" X 6" LAG SCREW PINIONS

(2) 1-1/2" X 12" REINFORCED RUBBER HOSE

(2) 1/2" X 2-1/2"
ROLLER PULLEYS

(2) 1/4" X 2" ROLL PINS

(2) 1-1/2" X 11-7/8" DOWEL ROLLERS

3/4" X 10-5/8" X 36"
PLYWOOD TABLE

(2) 1" X 13" 16-GAUGE TUBULAR STEEL ROLLER FRAME

1/8" X 1" ROLL PIN

1/4" X 1" X 10" FLAT STOCK CRANK ARM

1" X 3-1/4" DOWEL HANDLE

(4) 1/4" X 3-1/2" BOLTS

(8) 1/4" X 2" BOLTS

COUNTERSINK HEADS

3/8" X 4" BOLT

(2) 5/16" X 8" THREADED ROD HINGE PINS

3/4" X 4-3/8"
STEEL ROD CLEVIS SHAFT

(2) 1/4" X 2" BOLTS

(4) 1" X 4-3/4" 16-GAUGE
TUBULAR STEEL HINGE POSTS

(2) 1" X 35" 16-GAUGE TUBULAR STEEL TABLE FRAME

(4) 1/2" X 12"
THREADED ROD STANCHIONS

(4) 5/16" X 1-1/2" BOLTS

3/4" X 3-3/4" STEEL ROD CLEVIS SHAFT

(2) 1/4" X 1" BOLTS

(3) 1" X 14" 16-GAUGE
TUBULAR STEEL BASE FRAME

5/16-18 THREAD

(12) 5/16" NUTS

(4) 1/8" X 1" X 1-1/2"
ANGLE IRON HINGE BRACKETS

BELT GUARD TOP VIEW

4-1/4"

(2) 5/16" X 6" THREADED ROD HINGE PINS

1-7/8"

(2) 1" X 21" 16-GAUGE TUBULAR STEEL BASE FRAME

1/2"

3/8" X 22" THREADED ROD TABLE CONTROL

3" VALVE HANDWHEEL

(2) 3/8" X 3" BOLTS

machine bolts that serve as mounting pivots.

In preparation for using the sander, it's important that you set it up correctly. The roller frame must first be leveled by adjusting the nuts on the four ¹/₂" stanchions, and the tension on the pinion guides set so the rollers distribute equal (but not too much) pressure on the work. When wrapping the sanding belt around the drum, do it in a spiral, or "barber pole," pattern, and use a contact adhesive so you'll be able to change the belt easily. Since the drum must rotate toward the workpiece as it's being fed, wrap the belt in that direction, so it'll tend to tighten rather than loosen as it spins. (If necessary, secure the ends of the belt with staples sunk near the drum's edges.)

For safety's sake, never operate the sander without its drum and belt guard attached, and don't stand directly in front of the work as you crank it in, since it could kick back on you. Also, make a habit of using closed coat sanding belts, which can handle high speeds.

Even an occasionally used project is worth building right; take the time to make this one worthwhile, and its performance will reflect your extra effort.

PART THREE

Sticking Things Together

The basis of the human
genius for construction, uniting
one element with another,
lies in tight fits, worthy adhesives
and steady pins.

5 Easy Piece-Togethers

Perfect joints for modern glues and fasteners

For centuries, cabinetmakers, shipwrights and other professional woodworkers joined individual pieces of wood at various angles without recourse to glue or hardware. Moreover, their joints *stayed* joined.

At its best, this old-time nailless, screwless, glueless joinery was art masquerading as craft. Even more wondrous, the exacting work was done with hand tools; electricity and the whirring gadgets it would make possible—power jointers, routers and circular saws, for example—were as unthinkable to the old-time cabinetmaker as rocketing to the moon.

But before we hang our twentieth-century heads in comparative shame, consider that same bit of history from a different angle. Self-locking joints were devised because woodworkers of the time had no other choice. When the best glue available wasn't very good; when the only fasteners were wood slip feathers (splines), dowels and handmade nails, and the nails were difficult or impossible to come by; when you needed a chest, cabinet, wagon box or ship rib that would stay together under the strain of weight and use—then you did what you had to do. You cut and fit complicated slot-and-key tension joints that would hold, come hell or high water.

When woodworkers today choose to join two pieces of wood so exactly, they are generally motivated by challenge. If such vintage craftsmanship is what you're after, more power to you. But you no longer *have* to do it the hard way. Modern glues and fasteners make it possible to attain woodworking goals with a minimal investment of

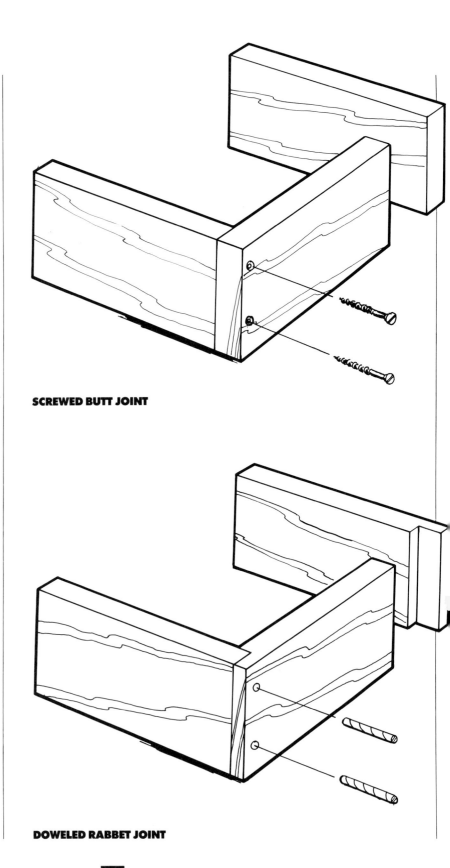

SCREWED BUTT JOINT

DOWELED RABBET JOINT

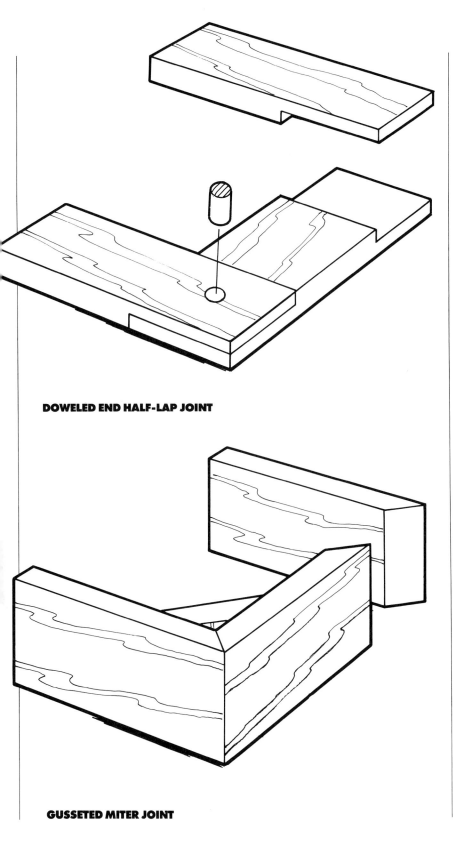

DOWELED END HALF-LAP JOINT

GUSSETED MITER JOINT

time and money, and without sacrificing appearance, strength or personal satisfaction. While there may be less glory in not doing things the hard way, there shouldn't be any shame, either. The simplest, most utilitarian wood joints can be cut with basic hand tools—or, if you have it, the fanciest power equipment.

Butt Joint

The butt joint is exactly what its name implies: two pieces of wood (members) butted together. It is most commonly used for 90° joints—either where two members meet at a corner, as in an L, or where the end of one member butts up against the face of a second at some point other than an end, as in a T. For example, a simple bookcase with two sides, a top, a bottom and one center shelf will typically employ six butt joints: one at each corner, and two more where the ends of the center shelf join the sides.

The butt joint requires no notching—just cutting to length and squaring the members where they join. However, simplicity of construction is offset by structural weakness. Therefore, all butt joints are generally glued *and* reinforced with hardware (dowels, slip feathers, corrugated fasteners, nails or screws).

Rabbet Joint

A rabbet is an end or edge joint in which the face of one member is notched to accept the end or edge of the second member. Because the joined members contact each other on two planes—rather than just one, as with the butt joint—the rabbet is much stronger. And since the seam doesn't show when viewed from the side, the rabbet is also an attractive (that is, unobtrusive) joint to use in the construction of cabinets, drawers, boxes, chests and other furniture (including items made of plywood).

The rabbet is also easy to lay out and cut. Rabbet joints should always be glued and, in most instances, further strengthened with some sort of fastening hardware.

End Half-Lap Joint

End half-laps are commonly used to join the corners of flat, rectangular structures with members of equal thickness—such as frames for pictures, doors and windows.

To lay out an end half-lap, measure back from the end of one member a distance equal to the width of the second, and vice versa, scribing squared shoulder lines all the way around both members. Next, scribe cheek lines on both members at the midpoints of their edge depths, *measuring from the faces* rather than from the backs or from one face and one back.

To assure tight-fitting joints, make all cuts on the scrap sides of the guidelines, rather than down their centers. When the two members of the half-lap are fitted together, they should form a square corner with faces and backs flush.

For low-stress structures such as picture frames, glue is sufficient to hold an end half-lap; other projects may require the joint to be reinforced with hardware fasteners.

Miter Joint

A miter joint involves beveling the ends of two members, generally at 45° angles, to form a square corner that reveals no end grain. Because of its clean appearance, the miter joint is an excellent choice for door casings and picture frames (where all members lie flat), as well as for chests and decorative boxes (where all members stand on edge).

Fabricating a miter joint is as easy as marking and cutting each joined end at 45°. With a steady hand, this can be accomplished with a handsaw or a portable circular saw. But a miter box—which holds a rib-backed handsaw in a jig that's adjustable through a wide range of angles—makes the cutting both easier and more precise. (The same thing can be accomplished, of course, and faster yet, with a radial arm or circular power saw.)

Since no notching is involved, the miter joint is actually nothing more than an angled butt joint. Consequently, it shares the butt's structural weakness and must be not only glued, but strengthened with slip feathers, dowels, nails, screws or corrugated fasteners.

Mortise and Tenon

Of the portfolio of joints held by our cabinetmaking forebears, only the mortise and tenon is indispensable today—not because it's the strongest but because it doesn't

Mortise-and-Tenon Joint

Lay out mortise around the center line. Bore holes slightly deeper than tenon length.

Remove the excess wood and clean the mortise using a mortising chisel.

Lay out the tenon and make cuts to the proper depths.

Remove wood on either side of the tenon and smooth with a razor-sharp chisel.

More Ways to Make Connections

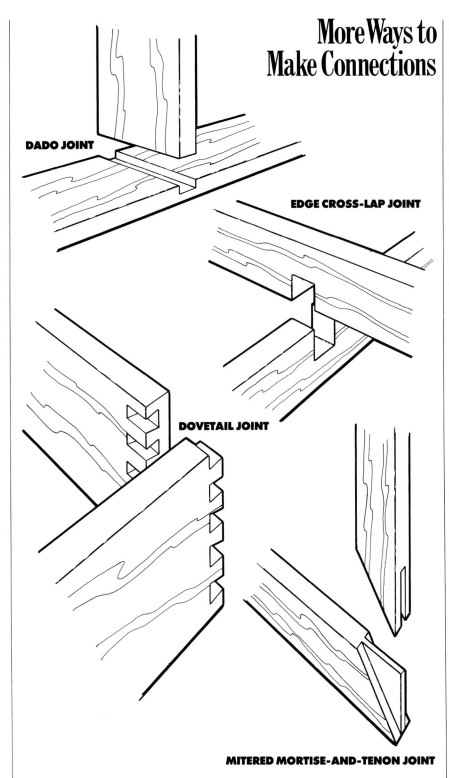

DADO JOINT

EDGE CROSS-LAP JOINT

DOVETAIL JOINT

MITERED MORTISE-AND-TENON JOINT

require glue. For that reason, mortise-and-tenon joints are essential for building furniture that can be disassembled for moving. If glued, the mortise and tenon offers unparalleled strength.

There are many variations on the mortise-and-tenon joint, but each involves a hole (mortise) into which fits a tenon (pin). The hole is usually cut square by drilling holes and then trimming the corners with a mortising chisel. The pin may be the full size of the member or may be cut down with a saw. A popular variation for knock-down furniture is to use a tenon that extends all the way through the receiving member; a dowel or tapered pin is then pushed through a hole in the tenon to secure the joint.

Joint Reinforcement

In many applications, butt, half-lap and miter joints need to be reinforced, and dowels offer an effective and attractive solution. In purely structural situations, nails or screws are far simpler, but dowels can be hidden or left exposed for an attractive effect.

Dowel rods can be purchased smooth or with spiraled grooves—like the rifling of a gun barrel in reverse. Of the two, spiraled dowels are preferable (though more expensive), since the channels between the grooves allow compressed air to escape while protecting the glue from being squeegeed off as a pin is driven into its hole. (An economical alternative is to cut a shallow groove down the length of a smooth dowel.)

Most important when using dowels is to carefully align the members and drill the dowel holes through *both members at the same time.* This will guarantee proper joint alignment when the dowels are driven home. A dowel pin should be cut slightly shorter than the total (combined) depth of its hole.

All five joints can be made both stronger and tighter if the sawn ends of the joined members are dressed smooth before gluing. When joints are to be glued but not reinforced with hardware fasteners, they should be carefully aligned and firmly clamped until the glue has dried.

Depending on the project and its intended use, butt, dowel, rabbet and miter joints can all be further strengthened by gluing a reinforcing block to the inside corner of each joint.

A Glues Gallery

Learn to choose the right adhesive from modern technology's fantastic selection.

ACRYLIC RESIN

WHITE GLUE (PVA)

HOTMELT STICKS

RESORCINOL

CONSTRUCTION

NEOPRENE

EPOXY

ALIPHATIC RESIN

SILICONE

LIQUID HIDE

Franklin

**Franklin
Hide Glue**

The choice of fine
craftsmen everywhere

NET 8 FL OZ (236 ML)

Franklin

**Titebond
Wood Glue**

For professional
woodworking results

NET 16 FL. OZ. (1 PT. 473 ML.)

MARKETED BY
DAP

DOW CORNING
100% SILICONE RUBBER

GENERAL PURPOSE
SEALANT
WHITE

• RE-SEALABLE NOZZLE & CAP
• PERMANENTLY FLEXIBLE
• WATERPROOF SEAL
• 20 YEAR LIMITED WARRANTY
CAUTION: ON CONTACT, UNCURED
SEALANT CAUSES IRRITATION.
Read precautions on back.)

NET 10.3 U.S. FL. OZ. (305 mL)

EXTRA STRENGTH
KRAZY GLUE GEL

CYANOACRYLATE FOR SMOOTH MATERIALS

Krazy Glue for
Wood & Leather

CYANOACRYLATE FOR POROUS MATERIALS

PLASTIC RESIN

ELMER'S
THE HOME SOLUTION

NEW
PREMIUM QUALITY
NON-FLAMMABLE SOLVENT

**CONTACT
CEMENT**

• DRIES IN 15
MINUTES
• EASILY APPLIED
BY BRUSH OR
ROLLER
• ALLOWS 3 HOURS
FOR ASSEMBLY

DANGER: TOXIC. VAPORS HARMFUL.
USE ADEQUATE VENTILATION.
SKIN AND EYE IRRITANT.
READ CAUTIONS ON BACK PANEL.

NET 32 FL. OZ. (1 QT.) (0.946 LITER)

**Plastic Resin
Glue**
Weldwood®

■ Makes joints stronger than
the wood itself
■ Highly water resistant
■ Ideal for all interior wood
applications

**WARNING! STRONG SENSITIZER
MAY CAUSE SKIN IRRITATION**
(Read other cautions on back panel)

NET WT. 8 OZ (227 g)

CONTACT CEMENT

The man who teaches a fool is gluing pot-sherds together.
—*Ecclesiasticus, Chapter 22*

Maybe Sirach's son was just having a bad day when he wrote his Apocrypha. More likely, though, he'd not yet discovered Super Glue. Back then, bitumen, tree pitch, beeswax and even glues extracted from animal bones were routinely used to stick things together. Sophisticated adhesives have been around for over 3,000 years. But the pot would have to wait until the middle of the twentieth century for resolution.

Today we've got an adhesive for almost every bonding need. The trick is to figure out which one is right for the task. You might not guess it from the variety of labels on the hardware store shelf, but most consumer-use glues can be divided into about a dozen generic categories. With the information that follows, you'll be able to interpret those labels and pick the right one. No more will you fear that your handiwork—and your composure—will come unglued.

Polyvinyl acetate (PVA) is by far the most popular all-purpose adhesive. Better known as white glue, it can be used to make repairs or to start a project from scratch. PVA works on paper, wood, broken china figures or even costume jewelry. The adhesive dries clear, leaving little evidence of its presence. Be aware, though, that not all white glues are the same. Some are watered down for a youngster's use, while others (Weldwood construction grade, for example) can withstand forces of up to 3,000 pounds per square inch (psi) when used to bond two blocks of hardwood, making the glue joint stronger than the wood itself. Although white glue is not generally considered water-resistant, its tolerance to moisture does improve with age.

Aliphatic resin, a favorite with woodworkers, comes in a plastic squeeze bottle under a variety of brand names, such as Titebond Wood Glue. It can be identified by its creamy yellow color.

Aliphatic resin has virtually the same properties as PVA, with the exception that it's stickier when wet. This makes a gluing job somewhat easier, since the parts won't slip quite so readily. Aliphatic resin can be diluted with water—in furniture assembly, for example—which allows the resins to soak deep into the pores of the wood, adding

Surface preparation is the key to a strong joint. To achieve a sound glued joint between two pieces of wood, for example, the mating surfaces should be clean and have an exact fit. Use only enough glue to cover the material surface, and maintain clamping pressure until fully set.

strength. Since it dries to a pale amber, it must be carefully wiped from wood surfaces that will show (use a damp cloth, and work while the glue is still wet).

Liquid hide glue is the fabled "horse glue" of early cabinetmakers. This adhesive, which really *is* made from animal hides, is characterized by a tan-to-brown color that requires careful application to avoid visibility. It's slow to grab and slower to set. For obvious reasons, horsehide glue also has a more distinctive odor than other adhesives. Though liquid hide glue forms a strong wood joint that is virtually unaffected by heat—a characteristic that made it the mainstay of old-time cabinetmakers—it's rapidly being replaced by aliphatic and plastic resins. Either woodworkers are succumbing to the allure of easy-to-use modern adhesives, or there's a shortage of horses being put out to that big pasture up above.

Plastic resin, basically of the urea-formaldehyde variety, is a powdery substance sold in a can and mixed with water. This powerful wood glue is the standard adhesive in furniture factories and a favorite of progressive cabinetmakers. During curing, plastic resin changes from a watery goo into an adhesive that's highly resistant to both moisture and heat, though it shouldn't be used on outdoor projects or objects that are in constant contact with water. Plastic resin has a pot life of four hours.

Resorcinol resin is identical to plastic resin, with one big addition: It's completely waterproof. Resorcinol is the only adhesive mentioned in this article that makes an absolutely watertight joint. Consequently, it's the glue of choice for outdoor work: boats, docks, lawn furniture, even water-skis.

Like plastic resin, this adhesive is used only in woodworking and forms the strongest bond of any glue. Resorcinol is easily identified by its two-can packaging. One container holds a powdered catalyst; the other, a liquid resin. Resorcinol has a pot life of about four hours.

Epoxy was one of the first commercial products to evolve from the space age. It is by far the most versatile of all adhesives, with

the ability to bond almost any two materials—dissimilar or alike. Epoxy comes in two parts, a resin and a hardener, which are mixed in 50:50 proportions. There are three popular versions of epoxy available to the homeowner.

In the original two-tube combination, the resin and hardener are packaged in small, metal tubes similar to toothpaste tubes. You lay down two beads of equal length—one of resin and another of hardener—on a working palette, and then blend them to create the epoxy adhesive. Unlike early epoxy, which typically had a setting time of 12 to 24 hours, the new epoxies set up in a matter of hours or even minutes. Curing time, however, is still 24 hours.

In a second version of epoxy, the resin and hardener are dispensed as two clear liquids in a two-tube syringe. When you press the plunger, the resin and hardener combine as they are forced through a single spout. This epoxy is usually "quick-set," solidifying in five minutes or less.

Finally, there's epoxy putty; the resin and hardener resemble sticks of modeling clay and have about the same consistency. To mix, you slice off an equal portion of each and knead them together to form a pliable mass. This adhesive is often used as a filler

for patching metal pipes, gutters, broken masonry and auto bodies. Pot life is about three hours.

Cyanoacrylate is the newest of the adhesives. Sold under brand names resplendent with adjectives like *Super* or *Wonder*, this clear glue *will* fasten virtually any nonporous surface to another, with a tensile holding strength of thousands of psi, all within a matter of seconds. The Krazy Glue TV commercial showing a man suspended by his hard hat is no joke. Recently, cyanoacrylate compounds have been formulated that permit even porous items, such as leather and wood, to be glued. Cyanoacrylate is also a very thrifty glue. You need no more than one drop of adhesive for every square inch of gluing surface.

Glue Failure

Many glue joints fail because too much dependency is placed on the glue's filling power. You can't expect glue to bridge even a tiny gap with much strength. If the two surfaces don't fit exactly, a filler material, such as plastic wood or liquid porcelain (for mending broken ceramics and dishes), should be used prior to gluing.

Eastman Chemical developed the original formula for cyanoacrylate some 30 years ago and sold it under the trade name Eastman 910. This was a wild and wonderful compound, with tremendous strength and a relatively short setting time of about 10 minutes. Over the years, catalysts were added to the adhesive to reduce the setting time, which was eventually whittled down to mere seconds. After a little chemical fine-tuning to make the adhesive safe for general use, Super Glue hit the market. The rest is history.

While cyanoacrylate *is* a modern marvel, it's far from the glue-to-end-all it claims to be. Although the tensile strength of the glue bond is tremendous—up to tens of thousands of psi in some cases—the adhesive has virtually no shear strength. A slight blow perpendicular to the glue seam will snap the bond. Some of the newer formulas have better shear strength, but the problem remains. Moreover, cyanoacrylate won't work with some types of plastics, such as the kind used for eyeglass frames. Rather than attaching the parts, the solvents in the glue attack the plastic and neutralize the adhesive.

Acrylic resin is akin to epoxy in that it can bond virtually any two dissimilar materials together with very high holding strength. It also works well on both porous and nonporous materials.

Acrylic resin is sold as a two-part package, consisting of a primer and an adhesive. The primer is first brushed onto one surface, then a syringe is used to apply the adhesive to the second surface. Setting action begins when you press the two surfaces together. The glue dries within 60 seconds to a clear-to-tan color, depending on formulation.

Silicone adhesive is also the result of space-age technology. Originally introduced as RTV some 20 years ago, this sticky material dries to a resilient firmness and comes in a wide range of colors. Silicone adhesive is readily identified by its pungent vinegar odor, which comes from the acetic acid used in its solvent.

Like epoxy putty, silicone sealant can be used as a filler as well as a glue. It's commonly used to caulk and seal around bathtubs, and adheres well to glass, metal, porcelain, ceramic, painted surfaces and many types of plastic and rubber. While the adhesive is virtually impervious to water, it's not recommended for submerged applications, such as

Adhesives at a Glance

Adhesive Type	For Use With	Wet-Tack	Setting Time	Curing Time	Strength	Moisture Resistance	Heat Resistance	Color When Dry
White glue (PVA)	Wood, wood products	Under 2 min.	10–30 min.	24 hr.	High	Poor	Poor	Clear
Aliphatic Resin	Wood, wood products	10–60 sec.	5–10 min.	24 hr.	High	Fair	Good	Clear to amber
Liquid Hide	Wood, wood products	Slow	2–3 hr.	8–12 hr.	High	Poor	Excellent	Amber
Plastic resin (Two-part)	Wood, wood products	Up to 4 hr.	4 hr.	12–16 hr.	High	Excellent	Good	Light tan
Resorcinol (Two-part)	Exterior, wood products	Up to 4 hr.	12 hr.	24 hr.	Very high	Waterproof	Good	Brown
Epoxy F = Fast S = Slow	Metal, china, hard surfaces	Set time	F: 4–8 min. S: 4–6 hr.	12–24 hr.	Very high	Good	Good	Clear or gray
Cyanoacrylate	Two types: porous/nonporous	Very fast	10–30 sec.	24 hr.	Very high	Fair to good	Fair	Clear
Acrylic resin (Two-part)	Metal, china, hard surfaces	Set time	1–3 min.	5–20 min.	Very high	Good	Good	Amber t tan
Silicone	Glass, metal, ceramic, tile	Slow	5–10 min. or longer	24 hr.	Fair	Excellent	Excellent	Clear or color
Contact cement S = Solvent-Based W = Water-Based	Laminates to plywood, particle board	S: 15–30 min. W: 30–60 min.	On contact	24 hr.	Medium	Good	Good	Amber
Neoprene	Glass, metal, tile	8 min.	On contact	24 hr.	Medium-high	Excellent	Good	Light tan
Construction S = Solvent-Based W = Water-Based	Wall panels, ceiling tile	S: 8–12 min. W: 15–20 min	S: 15 min. W: 30 min.	24 hr.	Medium-high	S: Good W: Fair	S: Fair W: Good	S: Color W: Whi
Hotmelt glue W = White A = Amber	Porous surfaces (wood, etc.)	15–20 sec.	60 sec.	2 min.	W: Fair A: Medium	W: Excellent A: Good	W: Poor A: Poor	W: Whi A: Ambe

Comments

All-purpose wood/paper glue; clamping required

All-purpose wood/paper glue

Original "horse glue"; made from animal hides; hot-pot life of 4 hours

High-strength, woodworking glue; clamping required

Waterproof wood glue; clamping required

High-strength, general-purpose cement and putty

Very fast setting; very high tensile strength

Similar to epoxy

Resilient when dry

Bonds on contact; for use with wood and plastic laminates

Similar to contact cement

Usually comes in 11-ounce cartridges; bracing or nail tacking required

Used with hot glue gun

below the water line of a boat. Its excellent electrical-insulating properties make it a favorite in both electronic and electrical construction and repair. **Contact cement** is used for nonstructural bonding, such as laminating veneers and Formica plastics. Contact cement is the preferred choice for working with large surface areas, such as applying laminates to counter tops, cupboards and tables, because it's economical.

Contact cement comes in bottles (for small jobs) and quart or gallon cans. The adhesive is applied liberally, as if painting a house, to both surfaces and allowed to dry until it's tack-free, about 15 minutes. During the drying period, the solvent evaporates and causes molecular surface shrinkage with electrical polarization. When the two surfaces are brought into contact, the strong electrical forces create an instantaneous, unyielding bond that permits no margin for error. Once the two surfaces touch, there is no going back for a second try, should the parts be slightly misaligned.

Neoprene cement, such as Weldwood's Touch-N-Glue, is a rubbery substance used to mend metal or tile and to affix them to wood and other surfaces. Like contact cement, neoprene glue comes in a bottle or can and is applied liberally. The adhesive is initially applied to one surface, generally the smaller piece, which is pressed into position so that the glue transfers to the second surface. Then the parts are separated and allowed to dry for about eight minutes. After the drying period, the tile is again pressed into place, and the adhesive is allowed to cure for 24 hours. Unlike contact cement, neoprene glue is somewhat forgiving; you do have a second chance to position the part if you react quickly. Its excellent resistance to moisture makes it ideal for use in the bathroom, shower and in wet kitchen applications.

Construction glue usually comes in an 11-ounce dispenser cartridge for use with a hand-pump gun. It's a thick, tacky adhesive used for securing wall panels and ceiling tiles, during building construction and remodeling.

Construction glues are generally of two types: solvent-based and water-based. The former is normally used with wood paneling, tileboard, subflooring and dry wall. The lat-

Glue Economy

Super glues are great for attaching just about any two nonporous surfaces together with great strength. New cyanoacrylates also repair porous surfaces, such as wood and leather. Apply no more than one drop of adhesive for every square inch of surface; otherwise the bond will be weakened.

ter type is used with ceiling tiles, plastic paneling and other materials that may be affected by a solvent. While construction cement's holding strength is relatively high, the wet-tack time is slow (10 to 20 minutes), requiring that the object be braced until dry or nailed in position.

Hotmelt adhesive comes in solid, cylindrical sticks that you insert in a gun resembling an electric drill. It works best on porous materials and can replace staples, nails, tapes and other glues. There are two important limitations, however. Don't use hotmelt glue to replace structural fasteners where heavy loads are involved, or in any situation where the working temperature is likely to exceed 140°F.

A glue stick is heated to the point of melting in the gun, and a plunger extrudes the molten adhesive. The two surfaces need to be held together for only about 30 seconds while the glue cools. This adhesive remains slightly flexible after it sets, and lends itself well to applications like sealing cardboard boxes, fixing books, repairing shoes and boots, tacking loose carpet and making arts and crafts. Roughening smooth surfaces improves the bond. Hotmelt glue is often used to hold parts in position until a stronger, longer-curing adhesive has had time to set. It also makes a good filler, provided high strength isn't required.

Whatever glue you use, proper application is always the key to success. Pick the right glue, and follow the instructions on the product's label. If anything, increase the clamping time. Don't be seduced by the allure of "miracle" glues and assume that technology will substitute for technique.—*TJ Byers*

TJ Byers is a technical writer who has published numerous books and magazine articles.

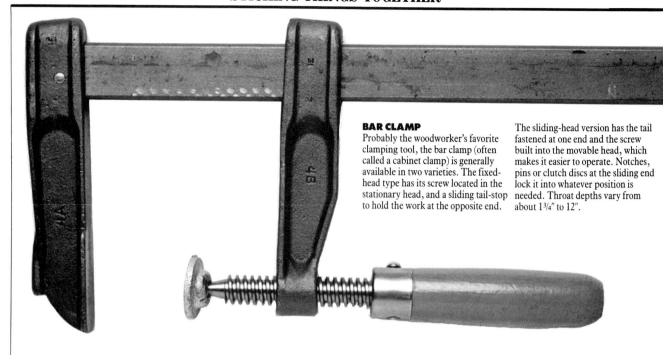

BAR CLAMP

Probably the woodworker's favorite clamping tool, the bar clamp (often called a cabinet clamp) is generally available in two varieties. The fixed-head type has its screw located in the stationary head, and a sliding tail-stop to hold the work at the opposite end.

The sliding-head version has the tail fastened at one end and the screw built into the movable head, which makes it easier to operate. Notches, pins or clutch discs at the sliding end lock it into whatever position is needed. Throat depths vary from about 1³/₄" to 12".

C-CLAMP

Also known as a carriage clamp, it comes in over a dozen varieties, including the three-way and multiple-spindle types. Its adjustable screw holds the work tightly against the fixed anvil. There are junior-, light-, medium- and heavy-service patterns; clamps with narrow throats have a greater load limit, with the exception of special deep-throat designs. A forged steel clamp has at least twice the strength (and price) of a similar-style malleable iron one.

Holding Your Own

Know what you're about when it comes time to get a grip on things.

Whether they click, screw, slide, spring or lever, they always come through in a pinch. Clamps: There are probably more types around—and more uses for them around the house—than you ever thought possible.

A clamp can be as simple as an iron weight on a board or as intricate as an instrument maker's beech cam clamp. It may be steel, brass, alloy, wood, plastic, nylon, canvas or a combination of several materials, and might wear jaws, bars, straps or corners. But regardless of how it's put together or what it looks like, its job is to hold work fast until you're ready to release it.

Chances are you'll never need some of the exotic clinchers that catch your eye on the hardware shelves. But even a modest workshop would be incomplete without at least a sampling of the down-to-earth varieties. Because a workpiece often needs to be held at more than one place to prevent pivoting, clamps are better bought in pairs, and best bought to complement each other. As an example, you might purchase one set with a deep throat and a limited (4" to 6") capacity, and another that can span a distance of several feet, such as pipe clamps. Together they should cover the lion's share of possibilities. (In case you're wondering, the throat depth is the distance between the center of the clamp pads and the inside of the frame; the capacity is how far the clamp's jaws or pads can open.)

If you're making your first purchase, the best all-around type is probably a bar clamp or a large C-clamp. The rogue's gallery of clamps that follows will help you decide about these and a host of others, so that you can make an intelligent purchase. Don't, however, go looking for a bargain unless it's a proven-quality item on sale; cheap imitations usually distort under pressure and are frustrating to use besides. Pay a premium, and you'll probably get an item that will last a lifetime. And that is surely a bargain.

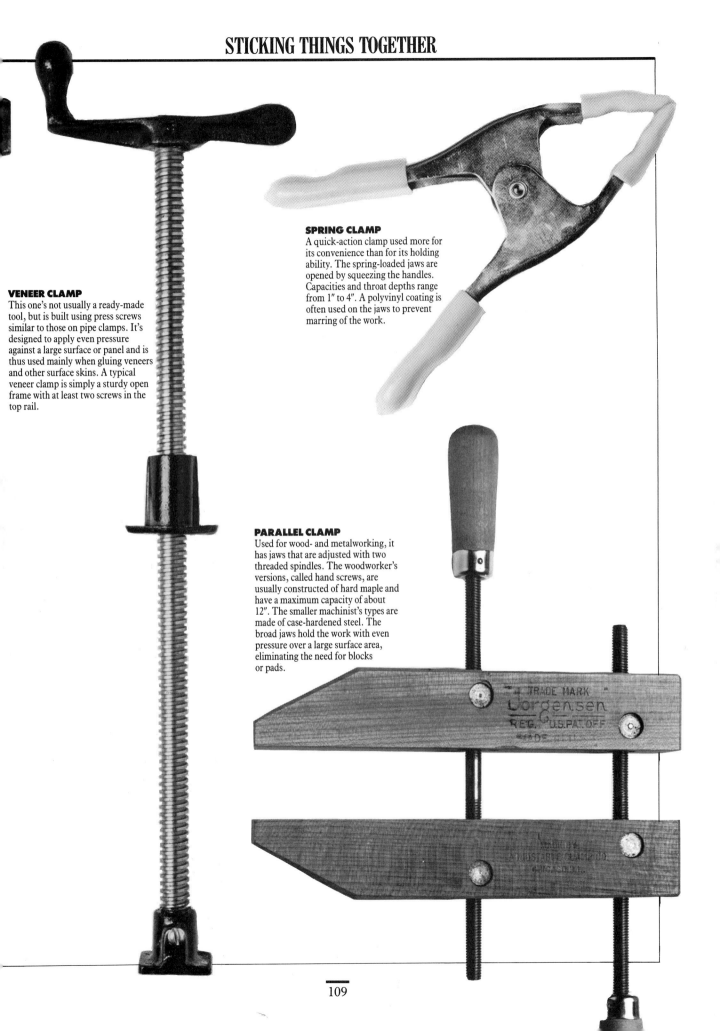

VENEER CLAMP
This one's not usually a ready-made tool, but is built using press screws similar to those on pipe clamps. It's designed to apply even pressure against a large surface or panel and is thus used mainly when gluing veneers and other surface skins. A typical veneer clamp is simply a sturdy open frame with at least two screws in the top rail.

SPRING CLAMP
A quick-action clamp used more for its convenience than for its holding ability. The spring-loaded jaws are opened by squeezing the handles. Capacities and throat depths range from 1″ to 4″. A polyvinyl coating is often used on the jaws to prevent marring of the work.

PARALLEL CLAMP
Used for wood- and metalworking, it has jaws that are adjusted with two threaded spindles. The woodworker's versions, called hand screws, are usually constructed of hard maple and have a maximum capacity of about 12″. The smaller machinist's types are made of case-hardened steel. The broad jaws hold the work with even pressure over a large surface area, eliminating the need for blocks or pads.

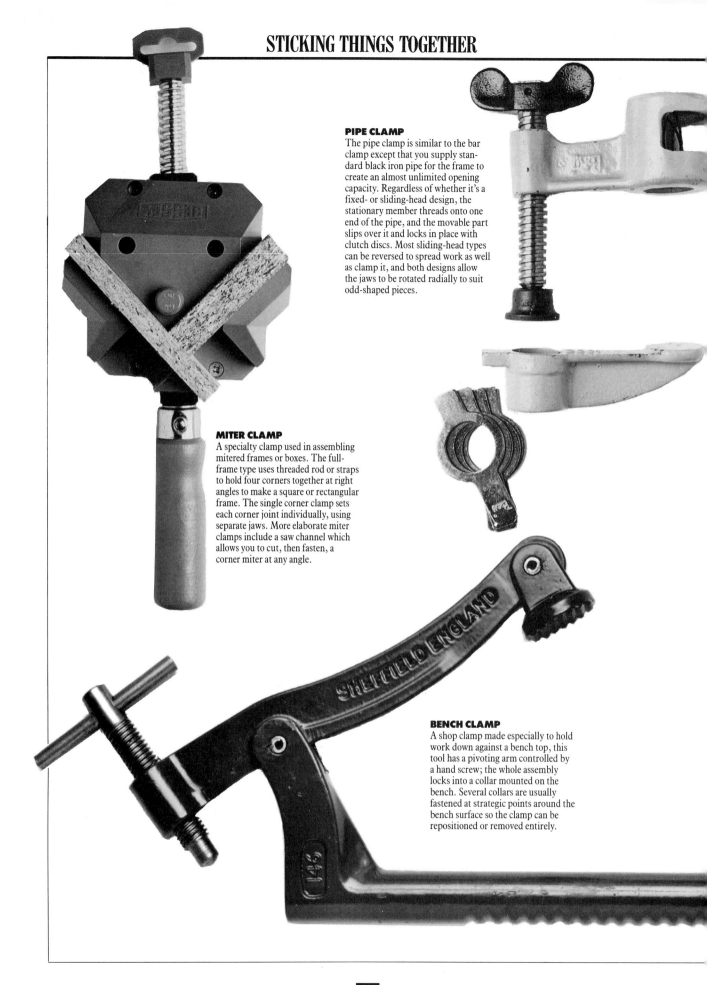

PIPE CLAMP

The pipe clamp is similar to the bar clamp except that you supply standard black iron pipe for the frame to create an almost unlimited opening capacity. Regardless of whether it's a fixed- or sliding-head design, the stationary member threads onto one end of the pipe, and the movable part slips over it and locks in place with clutch discs. Most sliding-head types can be reversed to spread work as well as clamp it, and both designs allow the jaws to be rotated radially to suit odd-shaped pieces.

MITER CLAMP

A specialty clamp used in assembling mitered frames or boxes. The full-frame type uses threaded rod or straps to hold four corners together at right angles to make a square or rectangular frame. The single corner clamp sets each corner joint individually, using separate jaws. More elaborate miter clamps include a saw channel which allows you to cut, then fasten, a corner miter at any angle.

BENCH CLAMP

A shop clamp made especially to hold work down against a bench top, this tool has a pivoting arm controlled by a hand screw; the whole assembly locks into a collar mounted on the bench. Several collars are usually fastened at strategic points around the bench surface so the clamp can be repositioned or removed entirely.

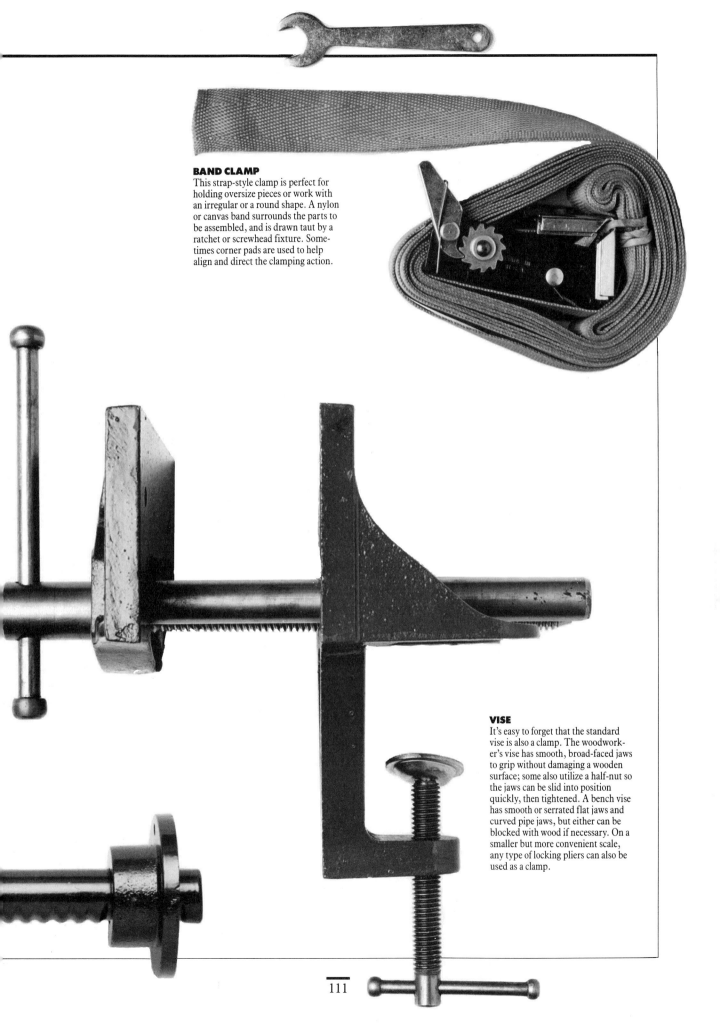

BAND CLAMP
This strap-style clamp is perfect for holding oversize pieces or work with an irregular or a round shape. A nylon or canvas band surrounds the parts to be assembled, and is drawn taut by a ratchet or screwhead fixture. Sometimes corner pads are used to help align and direct the clamping action.

VISE
It's easy to forget that the standard vise is also a clamp. The woodworker's vise has smooth, broad-faced jaws to grip without damaging a wooden surface; some also utilize a half-nut so the jaws can be slid into position quickly, then tightened. A bench vise has smooth or serrated flat jaws and curved pipe jaws, but either can be blocked with wood if necessary. On a smaller but more convenient scale, any type of locking pliers can also be used as a clamp.

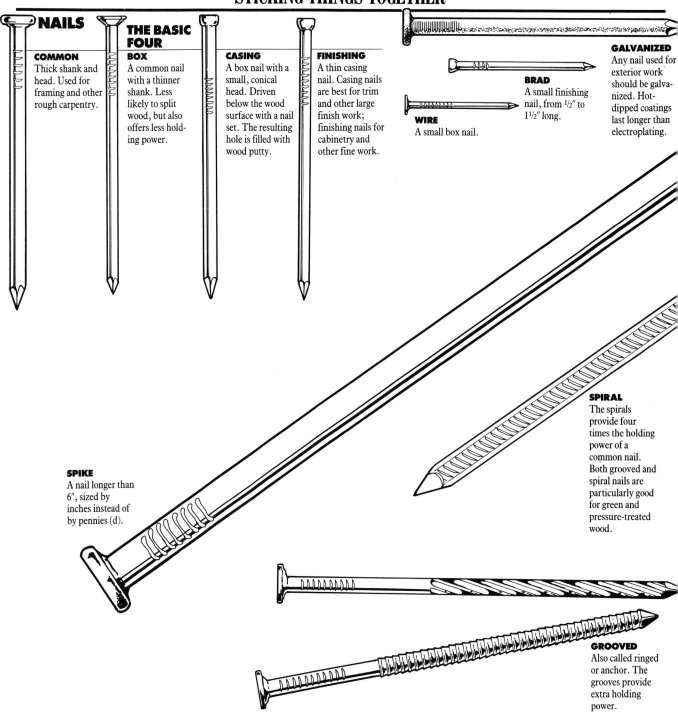

NAILS

THE BASIC FOUR

COMMON
Thick shank and head. Used for framing and other rough carpentry.

BOX
A common nail with a thinner shank. Less likely to split wood, but also offers less holding power.

CASING
A box nail with a small, conical head. Driven below the wood surface with a nail set. The resulting hole is filled with wood putty.

FINISHING
A thin casing nail. Casing nails are best for trim and other large finish work; finishing nails for cabinetry and other fine work.

WIRE
A small box nail.

BRAD
A small finishing nail, from $1/2''$ to $1 1/2''$ long.

GALVANIZED
Any nail used for exterior work should be galvanized. Hot-dipped coatings last longer than electroplating.

SPIKE
A nail longer than $6''$, sized by inches instead of by pennies (d).

SPIRAL
The spirals provide four times the holding power of a common nail. Both grooved and spiral nails are particularly good for green and pressure-treated wood.

GROOVED
Also called ringed or anchor. The grooves provide extra holding power.

Fascinating Fasteners

When it comes to nails, screws and bolts, *these* are the good old days.

Surely you've felt it. That unfortunate catch in the throat that comes as you push open the door of the nearest hardware shop. Funny, all you're doing is shopping for a few simple fasteners for a pet project. Why should you be nervous?

But then a tall salesman walks over (with the swagger belonging only to possessors of elaborate, arcane mysteries) and asks, "Can we help you?" You can answer that question confidently enough. "I need a few fasteners for a whozeewhatzit I'm building." It's the

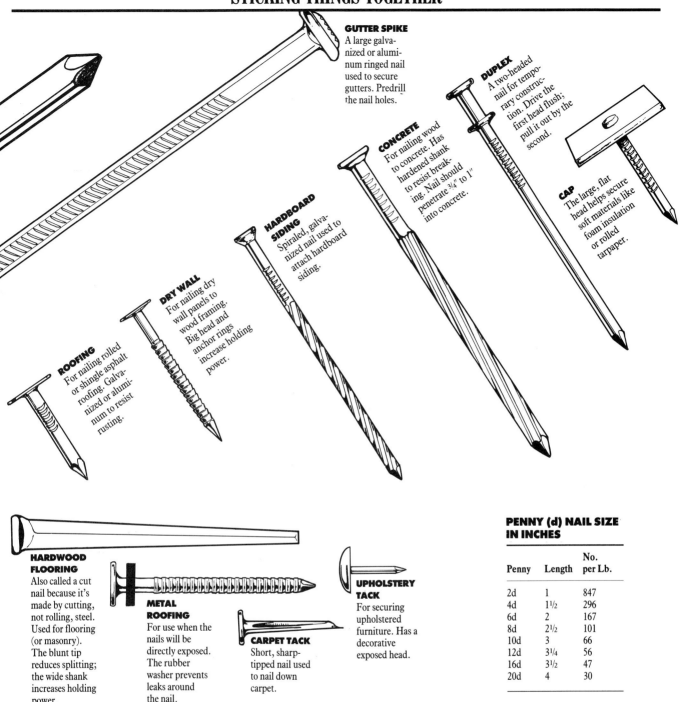

GUTTER SPIKE
A large galvanized or aluminum ringed nail used to secure gutters. Predrill the nail holes.

DUPLEX
A two-headed nail for temporary construction. Drive the first head flush; pull it out by the second.

CONCRETE
For nailing wood to concrete. Has hardened shank to resist breaking. Nail should penetrate ¾" to 1" into concrete.

CAP
The large, flat head helps secure soft materials like foam insulation or rolled tarpaper.

HARDBOARD SIDING
Spiraled, galvanized nail used to attach hardboard siding.

DRY WALL
For nailing dry wall panels to wood framing. Big head and anchor rings increase holding power.

ROOFING
For nailing rolled or shingle asphalt roofing. Galvanized or aluminum to resist rusting.

HARDWOOD FLOORING
Also called a cut nail because it's made by cutting, not rolling, steel. Used for flooring (or masonry). The blunt tip reduces splitting; the wide shank increases holding power.

METAL ROOFING
For use when the nails will be directly exposed. The rubber washer prevents leaks around the nail.

CARPET TACK
Short, sharp-tipped nail used to nail down carpet.

UPHOLSTERY TACK
For securing upholstered furniture. Has a decorative exposed head.

PENNY (d) NAIL SIZE IN INCHES

Penny	Length	No. per Lb.
2d	1	847
4d	1½	296
6d	2	167
8d	2½	101
10d	3	66
12d	3¼	56
16d	3½	47
20d	4	30

next question that stings you: "What type of fasteners are you looking for?" *Then* your Adam's apple starts to yo-yo and your words to sputter, like it's been a while since you've been breathing regularly.

What happened? You've been afflicted with the hardware store stammers. And for one simple reason: There are so confounded many different metal joiners on the market today that you can't possibly know which is best for the job at hand.

The accompanying portfolio of fasteners should give you a handle on the jargon of joiners. If you're anxious to be on your way to the store to pick up a few bags of miscellaneous common and finish 6-through-16d nails, dog ear this page and dig out your car keys. But to help you feel better about the bewilderment of facing too many fastener choices, perhaps we should peel back the pages of hardware history for a few moments and look at some of the problems and difficulties our forebears faced. It's a pleasant journey as well as an instructive one.

For Want of a Nail

"Nothing is impossible if you have enough nails" is the slogan of many a modern-day handyperson (and, alas, professional carpenter as well). The principle held all too true for American colonists. For them, the *scarcity* of those simple fasteners often resulted in very little being possible.

Nails were valuable things. Indeed, seventeenth-century landowners attracted

NAILS

SCREWS

CORRUGATED
Driven into the side of a mitered joint (like those on picture frames). Sometimes called a wiggle nail.

ELECTRICIAN'S STAPLE
A two-pointed, flat-surfaced nail used to secure electric cable.

FENCE STAPLE
A heavy-duty, U-shaped nail designed to hold barbed wire and other fencing.

CHICKEN WIRE STAPLE
A light-duty, two-pointed nail suitable for small-gauge fencing.

FLATHEAD*
Used when you want the head flush with the surface. Requires a countersunk hole for the head.

ROUND HEAD*
The head projects above the surface. Good for work when appearance is not a concern.

OVAL HEAD*
Head protrudes slightly from its countersunk hole. The deep slot makes it easy to insert and remove. Decorative.

LAG*
Stronger and longer than ordinary wood screws. The head is tightened with a wrench.

DRY WALL*
Has a Phillips slot, bugle head, case-hardened body and self-tapping threads. A dry wall screw can be power-drilled without a pilot hole.

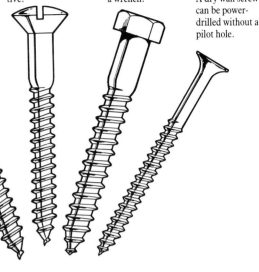

HANGER SCREW*
Self-taps (after drilling) into wood. Protruding end has machine thread to accept nut. Also called a table screw.

SLOTTED
The standard drive with a single slot.

PHILLIPS
A drive that uses a four-point recess.

HEX SOCKET
A drive that uses a six-sided internal socket.

DOWEL*
A double-pointed screw for joining wood end-to-end. Often used for long, lathe-turned pieces.

tenants with a special "signing bonus": enough nails for the tenants to build themselves a 16′ X 24′ home.

When said tenants left the property, they often tried to gain permanent possession of those nails by burning down the house. The Virginia General Assembly even passed a law in 1644 against burning buildings for their nails without prior authorization.

All nails of the time were individually hand-wrought from heated iron rod. The process was slow; Adam Smith estimated that a common smith could make but 200 to 300 (very poor) nails a day. The material was scarce, so most nails were imported from England. And the technology was so unevolved that a nail in a 1724 Wethersfield, Connecticut, house was indistinguishable from one taken from the Roman Forum.

All that changed with the Revolutionary War. One committee to the 1775 Continental Congress recommended unanimously that the colonies begin manufacturing three crucial necessities: gunpowder, steel and nails. The very act was practically seditious; Britain had tried to outlaw nail making. As William Pitt, the colonists' leading supporter in Parliament, stated, "If the horse flung a shoe, an American could not, of right, so much as make the nails required to set it." (Shades of the old verse, "For want of a nail . . .") Both government and private naileries sprang up, along with a modest business of smuggling British nails in from the West Indies.

Imported nails returned with indepen-

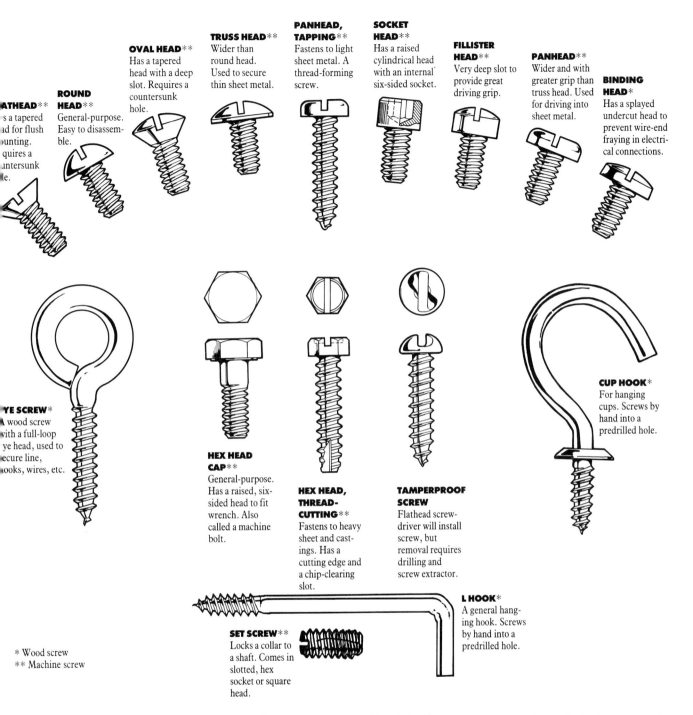

OVAL HEAD✳✳
Has a tapered head with a deep slot. Requires a countersunk hole.

TRUSS HEAD✳✳
Wider than round head. Used to secure thin sheet metal.

PANHEAD, TAPPING✳✳
Fastens to light sheet metal. A thread-forming screw.

SOCKET HEAD✳✳
Has a raised cylindrical head with an internal six-sided socket.

FILLISTER HEAD✳✳
Very deep slot to provide great driving grip.

PANHEAD✳✳
Wider and with greater grip than truss head. Used for driving into sheet metal.

BINDING HEAD✳
Has a splayed undercut head to prevent wire-end fraying in electrical connections.

ROUND HEAD✳✳
General-purpose. Easy to disassemble.

ATHEAD✳✳
s a tapered ad for flush ounting. quires a ntersunk le.

YE SCREW✳
A wood screw with a full-loop ye head, used to ecure line, ooks, wires, etc.

HEX HEAD CAP✳✳
General-purpose. Has a raised, six-sided head to fit wrench. Also called a machine bolt.

HEX HEAD, THREAD-CUTTING✳✳
Fastens to heavy sheet and castings. Has a cutting edge and a chip-clearing slot.

TAMPERPROOF SCREW
Flathead screwdriver will install screw, but removal requires drilling and screw extractor.

CUP HOOK✳
For hanging cups. Screws by hand into a predrilled hole.

L HOOK✳
A general hanging hook. Screws by hand into a predrilled hole.

SET SCREW✳✳
Locks a collar to a shaft. Comes in slotted, hex socket or square head.

✳ Wood screw
✳✳ Machine screw

dence, but soon that newly proclaimed stateside virtue, Yankee ingenuity, stepped forth, and an American invented the process of manufacturing nails by *cutting* them from iron bars. Cut nails were less likely to split wood, had better holding qualities and cost less, so they soon supplanted their handwrought kin.

Thomas Jefferson established one of the first full-scale naileries, using the labor of 10- to 16-year-old slave boys at Monticello, his Virginia estate. Jefferson was quite proud of his efforts. He wrote a friend in 1795, "My new trade of nail making is to me in this country what an additional title of nobility or the ensigns of a new order are in Europe." And, indeed, his nailery soon produced 10,000 or more nails a day and brought in each fortnight enough income to cover a quarter-year's grocery bill ($100 to $125). Unfortunately, Jefferson's enterprise ultimately failed. Its owner was away too often—with such sideline employment as serving as the nation's vice-president and president—to collect all the back debts. (Speaking of debts, many of the more successful naileries of the period were staffed by prisoners paying their dues to society.)

Midway through the 1800s, another innovation entered the scene: wire nails. First made in small sizes for cigar boxes and pocketbook frames, these American incarnations of a European invention were perfected around the 1870s. Wire nail machinery was one of the marvels exhibited at the Philadelphia Centennial Exposition of 1876.

NUTS

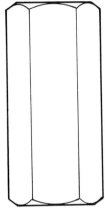

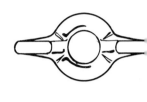

HEX
General-purpose.
Available in
heavy, regular
and finished.

ACORN
Covers end of
bolt for better
appearance or to
seal threads from
elements. Also
called cap.

COUPLING
For connecting
two rods or other
threaded fasten-
ers together.

FLANGE
Provides greater
bearing area for
nut without using
washer. Raises
nut above surface
of material to
prevent marring.

WING
Standard finger-
threaded nut.
Also available
with nylon lock.

BOLTS

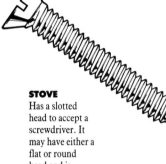

STOVE
Has a slotted
head to accept a
screwdriver. It
may have either a
flat or round
head and is
usually fully
threaded.

CARRIAGE
Used for very
strong joints in
wood. The
square neck
keeps the bolt
from rotating.

MACHINE
General-purpose.
Requires two
wrenches to
tighten, if used
with a nut. If not,
it's called a cap
screw.

**THREADED
ROD**
Buy, cut to
length and put a
nut on each end.
An easy way to
make a bolt you
need.

Though wire nails were cheaper to manufacture and easy to handle, they didn't crowd cut nails off the market. Even today, the stouter stakes are used for hardwood flooring and masonry. Wire nails did soon proliferate into a vast variety of shapes and sizes, such as those widely available today.

A Confusion of Screws

The screw, too, has had an uneven history. It started nobly enough when the Greek mathematician Archimedes invented "an inclined plane wrapped spirally around a cylinder," enclosed it in a tube and used it to bail out naval boats. (Today Archimedes' "water snail" is used to move grain.) The Romans invented the wood screw (often filing the threads by hand), and medieval torturers devised the diabolical thumbscrew (to *un*-fasten a prisoner's resistance). A few screws were often used to wrench on a knight's breastplate before the armored warrior went off to battle. The wrench was then attached to the suit, and pity the knight who lost his.

But the handy securer didn't really get much use for hundreds of years, partly because no two screws were alike. The first practical screw-making machine was invented in 1568 by the French mathematician Jacques Besson. That led to screws becoming a common component of firearms. But individual screws still varied widely. Finally, during the 10 years between 1800 and 1810, Britisher Henry Maudslay perfected a consistent screw-cutting lathe that turned

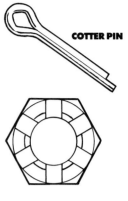

COTTER PIN

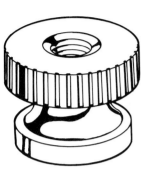

KNURLED
For finger-tightening in close locations or with electric terminals.

TEE
Used on wood or similar material where steel threads are needed. Prongs sink into material as bolt is tightened.

NYLON LOCK
Nylon insert self-taps to hold bolt and seal nut. Vibration-proof. Limited reusability. Not for high-heat applications.

CASTLE
Used with cotter pin (which passes through hole drilled in the bolt) to provide extra security.

WASHERS

FLAT
Standard washer. Prevents marring of material's surface. Eases tightening and loosening but does not help secure nut.

FENDER
A wide, flat washer useful for securing thin material or covering a large hole.

LOCK
The springy spiral pushes against nut and workpiece, providing good security. Should be used with flat washer.

EXTERNAL-TOOTHED
Used with large-head bolts. Will fracture in high-torque situations.

INTERNAL-TOOTHED
Same application as external-toothed, but prevents snags of nearby material.

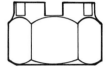

COUNTERSUNK FINISHING
Prevents having to drill a counter-sunk hole when installing a stove bolt or recessed screw.

out the same fastener first time, every time.

The only hitch? There was no standard for what the threads on screws should look like, so different manufacturers' products varied widely. This problem continued long after it should have been resolved. Indeed, when the city of Baltimore caught fire in 1904, fire companies from nine neighboring cities had to stand and watch: None of their fire hoses could thread onto Baltimore's hydrants. Even in World War II, America could not make British engines (until the U.S. facto-ries underwent a 10-month retooling process) and British mechanics couldn't fix American planes—because the two countries' screws didn't match.

Nuts and Bolts

The compatibility problem was even worse with nuts and bolts. Sometime in the fifteenth century, some sage figured out that you could add a nut to a screw and have an even more versatile fastener (easy to dis- and reassemble), but since each handmade bolt was unique, only the nut made with it would fit. People had to tie the two parts together until the unit was installed.

It took the Industrial Revolution's need for standardization of parts to propel progress toward uniformity. In 1801, Eli Whitney, the maker of the cotton gin, demonstrated the interchangeability of parts—a fundamental principle of factory assembly—to a group of Washington officials that included President Adams and that nail-making V.P., Jef-

WALL FASTENERS

ALL-PURPOSE

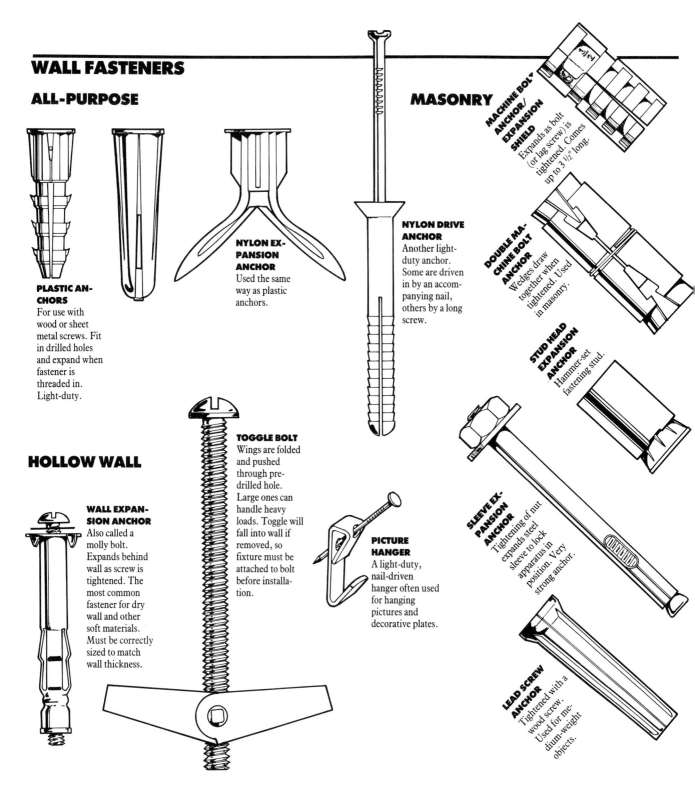

PLASTIC AN-CHORS
For use with wood or sheet metal screws. Fit in drilled holes and expand when fastener is threaded in. Light-duty.

NYLON EXPANSION ANCHOR
Used the same way as plastic anchors.

MASONRY

MACHINE BOLT ANCHOR/ EXPANSION SHIELD
Expands as bolt (or lag screw) is tightened. Comes up to 3 ½" long.

NYLON DRIVE ANCHOR
Another light-duty anchor. Some are driven in by an accompanying nail, others by a long screw.

DOUBLE MACHINE BOLT ANCHOR
Wedges draw together when tightened. Used in masonry.

STUD HEAD EXPANSION ANCHOR
Hammer-set fastening stud.

SLEEVE EXPANSION ANCHOR
Tightening of nut expands steel sleeve to lock apparatus in position. Very strong anchor.

LEAD SCREW ANCHOR
Tightened with a wood screw. Used for medium-weight objects.

HOLLOW WALL

WALL EXPANSION ANCHOR
Also called a molly bolt. Expands behind wall as screw is tightened. The most common fastener for dry wall and other soft materials. Must be correctly sized to match wall thickness.

TOGGLE BOLT
Wings are folded and pushed through pre-drilled hole. Large ones can handle heavy loads. Toggle will fall into wall if removed, so fixture must be attached to bolt before installation.

PICTURE HANGER
A light-duty, nail-driven hanger often used for hanging pictures and decorative plates.

ferson. Whitney arranged several piles of identical musket parts on a table. Then, picking a part at random from each pile, he quickly constructed a working musket. An idea was born and uniformity of such parts as nuts and bolts caught on.

Still, as with screws, for many years *my* uniformity didn't equal *your* uniformity. To solve that problem, Britain adopted Joseph Whitworth's standards for screw and bolt threads in 1881. All well and good, only America went for William Seller's stan-

dards, which were different. After World War II, in 1948, the United States, Canada and England adopted the new Unified Thread System (UTS). At the same time, however, the International Organization for Standardization (ISO) began work on a worldwide standard. That was adopted in 1964, or rather, *those* were adopted—there were two, the ISO Inch Screw Thread System (same as the UTS one) and the ISO Metric Screw Thread System. The latter has since been replaced by the ANSI (American

National Standards Institute) ISO system.

Confusing? And you thought going into a hardware store was bad.

So the next time you're facing all those bins of fasteners, with their puzzling shapes and polysyllabic names, relax. Reflect on the past a moment, with its scarcity of some fasteners and nonuniformity of others. Then you'll realize what a blessing it truly is to have so many useful and highly functional nails, screws and bolts right at your fingertips.

Recommended Hole Sizes for Bolts and Screws

Size of Screws or Tap (No. or Frac.)	Dec. Equiv.	Tap Drill* No. of Threads Per Inch	Tap Drill* Drill Size	Tap Drill* Dec. Equiv.	Tap Drill* Closest Fraction Drill Size	Body Drill* CLOSE FIT Drill Size	Body Drill* CLOSE FIT Dec. Equiv.	Body Drill* FREE FIT Drill Size	Body Drill* FREE FIT Dec. Equiv.	Pilot Drill Size* Hard Wood	Soft Wood	Frac.	Sheet Metal Screws Pilot Drill Size*	Shank Clear. Drill Size*	Lag Screws Pilot Drill Size*	Shank Clear. Drill Size*	Decimal Equivalents Frac.	Dec. Equiv.
0	.060	80	3/64	.0469	3/64	52	.0635	50	.0700	70		1/16	66	1/16			1/64	.0156
										1/32			1/32				1/32	.0312
1	.073	64	53	.0595	1/16	48	.0760	46	.0810	66	71	5/64	57	5/64			3/64	.0468
		72	53	.0595	1/16					1/32	1/32		3/64				1/16	.0625
2	.086	56	50	.0700	5/64	43	.0890	41	.0960	56	65	3/32	53	3/32			5/64	.0781
		64	50	.0700	5/64					3/64	1/32		1/16				3/32	.0937
3	.099	48	47	.0785	5/64	37	.1040	35	.1100	54	58	7/64	50	7/64			7/64	.1093
		56	45	.0820	3/32					1/16	3/64		1/16				1/8	.1250
4	.112	40	43	.0890	3/32	32	.1160	30	.1285	52	55	1/8	45	1/8			9/64	.1406
		48	42	.0935	3/32					1/16	3/64		5/64				5/32	.1562
5	.125	40	38	.1015	7/64	30	.1285	29	.1360	49	53	1/8	42	1/8			11/64	.1718
		44	37	.1040	7/64					5/64	1/16		5/64				3/16	.1875
6	.138	32	36	.1065	7/64	27	.1440	25	.1495	47	52	9/64	40	9/64			13/64	.2031
		40	33	.1130	1/8					5/64	1/16		3/32				7/32	.2187
8	.164	32	29	.1360	9/64	18	.1695	16	.1770	40	48	11/64	32	11/64			15/64	.2343
		36	29	.1360	9/64					3/32	5/64		7/64				1/4	.2500
10	.190	24	25	.1495	5/32	9	.1960	7	.2010	33	43	13/64	30	13/64	31	13/64	17/64	.2656
		32	21	.1590	11/64					7/64	3/32		1/8		1/8		9/32	.2812
12	.216	24	16	.1770	3/16	2	.2210	1	.2280	30	38	7/32	22	7/32			19/64	.2968
		28	14	.1820	3/16					1/8	7/64		5/32				5/16	.3125
1/4	.250	20	7	.2010	13/64	F	.2570	H	.2660						17	1/4	21/64	.3281
		28	3	.2130	7/32										11/64		11/32	.3437
5/16	.3125	18	F	.2570	17/64	P	.3230	Q	.3320						1	5/16	23/64	.3593
		24	1	.2720	9/32										7/32		3/8	.3750
3/8	.375	16	5/16	.3125	5/16	W	.3860	X	.3970						H	3/8	25/64	.3906
		24	Q	.3320	11/32										17/64		13/32	.4062
7/16	.4375	14	U	.3680	3/8	29/64	.4531	15/32	.4687						P	7/16	27/64	.4218
		20	25/64	.3906	25/64										21/64		7/16	.4375
1/2	.500	13	27/64	.4219	27/64	33/64	.5156	17/32	.5312						U	1/2	29/64	.4531
		20	29/64	.4531	29/64										3/8		15/32	.4687
																	31/64	.4843
																	1/2	.5000

*NOTE: Drill sizes are given in either numbers or fractions.

Eye Screws

No. of Wire Gauge	Decimal	Closest Fraction	Large Eye I.D. Inch	Medium Eye I.D. Inch	Small Eye I.D. Inch	Overall Length Inch
000	.362	3/8 (.375)	1 1/8			3 7/8
0	.306	5/16 (.3125)	13/16			2 7/8
2	.262	17/64 (.2656)	23/32			2 5/8
4	.225	15/64 (.2343)	39/64	31/64	19/64	2 3/16–1 15/16
6	.192	13/64 (.2031)	17/32	7/16	17/64	1 15/16–1 5/8
8	.162	11/64 (.1718)	15/32	25/64	15/64	1 5/8–1 3/8
10	.135	9/64 (.1406)	13/32	19/64	7/32	1 3/8–1 3/16
12	.105	7/64 (.1093)	3/8	1/4	3/16	1 3/16–3/4
14	.080	3/32 (.0937)	11/32	1/4	5/32	1 1/16–5/8

Nail Size

Penny Number	Length (Inches)	NUMBER PER POUND Common Nails	Box Nails	Finishing Nails
4d	1 1/2	316	437	548
6d	2	181	236	309
8d	2 1/2	106	145	189
10d	3	69	94	121
12d	3 1/4	64	87	113
16d	3 1/2	49	71	90
20d	4	31	52	62
30d	4 1/2	20		
40d	5			
50d	5 1/2			
60d	6			

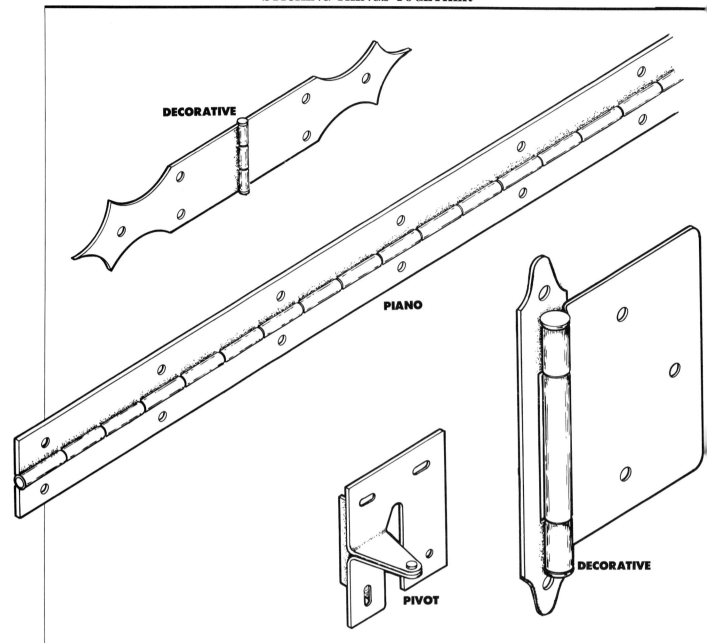

DECORATIVE

PIANO

PIVOT

DECORATIVE

Hinges

The lowdown on a pivotal subject for cabinetmakers

Love may make the world go round, but hinges make things swing. Whether used to disguise a dainty jewelry-box lid, to decorate a kitchen cabinet or to bolster a massive security gate, hinges play important roles in construction and cabinetry.

Shopping for a hinge, however, can be a confusing and frustrating experience. The typical hardware store might stock more than 150 different types, and finding the right one for the job can make you dizzy. Fortunately, hinges aren't as complex as they might first appear. You can categorize them by dividing them into three simple groups according to the geometry of the door to which they are attached: flush, overlay or lipped. Beyond that it's mostly a matter of size and style. However, categorization is hardly ever final, so it's also worth talking separately about a couple of specialty hinges.

Flush Hinges

Flush hinges are used to mount doors on the same plane as the attachment point. This configuration is popular in both contemporary and traditional designs, and it's, therefore, easily the most common general hinge category.

Butt hinges are commonly used for large and/or heavy doors, such as entry and interior house doors and outdoor gates. Butt hinges install between the edge of the door and the edge of the supporting wall, and may be recessed into the doorjamb and door to reduce the size of the mounting gap. There are two major types, *loose* and *fixed pin*. The former's pivot pin can be pushed out to separate the two hinge plates, so that a door can be removed without unscrewing the hinge plates from the door and wall. The latter's pin is set permanently in place.

Piano, or *continuous, hinges* are butt hinges

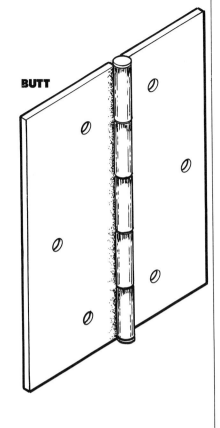

BUTT

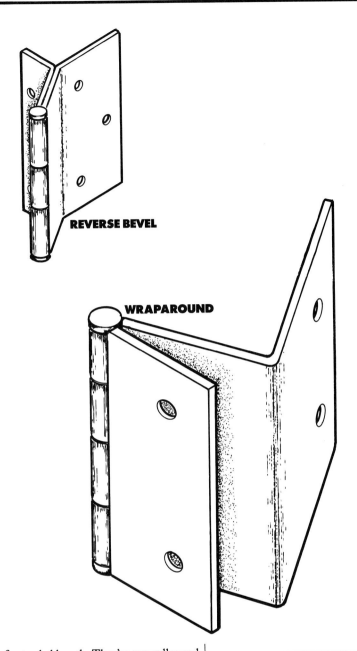

REVERSE BEVEL

WRAPAROUND

of extended length. They're generally used on large objects, such as trunk lids, where the rigors of opening and closing a heavy door at odd angles could cause a butt hinge to pull loose. Piano hinges usually run the length of the seam and are seldom recessed. They are sold in standard lengths (3′ is a size that you'll commonly find at hardware stores) and can be cut with a hacksaw to fit a particular application.

Decorative hinges are often used on kitchen cabinets, garden gates and other places where visual enhancement is desired. Unlike the butt hinge, the decorative hinge attaches to the outside surfaces of the door and the cabinet wall and leaves no seam gap. The design of this hinge can range from mundane to ornate.

Overlay Hinges

Overlay hinges are used to attach doors that are not on the same plane as the attachment point. In some cases, the offset is necessary for the door to make contact with a surface in a different plane from the attachment point; in other designs it's used to highlight the presence of the door. An overlay door always has its back side parallel to the front side of the stationary surface.

Reverse bevel hinges are used to anchor a door with an attaching edge cut at an acute angle to a square mounting surface. In this design, the front surface of the door is larger than the back, creating the illusion of a hidden hinge.

Pivot hinges consist of two angled brackets, one horizontal and one vertical, that are attached to each other at a forward pivot point. The hinge mounts with one bracket on the front surface of the stationary base and the other on the top, perpendicular, edge of the door. It is possible to partially conceal a pivot hinge by cutting into the edge of the door.

Wraparound hinges are the overlay equivalent of a butt hinge and allow the door to overlap the front of the base. They have a simple butt design with a 90° bend to both hinge plates, so that the hinge mounts between the front surface of the stationary base and the back side of the door. The hinge isn't concealed, and the pivot joint becomes a highlight.

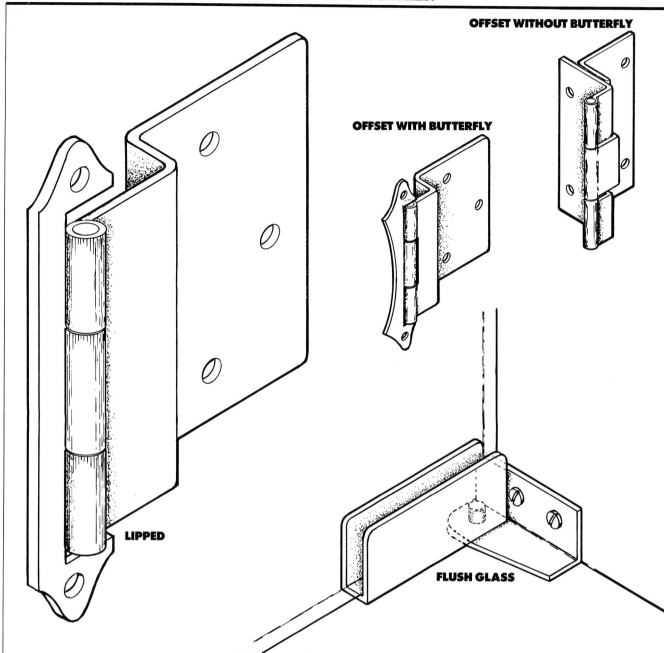

OFFSET WITHOUT BUTTERFLY

OFFSET WITH BUTTERFLY

LIPPED

FLUSH GLASS

Lipped Hinges

The lipped hinge is a cross between the flush hinge and the overlay hinge, in which the door is partially recessed into the door cavity. Lipped doors are very popular with cabinetmakers because they allow a wide latitude of door exposure, some support for the door when closed and a less primitive appearance than a full-overlap door. All lipped hinges are offset.

Offset hinges with butterfly are partially concealed but have a decorative exposure. The decorative part of the hinge attaches to the outside stationary edge, while the door portion is contoured to fit along the back side of the door.

Offset hinges without butterfly are the lipped equivalent of the wraparound hinge. In this design, the cabinet flap is bent to wrap around the instep of the stationary edge so that the hinge appears as a butt hinge.

Window Hinges

Glass doors are unique in that they can't accept conventional fasteners because of the brittleness of the material. Two types of hinges, overlay and flush, are used to mount them, but the latter is much more popular with amateurs.

Overlay glass hinges require a hole to be cut in the glass door. Cutting holes in glass, however, is not a job for the neophyte, so we will do no more than mention the

availability of this type of window hinge.

Flush glass hinges don't require a hole to be cut in the glass. Instead, the hinge slips over the edge of the glass and is held in place by the pressure of two retainer screws. Installing this hinge requires that a hole first be drilled in the frame of the cabinet and a hinge insert (for the pivot) be installed. The hinge is then positioned into the insert, the glass door is slid into place, and the retainer screws are tightened.

Concealed Hinges

Throughout this discussion, ways have been suggested to hide the hinge from view. In Early American style cabinetwork, the hinges are often important visual parts of the

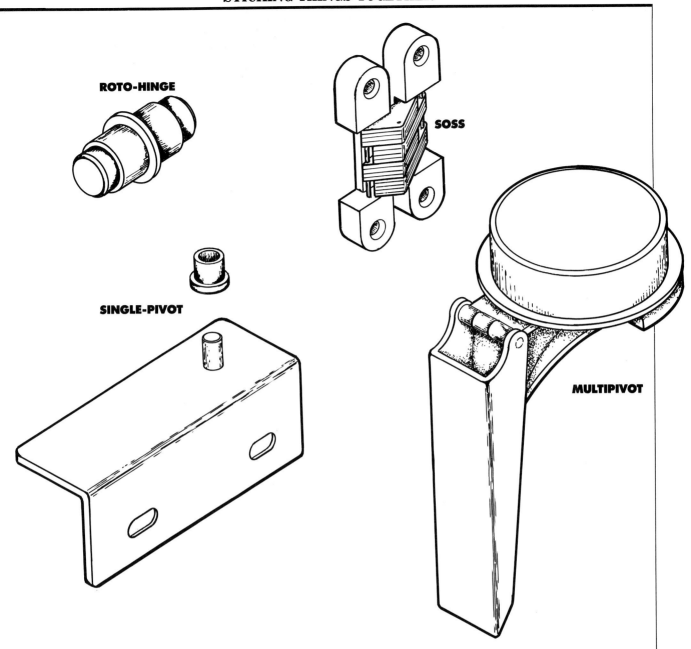

ROTO-HINGE

SOSS

SINGLE-PIVOT

MULTIPIVOT

design, but modern and European cabinet-makers generally prefer to hide them.

Soss hinges are recessed into the edges of a flush-mounted door and its adjacent suspension edge. They require a bored hole and shallow mortising for installation. These hinges are not adjustable, and they must be precisely installed, but they're strong and operate smoothly.

Single-pivot hinges are used with flush-mounted doors. Unlike the overlay pivot hinge, the concealed single-pivot hinge consists of two pieces: a vertical pivot pin attached to a plate secured to the back surface of the door and a nylon bearing that fits into a hole drilled into the horizontal edge of the cabinet. The metal door pivot fits into the nylon insert, thereby allowing the door to swing off center from the pivot point.

Multipivot hinges (popularly known as European hinges) are ideal for carcass (box) cabinetry. Models are available for overlay and flush doors that are perpendicular to the supporting edge—the hinge attaches to the inside corner of the cabinet, remaining out of sight until the door is opened; and for flush doors that are parallel to the supporting wall—the hinge attaches to the inside surfaces of both the door and stationary base. Multipivots are usually adjustable, allowing fine-tuning, and many permit door removal without detaching the hinge.

Roto-Hinge, a trademark of Abra, Inc., is the ultimate concealed hinge. This completely invisible hinge consists of two hardwood disks, separated by a washer and held together by a steel rivet. The wooden disks rotate independently about the rivet in a manner similar to a single-pivot hinge. A bore hole the size of the hinge is drilled into the mating edges of a flush door and the cabinet at the point of pivot, and the hinge is glued into place. These hinges aren't adjustable, and once installed, a Roto-Hinge cannot be removed or replaced.

There you have it: everything you wanted to know about hinges but didn't know to ask. Next time you go shopping for hinges, you'll be able to enjoy and appreciate their diversity. Better yet, you'll come home with the right item. —*TJ Byers*

TJ Byers is a technical writer who has published numerous books and articles.

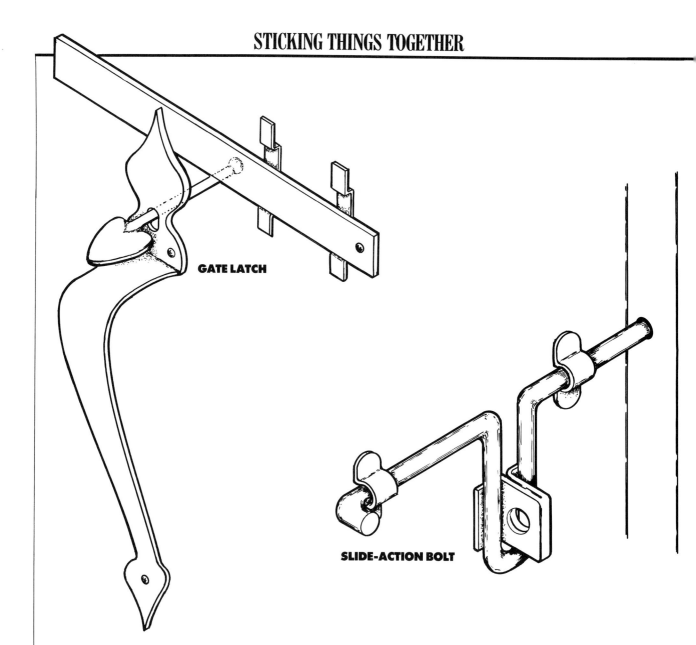

GATE LATCH

SLIDE-ACTION BOLT

Latches

Sorting out the choices, from catches to locks

Carpenters may call them *locks*. Cabinetmakers might prefer the term *catches*. To anyone else, they could simply be *latches*. Whatever their description, catches, latches and locks have been with us since long before screws and nails were commonly available. Ancient Egyptians developed intricate latching devices to secure palace doors; the Romans —and, subsequently, Europeans of the Middle Ages—made use of metals, and placed *wards* in their locks, which allowed access only to match-cut keys. By the late eigh-

teenth century, locking mechanisms had reached a sophistication close to today's.

The problem with choosing a latch, however, lies not as often in how complicated its design, but rather in the wide variety of locks and latches available—a selection which truly numbers in the hundreds. Adding to the confusion is the variation in nomenclature between latching devices with a similar purpose.

Fortunately, much of the misunderstanding can be eliminated by grouping the hardware according to its application, which can be broadly categorized to include three areas: outdoor gates and doorways, entry doors, and interior cabinets and cupboards.

Types of Latches

There are a number of applications for locks and latches outside the home itself.

Consider the garage door, the garden gate and the storage shed—all of which require locking, or at least latching, devices. Too, there may be a barn-type door or a driveway gate that also needs an easy to use but secure fastener.

The most popular outdoor latch is the *mechanical bolt*. It's simply a metal bar or rod that, when engaged, holds the door fast (usually in the closed position) by securing the unhinged edge to the doorjamb or other stationary point. Central to the construction of a bolt latch is the latching pin—that part of the assembly which actually engages with an outside catch to hold the door secure. The pin, or bolt proper, is moved with a handle called a lever. Generally, the travel of the bolt or pin is limited by stops placed on either side of the lever.

Closer to home, there are entry doors for both indoor and outdoor use. These familiar

BARREL BOLT

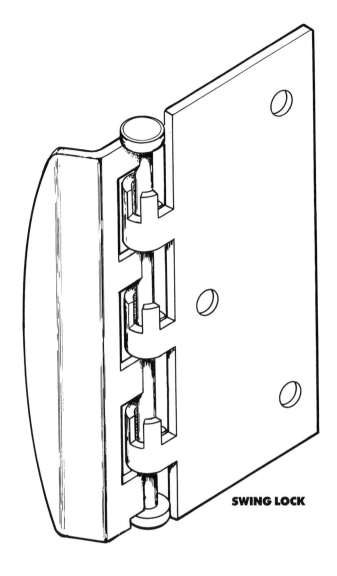

SWING LOCK

hinged doors are secured with mechanical latches called *locksets*, which may or may not contain locking mechanisms.

Inside entry doors separate bedrooms, baths and utility rooms from the main living area. Closets and pantries use *passage sets* which cannot be locked. Bedrooms and baths are usually equipped with *privacy locksets*—keyless latches that are locked and released from inside the room. Outside entry doors, on the other hand, must provide security for the building, so they require *entry locksets* which are opened by key from the outside.

Inside the house are a multitude of cabinets and cupboards that are held shut with what cabinetmakers prefer to call catches rather than latches. Catches fall into three categories: friction, magnetic and mechanical. Both *friction* and *magnetic catches* work well for most residential cabinet installations because of their simple push-pull design.

Mechanical latches find fewer cabinet applications because of their more complex release mechanism; cupboard turns and child-proof safety catches are notable exceptions.

Outside Doors and Gates

Barrel bolts are characterized by their one-piece construction. In barrel-bolt design, the latching pin is contained inside a metal tube, called a barrel, that allows the pin to slide back and forth. Limiting the pin's travel, and serving as the handle, is a center-fastened lever that rides inside a slot cut along the length of the barrel. In most barrel bolts, the latching pin is free to rotate inside the barrel, a feature that allows the lever to serve as a lock when flipped downward into a notch cut perpendicular to the barrel slot.

The barrel bolt is attached to the face of the door or gate perpendicular to the stile and

is positioned so the tip of the latching pin is flush with the gate edge when in the retracted position. Depending on design, either a hole drilled in the gate post or a surface-mounted metal keeper serves as the latch's catch.

Slide-action bolts can be found on many garage doors. The latch consists of a metal rod bent in an exaggerated U-shape that serves as both latching pin and handle. A single metal plate with up-bent tabs, or two individual saddles, holds the latching pin in place and limits its travel; a lower tab is used as a positioning stop for the lever.

In use, the lever is lifted to clear the bottom tab and the latching pin is slid into position. A drilled plate or a hole in the doorjamb serves as the catch. Once engaged, the lever is lowered so that it straddles the positioning tab. A hole is normally drilled in the tab to accept a pin or padlock; when this hole is used, the narrow U-shaped lever is un-

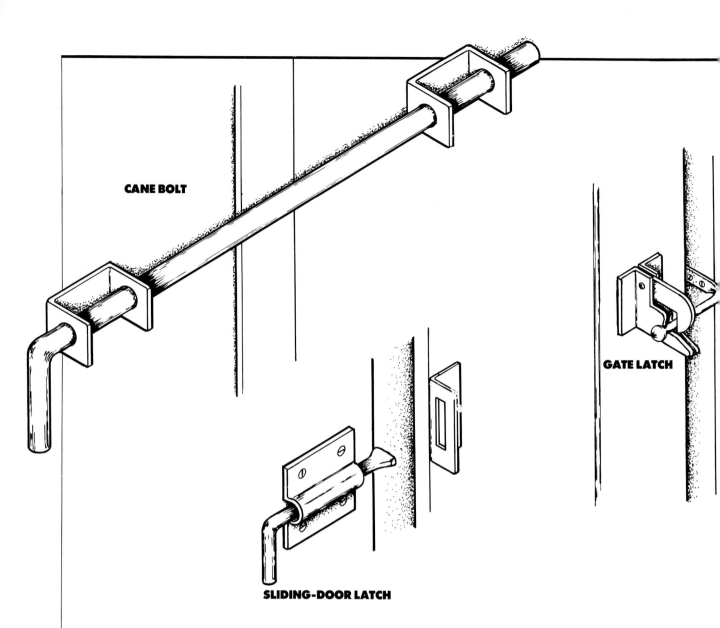

CANE BOLT

SLIDING-DOOR LATCH

GATE LATCH

able to clear the tab, thus preventing movement of the bolt.

Cane bolts are used to secure very large double doors, such as barn doors and driveway gates. There are three pieces to a cane bolt assembly: a latching pin and two saddles. The latching pin is nothing more than a long metal rod with a 90° bend at one end that serves as the handle. The saddle is a U-shaped piece of sheet metal with holes drilled in the tabs to accommodate the latching pin. A saddle is mounted to each of the doors, and the latching pin is thrust through all four saddle holes to form a dead bolt. In some designs, the saddles are simply surface-mounted loops used in pairs on each door.

A common variation is the cane bottom bolt, which is the same piece of hardware mounted vertically to the unhinged stile of each door. When used in this fashion, a hanger holds the rod up when the door is free, and a keeper installed in the floor secures the door when the rod is lowered.

Sliding-door latches are similar to the slide-action bolt, but are designed for sliding rather than swinging doors. The bolt is in the shape of an L, with its horizontal portion (the latching pin part) secured to the front of the door by a metal plate with two up-bent tabs or a standard barrel. Unlike most barrel bolts, the lever (the bent part of the L) is not constricted by limiting tabs and is sometimes removable.

The end of the latching pin is flattened so that it has a broad face, or blade, set perpendicular to the bend of the lever. On the door-jamb is a metal catch plate with a vertically slotted hole cut in it. When the latching pin is rotated 90°, its oblong tip easily engages with the slot of the catch when the bolt is thrown. Returning the lever and pin to its original angle turns the blade sideways to the

catch slot, thus preventing it from becoming disengaged.

Gate latches are unique among outside locks in that they are self-latching. The latching part of the mechanism, called the catch, consists of two components, one stationary and the other movable. The stationary ramp is a folded piece of sheet metal that looks like a knife-blade can opener when viewed from the side. Fastened to the top of this piece, a flat metal hook called a clasp moves up and down on a rivet.

A metal rod that aligns with the catch ramp is attached to the gate. When this rod strikes the front of the catch, the movable clasp is forced upward by a curvature in its edge, allowing the rod to penetrate the latch. Once the rod is clear of the clasp, its weight causes the hook to fall, capturing the rod. The catch is released by raising the clasp.

Another gate latch design uses a floating

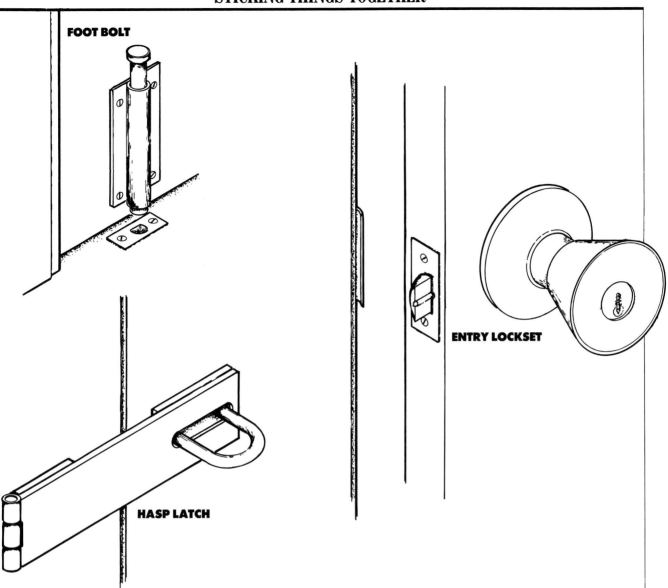

FOOT BOLT

HASP LATCH

ENTRY LOCKSET

latch bar held within a plate fastened to the gate. The gate post is equipped with a metal ramp that has a notch cut into its upper surface. When the gate is closed and the latch bar reaches the limit of the ramp, it falls into the notch, securing the gate.

The addition of a thumb latch makes the gate latch more convenient by providing a thumb lever and handle for easy opening of the gate. The thumb lever is attached to a metal bar that pushes against the clasp or latch bar of the catch. When the lever is depressed, the metal bar raises, and the clasp is opened.

Hasp latches are by far the simplest of all locking devices. A hasp consists of a hinged metal strap and a U-shaped catch called a staple. The shorter leaf of the hasp is fastened to the front of the door or gate, while the slotted longer leaf is free to pivot. The staple mounts to the gatepost or doorjamb so that the slot in the hasp fits over the staple. A pin or padlock inserted through the staple secures the hasp flap and prevents the door from opening. Sometimes the staple is designed with ears and made to pivot so the hasp can be latched without a padlock.

Entry Doors

Entry locksets are essentially self-latching barrel bolts. The latch bolt of the lockset is placed in a closed-end barrel containing a spring, which forces the bolt outward in the engaged position. A full chamfer or bevel is ground into the end of the bolt on the side facing the doorjamb.

Attached to the jamb is a curved piece of metal with a central hole, called a strike. When the door is being closed, pressure is applied to the chamfered edge of the latch bolt by the curved surface of the strike, forcing the bolt to retract into the barrel. Once past the face of the strike, the bolt springs back to its extended position and into the latching hole, securing the door. An offset arm attached to the knob shaft retracts the bolt to disengage the latch.

The entry lockset differs from the passage and privacy sets only in that it contains a keyed lock cylinder which prevents the knobs from being turned when the lock is engaged. Entry locks also have a deadlocking pin built into the latch bolt which prevents the bolt from being forcefully retracted when the door is closed and locked.

Foot bolts are used to secure the bottom edge of an entry door and are particularly popular on French, or double-wide, doorways. The foot bolt is essentially a barrel bolt that mounts on the inside surface of the door perpendicular to the bottom rail. A metal keeper or a hole drilled in the floor engages

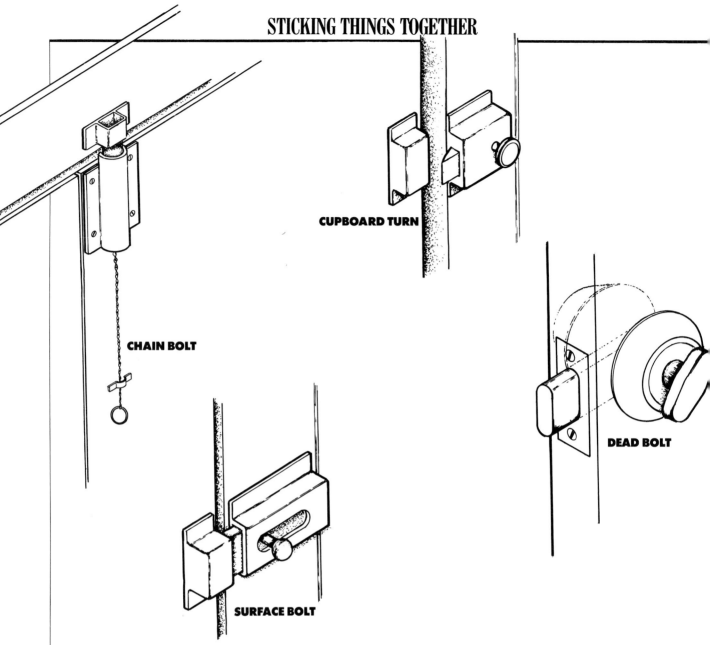

CHAIN BOLT

CUPBOARD TURN

DEAD BOLT

SURFACE BOLT

the latching pin to hold the door secure.

Chain bolts are the upper-rail counterparts to foot bolts. On large doors, a single foot bolt may not be sufficient to keep the door secure. To provide another latching point, a barrel-type chain bolt is fastened at the top of the door and matched to a keeper, a strike plate or a hole drilled in the door header. The latching pin is spring-loaded so the bolt self-latches. Because it's not always easy to reach this latch, a pull chain is attached to the latching pin to disengage the bolt.

Dead bolts come in two varieties. The mortise types are heavy-duty sliding bolts which are mounted within a pocket cut into the door stile and aligned with a drilled strike or a hole in the doorjamb. The bolt or latching pin is activated by a keyed or keyless rotary knob or by interior and exterior locking cylinders. A connecting shaft with an offset arm moves the bolt in and out.

Surface-mounted dead bolts are easier to install, and can be specially made slide-action hand bolts, or encased designs that operate with rotary knobs or keys and utilize either horizontal or vertical bolts. Both are fastened to the inside of the door and require matching strikes to function correctly.

Swing locks are relatively new and are primarily security devices rather than utility latches. The swing lock is essentially a butt hinge that attaches to the unhinged doorjamb just above the lockset strike, with the pivot facing the inside of the room. Only one leaf is attached; the other is free to swing about the pivot. Notches cut into the pivot knuckles act as the locking mechanism. When the leaf is swung against the door, it falls into these notches, preventing any further movement. The closed door cannot be opened until the swing lock is released by lifting up on the leaf and disengaging the notches.

Cabinets

Surface bolts, sometimes called cabinet bolts, are finished barrel bolts with internal springs that hold the latching pin in any position, no matter how the latch may be oriented. The bolt lever, which also serves as the handle, rides in a groove cut along the length of the barrel and prevents the latching pin from slipping out of the barrel. The pin, or bolt, is usually either a half-round or half-oval steel rod.

A metal strike mounted to the cabinet jamb accepts the latching pin and holds the door fast. Strikes that mount in the jamb of the door are called mortise strikes; those that mount on the face of the cabinet are called rim strikes.

Cupboard turns are self-latching mechanical bolts for cabinets. The latching pin of the

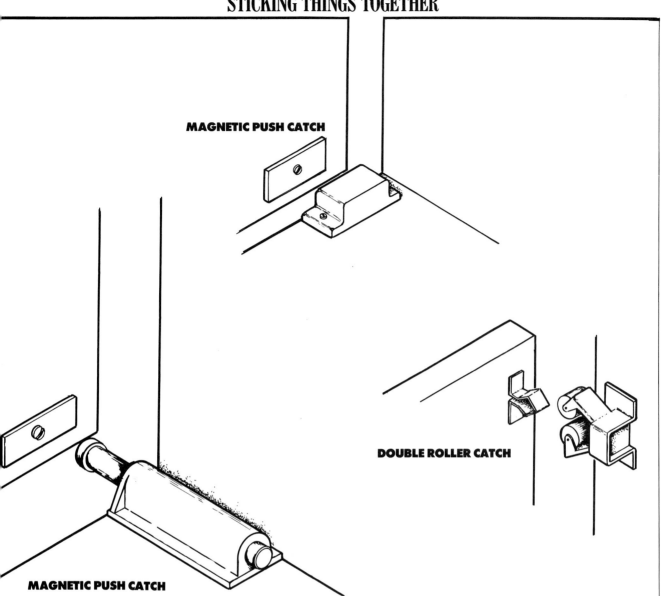

MAGNETIC PUSH CATCH

DOUBLE ROLLER CATCH

MAGNETIC PUSH CATCH

cupboard turn is set in a closed-end barrel against a spring. A full chamfer ground into the end of the pin provides the taper needed to make the latch self-locking. When the cupboard door is pushed against the strike, the pin is forced inside the barrel. Once the latching pin has cleared the strike's leading edge, spring tension forces the pin into a pocket in the strike, thus latching the door. Both mortise and rim strikes are common. An offset cam attached to a twist knob retracts the latching pin to open the door.

Magnetic catches consist of a metal strike plate mounted to the inside surface of the cabinet door and a magnetic catch mounted opposite the strike inside the cabinet or under a shelf. When the door is closed, the magnetic field holds the strike secure with a pull of up to 10 pounds. A slight tug is enough to release the door. Some designs use floating, self-aligning magnets that allow full sur-

face contact with the metal strike plate.

Touch catches are unique in that they fasten and release with a push, thus eliminating the need for cabinet knobs. One type has a magnet mounted on the end of a plunger that slides inside a spring-loaded barrel and is linked to a toggle mechanism. A metal strike is mounted to the inside of the door across from the magnet. Pressing on the door initially forces the plunger in, causing the toggle to engage and hold the plunger in the depressed position. In this mode, the magnet and strike are in alignment and magnetic pull keeps the door closed. A second push on the door and plunger disengages the toggle, and the plunger pops out far enough to cause the magnet to break its hold on the strike, releasing the door.

The mechanical variation has a roller mounted on the end of a spring-loaded lever that's also controlled by a toggle. The strike

in this case is a hooked tang fastened to the door opposite the cabinet-mounted latch. The travel of the roller lever is enough that it engages the door tang securely on the first push and releases it easily on the second.

Friction catches come in a wide variety of shapes and styles. Typical of a friction catch design is the roller catch. The latch portion of the catch is a pair of plastic rollers mounted in a spring-loaded, U-shaped metal frame. A shouldered tang, or strike, mounts to the inside surface of the door in alignment with the latch. When the two are engaged by closing the door, the strike slides into the space between the rollers, forcing them to grip the shoulders. A suitable pull force disengages the strike as it slips free of the rollers. Other friction latch designs reverse the positions of the rollers and strike, replace the rollers with a spring clamp or use a recessed spring-loaded bullet and a dimpled strike.

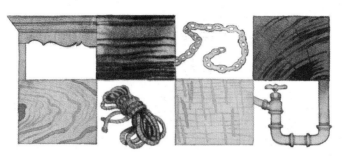

PART FOUR

Boards & Trims, Ropes & Runs

The trouble with
hardware, but also its glory, is
that every aspect of it requires a
special language, words that
describe the ware as well as the
process in which it is
employed.

Go With the Grain

Warm and workable, wood still continually challenges the crafts-man with its staunch independence.

Wood has been a staple of every culture since humans learned to use their thumbs. Even today, in a profusion of miracle metals and corporate composites, wood holds its own as a valuable commodity.

Economically, we've come to depend upon the timber; environmentally, we're learning to respect the tree it's cut from; aesthetically, we virtually demand the finished product. Yet, to many, wood is a puzzle whose pieces are widely scattered.

The frontier nature of logging and the raw power of the sawmill represent the familiar and fabled adventure. But the process that puts the timber in your kitchen table is a well-oiled system that melds time-honored tradition with state-of-the-art engineering to produce a product that spans a tremendous range and fills needs unsatisfied by anything else on this earth.

Lumber

Wood sawn from trees by section and sold by dimension is known as lumber. This wood is available as softwood (cut from needle-bearing conifers like pine, fir, hemlock, cedar, redwood) and hardwood (sawn from deciduous, or leaf-bearing, trees such as oak, maple, walnut and cherry). There are two methods of mill sawing. The most common is plain, or flat, sawing, in which cuts are made tangent to (they follow) the tree's growth rings, yielding a face-grain board. Quartersawing, a somewhat less economical method, entails making cuts perpendicular to the growth rings and produces straight-grained wood with better warp resistance.

All lumber is sized and priced by its rough mill-sawn dimensions, but the finished product may be diminished in size by up to one-third after the surface-planing process is complete. Hence, a nominal 2 X 6 measures only $1^1/_2''$ X $5^1/_2''$ in actual dimension.

A piece of lumber less than 2″ thick and from 2″ to 16″ wide in nominal dimension is a board. Boards less than 6″ wide are called strips. Dimension lumber used for framing work is between 2″ and $4^1/_2''$ thick and up to 16″ wide. Timbers measure at least 5″ on

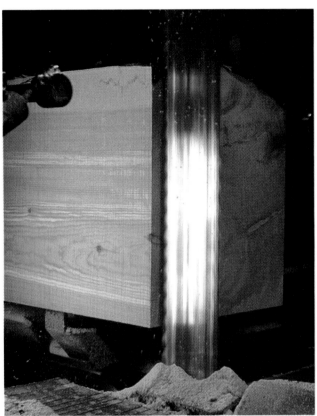

Left: Rivers are the highways of western lumber. Above: Lumber milling in an automated operation.

any surface. Normally, lumber is available in 6' to 20' lengths in 2' multiples.

Lumber is sold by the board foot, each unit being equivalent to a rough board measuring 1" thick, 12" wide and 12" long—144 cubic inches of wood all told. Wood less than 1" thick is counted as a full inch, and stock over 1" is figured by the next larger 1/4". Thus, an 8'-long 1 X 6 contains four board feet, as does a strip measuring 1 3/8" X 2" X 16'. To figure board feet, multiply thickness by width in inches, then multiply by length in feet and divide by 12. Often, retail dealers sell lumber by the lineal, or running, foot which is the standard practice for moldings and other factory-shaped wood. Discount houses even sell by the piece.

Wood is graded according to quality, which is determined by the size of the board and the number and significance of defects such as knots, checks and shake, pitch pock-

ets and wane (rounded edges). Both hardwood and softwood are further graded by intended use, which takes species, structural integrity and appearance into account.

Softwood

Softwood grades exist for both construction and remanufacture use. Lumber for remanufacture is supplied exclusively to industry and is divided into shop grades, industrial clears and specific product stock. Construction lumber is for consumer use and is broken down into three general categories:

Stress-graded includes typical framing members, and timbers, posts, decking and stair stringers. This "American Standard" lumber must meet the criteria of the National Grading Rule.

Non-stress-graded includes yard lumber and wood used for general building purposes, such as boards, battens, lath and planks. The boards are known as commons and are separated into five different grades depending upon the species and the lumber-manufac-

turing association concerned. No. 1 grade has tight knots and minor blemishes and is used for paneling, shelving and finish work; No. 2 has larger knots and noticeable blemishes and is suitable for flooring and rustic paneling; No. 3 has knotholes and visible flaws and is good for sheathing and fencing; No. 4 is a low-quality board with adequate strength for subflooring and concrete forms; No. 5 is the lowest grade of board, used for crating because of its appearance and limited strength. Some species, such as Idaho (western) white pine, are graded by name (colonial, sterling, standard, utility and industrial), but because of differences in species characteristics, grade numbers and names are not necessarily interchangeable.

Appearance lumber is non-stress-graded but visually appealing and is suitable for working, shaping and fine finishing. Most appearance, or "select," grades are noted by letters and are separated into three categories. Grade B & Better allows only a few minor surface imperfections and is chosen for superlative finish work; C Select is the most readily available and has limited defects, which makes it suitable for quality trim and cabinetwork that use a natural finish; D has surface imperfections that can be covered with paint. A certain number of species are graded by number and description (1 and 2 clear) and others use names (prime, supreme, choice and quality).

Hardwood

Hardwood lumber is graded in three categories: factory, dimension parts and finished market products. Factory grades are based on the proportion that can be cut into usable pieces, or cuttings, which are divided further into three project grades.

Firsts and seconds (FAS), a combination of the two best cutting grades, is limited to boards whose poorest side yields at least 83% clear wood. All first and second boards must be at least 6" wide and 8' long.

Selects, quality project wood with the good side equivalent to an FAS board, must be at least 4" wide and 6' in length.

No. 1 common, or "shorts," is the lowest grade of project hardwood. Boards must yield at least 66% clear wood on the poor side and can be no less than 3" wide and 4' long.

Note that hardwood comes in random

Wood		Hardness	Hardness No.*	Figure (Plain-sawn)	Figure (Quarter-sawn)	Machining	Finishing	Uses
Maple (Sugar)		Hard	41	Faint growth ring, some curly, wavy or circular	Occasionally curly or wavy	Good	Moderate	Stable and hard; furniture, flooring and wood products; water or wiping stain, or natural finish
Oak (White)		Hard	40	Conspicuous growth ring	Growth ring stripe, flake	Good	Moderate	Heavy and decay-resistant; furniture, heavy construction and flooring; non-grain-raising stain or natural finish
Pine (White)		Soft	25	Faint growth ring	None	Good	Low	Stable and workable; furniture, trim and millwork; water or oil stain, or paint finish
Pine (Yellow)		Medium	34	Conspicuous growth ring	Growth ring stripe	Moderate	Moderate	Reasonably heavy and strong; construction, plywood, trim and flooring; water or oil stain, paint or natural finish
Poplar (Yellow)		Soft	29	Faint growth ring	None	Good	Low	Moderately strong; furniture frame, trim, plywood and general use; non-grain-raising stain or paint finish
Redwood		Soft	29	Growth ring, some burl	Growth ring stripe, some burl	Moderate	Low	Durable and decay-resistant; construction, outdoor furniture and siding; paint or natural finish
Spruce (Sitka)		Soft	28	Growth ring	Faint growth ring stripe	Moderate	Low	Good strength-to-weight ratio; aircraft and boat construction, millwork and sounding boards; water or oil stain, or paint finish
Walnut (Black)		Medium	36	Growth ring, some burl, curly or wavy	Growth ring stripe, some burl, curly or wavy	Good	Low	Stable, strong and durable; furniture, cabinetwork, gunstocks and paneling; water stain or natural finish
Willow (Black)		Soft	24	Wide growth ring	Growth ring stripe, some fleck	Moderate	Moderate	Light and soft-textured; construction, paneling and furniture; non-grain-raising stain or paint finish

*Reflects machining properties and splinter or split resistance in addition to ease of working with hand tools.

Properties & Characteristics of Some Common Woods

Name	Hardness	Density lb. per cu. ft.	Grain Figure Plainsawed	Grain Figure Quartersawed	Working Quality*	Warp Tendency	Comments
Ash (White)	Medium	35	Conspicuous growth ring, some burl	Plain growth ring stripe, some burl	Difficult	Moderate	Strong, grainy, shock-resistant, steam-bendable; used for handles and furniture; natural finish
Beech (American)	Hard	40	Faint growth ring	Small flakes	Good	High	Strong, shock-resistant, steam-bendable; flooring and furniture; natural finish
Butternut	Soft	25	Faint growth ring	None	Good	Low	Light, coarse-textured; cabinetwork and trim; water stain or natural finish
Cedar (Aromatic)	Soft	23	Faint growth ring	Faint growth ring stripe	Moderate	Low	Light, soft, decay-resistant; chests and paneling; natural finish
Cherry (Black)	Medium	36	Faint growth ring, some burl	Some burl	Good	Low	Strong, dense; furniture and woodworking; water stain or natural finish
Cypress (Bald)	Soft	29	Irregular growth ring	Growth ring stripe	Moderate	Moderate	Durable, decay-resistant, splinters easily; construction and paneling; stain or natural finish
Douglas Fir	Soft	26	Conspicuous growth ring	Growth ring stripe	Difficult	Moderate	Strength varies; construction, plywood and general use; wiping or oil stain, or paint finish
Mahogany (Honduras)	Medium	35	Subdued growth ring	Visible ray pattern	Good	Low	Stable and attractive; furniture, paneling and marine applications; water stain or natural finish

Proper stacking prevents newly sawn lumber from warping.

Softwood Dried Lumber Dimensions *
Thickness (inches)

Strips**		Boards		Dimension		Timbers	
Nominal	Actual	Nominal	Actual	Nominal	Actual	Nominal	Actual
3/8	5/16	1	3/4	2	1 1/2	5 and	1/2 less
1/2	7/16	1 1/4	1	2 1/2	2	greater	than
5/8	9/16	1 1/2	1 1/4	3	2 1/2		nominal
3/4	5/8			3 1/2	3		
				4	3 1/2		
				4 1/2	4		

Face Width (inches)

Strips, Boards, Dimension*

Nominal	Actual	Nominal	Actual	Nominal	Actual	Nominal	Actual
2	1 1/2	6	5 1/2	10	9 1/4	16	15 1/4
3	2 1/2	7	6 1/2	11	10 1/4		
4	3 1/2	8	7 1/4	12	11 1/4		
5	4 1/2	9	8 1/4	14	13 1/4		

*Kiln- or air-dried lumber with a moisture content of 19% or less, surfaced on four sides. Not all sizes indicated are standard stock or readily available.
**Boards less than 6″ wide are referred to as strips.
***Timbers, which have a nominal width of 5″ or greater, have an actual width 1/2″ less than nominal.

Hardwood Lumber Thickness Standards

Rough (inches)	Surfaced Two Sides (inches)	Rough (inches)	Surfaced Two Sides (inches)	Rough (inches)	Surfaced Two Sides (inches)
3/8	3/16	1 1/4	1 1/16	3	2 3/4
1/2	5/16	1 1/2	1 5/16	3 1/2	3 1/4
5/8	7/16	1 3/4	1 1/2	4	3 3/4
3/4	9/16	2	1 3/4		
1	13/16	2 1/2	2 1/4		

widths, with specified minimums assigned by grade. Standard lengths range consecutively from 4′ to 16′. Hardwood is sold as rough (unplaned) or as S2S (surfaced on two sides—top and bottom). Thickness is measured in 1/4″ increments from 1″ to 4″ and expressed as a fraction, so a 5/4 board is nominally 1 1/4″ thick.

Plywood Products

Plywood is a manufactured wood panel made of thin layers, or veneers, glued so adjacent grains run perpendicularly to one another. Normally, panels have an odd number of plies, but sheets with thicker layers may have four or six plies. The outer layers are known as face and back veneers, the inner ones are cores, and the layers just below the surface are called crossbands.

The standard panel size is 4′ X 8′, and its thickness may be 3/16″ or a size from 1/4″ to 3/4″ in 1/8″ increments. Thicknesses of 1″ to 3″ and lengths of 10′ and 12′ are also available by special order.

Plywood's main advantage is that it's dimensionally stable and has nearly equal strength along its width and length. The properties of any given panel depend upon the species of wood used, the placement of plies, the type of glue used and the gluing process. The grade is established by the quality of the face and back veneers.

Generally, two classes of plywood are offered to the consumer—softwood and hardwood. Softwood plywood is more common because it's mainly intended for construction, though some grades are meant for finish work. Most softwood panels are domestically produced from Douglas fir, western hemlock and larch, pine and even redwood. Hardwood plywood is made largely for appearance, of both domestic and imported woods. Oak, birch, cherry, teak, mahogany and walnut veneers aren't uncommon.

Plywood is also manufactured for specific applications such as textured, grooved, or brushed siding, concrete form work, marine construction and floor underlayment.

Plywood standards are established by the manufacturers' associations under the guidance of the U.S. Department of Commerce. Inspection stamps on the back of each panel indicate the grade of the face and back veneers, the species group number (lower numbers indicate stiffer panels), interior or exterior application, the mill code and product standard and the association stamp.

Plywood Grades
Softwood

Grade	Characteristics
N	Smooth surface suitable for a natural finish, all heartwood or sapwood. Free of open defects.
A	Smooth and paintable with no more than 18 neatly made repairs. Suitable for an acceptable natural finish.
B	Solid surface with circular repair plugs, tight knots and minor splits permitted.
C Plugged	Improved C veneer with splits limited to $1/8''$ in width. Knotholes and borer holes limited to $1/4'' \times 1/2''$.
C	Knotholes to $1''$ and tight knots to $1\frac{1}{2}''$. Limited splits permitted.
D	Knots and knotholes to $2\frac{1}{2}''$. Limited splits permitted.

Hardwood

Grade	Face Veneer	Allowable Defects
1	Premium (book-matched)	Burls, pin knots, slight streaks, small patches.
1	Good (unmatched)	Burls, pin knots, slight streaks, small patches.
2	Sound (painting grade)	Appearance defects and smooth patches permitted.
3	Utility (natural)	All natural defects within maximum defined size.
4	Backing (construction)	Unlimited defects with structural integrity intact.

Characteristics of Heartwood Decay

Extremely Resistant	Fairly Resistant	Moderately Resistant	Hardly Resistant
Locust (black)	Cypress (old)	Cypress (young)	Ash
Mulberry (red)	Cedar	Douglas Fir	Beech
Osage Orange	Cherry (black)		Birch
Yew (Pacific)	Chestnut (American)		Butternut
	Juniper		Maple
	Mahogany (Honduras)		Oak (red)
	Mesquite		Pine (white)
	Oak (white)		Pine (yellow)
	Redwood		Poplar (yellow)
	Sassafras		Spruce
	Teak		Willow
	Walnut (black)		

Hardboard

Hardboard—the thin, brown sheet material often known by one of its proprietary names, Masonite—is a quality manufactured wood product that utilizes tailings and scrap material. Wood chips are converted into individual fibers, then compressed into wet mats. Binding agents and other materials

Lumber Grade

Nearly all grade stamps, with the exception of those used for heavy timbers, include at least the following elements:

1. Certification mark: Indicates the association or agency responsible for inspection at the mill.

2. Mill identification: The company name, logo or assigned mill number.

3. Grade designation: The grade name or abbreviation, sometimes indicated by number.

4. Species identification. Indicates an individual species or otherwise the species group.

5. Seasoning condition: Specifies the moisture content at surfacing; S-DRY indicates 19%, MC 15 means 15%, and S-GRN indicates unseasoned lumber over 19%.

may be added to the natural adhesives already in the wood, then heat and pressure are used to form the raw cellulosic material into hard sheets.

Though hardboard is available in many different forms, the two common types are standard (tan brown, light in weight and smooth on one side) and tempered (dark brown, strong and somewhat water-resistant because of the oiling and baking process it goes through). Tempered hardboard is available with one side or both sides smooth.

For special applications, hardboard floor underlayment, paneling and siding can also be ordered. The sheathing grades may be embossed, striated, perforated or prefinished with wood grain, vinyl or a variety of other coatings. Because a hardboard sheet's cut

edge tends to be ragged, there are a number of trim moldings, joints, clips and locking strips available to secure a panel section to a variety of surfaces. Though it doesn't fasten easily to itself, adhesives can be used to secure it to wood, metal and other materials.

Retailers usually sell hardboard in 4' widths and 8' lengths. Panels 2' and 5' wide and lengths from 4' to 16' can be specially ordered. The most common thicknesses are $1/8"$, $3/16"$ and $1/4"$, though $5/16"$ is also made.

Glue-Laminated Lumber

As good timber becomes less available (and as adhesives become more reliable), the market for glue-laminated structural members increases. These members come in the form of wood timbers (straight or curved) and wood-plywood combinations, such as box beams, I-beams and stressed-skin panels.

Essentially, both types use the same construction: Wood or plywood is layered together and bonded under heat and pressure with adhesive to form an engineered structural unit. Laminated timbers are used to make arches, joists and framing parts, while the wood-plywood combinations are more likely to be applied where strength and surface coverage are important.

The advantages of laminated lumber are that large pieces can be made from readily available smaller ones, that the members can be designed and engineered to suit specific requirements and that defects such as cracks are of little importance. There are, however, some additional costs involved in preparing and gluing the wood and in making certain the finished product is of good quality.

Glue-laminated lumber is not normally kept in yard stock but must be specially ordered. It is, however, readily available in most locations through conventional lumber dealers.

Decay-Resistant Woods

Nearly all wood, especially that exposed to the elements, faces eventual decay. Short of repeated painting or chemical treatment, most species will succumb to some type of fungi-induced rot in time.

Pressure-treated lumber is ideal for greenhouse construction.

If that sounds ominous, consider that there are at least three kinds of fungi that inhabit wood. These parasitic organisms can survive as long as four conditions are suitable: temperature, oxygen, moisture and food supply. By restricting any one of these essentials, it's possible to retard or halt decay.

Temperature control is impractical because the range in which the fungi thrive—75°F to 90°F—is also the human comfort range. Likewise, only water-logged wood is saturated enough to deprive the organisms of necessary oxygen, and most wood can't be used in that state.

Conversely, moisture control works fairly well because construction and appearance lumber is kept at a moisture content below the fungi-sustaining threshold of 20%. But by far the best course of action is to select a wood species that is naturally decay-resistant owing to extractives in the heartwood that are either repellent or toxic to fungi. The second table compares the decay resistance of some available woods.

Treated Wood

Treated wood is a common material for outdoor construction or in environments where exposure to water or weather is severe. For most applications, protection against decay and insects is the prime concern; other situations may call for special treatment against fire or underwater exposure.

There are three main types of preservative treatments: the preservative oils such as creosote and other coal-tar products; oil-based organic solvent solutions containing chlorinated phenols; and waterborne salts such as ammoniacal and chromated copper arsenate. For residential use, the waterborne treatments are most popular because they leave the wood fairly clean and paintable, although a process that introduces pentachlorophenol with liquid petroleum gas has been able to achieve this as well.

Two methods are used to implant the preservative within the wood product. The pressure process forces the solution into the wood under specific pressure, and generally allows close control over penetration and retention. The less-involved nonpressure processes include brushing, dipping, soaking and a variety of thermal, diffusion and vacuum treatments. The pressure method is consid-

ered superior, but for certain applications, the other processes are suitable.

Treated lumber is graded the same way as untreated wood. The chemical treatment does not affect the wood's grade designation. The degree of treatment, however, is indicated by its retention level, measured in pounds per cubic foot, and applies to how the wood is to be used. For aboveground applications, a minimum retention level of .25 lb./cu. ft. is recommended. Belowground use requires up to a .60 lb./cu. ft. level, and marine applications need a 2.5 lb./cu. ft. level. Depending on the preservative used and the method of treatment, the life expectancy of treated wood can range from four and a half to 60 years.

Wood-Based Particleboard

Sheets and panels made from processed wood residues are known by a variety of names: particleboard, flakeboard, waferboard and oriented strand board (OSB). Within the industry, panels made of small wood particles are referred to as particleboard. Larger-particle flakeboard is broken down into two subcategories of products made from specific sizes and types of flakes and exterior glues: waferboard, produced from wide-flaked aspen; and OSB, manufactured with the strands in adjacent layers oriented perpendicularly to each other.

In the manufacturing process, wood derived from planer shavings, logging residue, sawdust or mill waste is physically prepared or reduced, then dried and screeded to specific size categories. The particles are then mixed with adhesive binders, and fed into a drum or press where they're heated and formed into panels. Depending upon the finished product desired, the raw material can be layered or aligned before the sheets are pressed, trimmed and sanded.

There are two panel types in general use. Interior-grade Type 1 is made with urea-formaldehyde resin; and Type 2, for protected exterior applications such as sheathing and subfloor, is manufactured using a phenol-formaldehyde binder. Further, three density levels—high, medium and low—exist in each category to serve as a comparative grade certification. Particleboard comes in thicknesses of $1/8"$ to $1 1/4"$, and in sizes from 4' to 8' wide and 8' to 60' long.

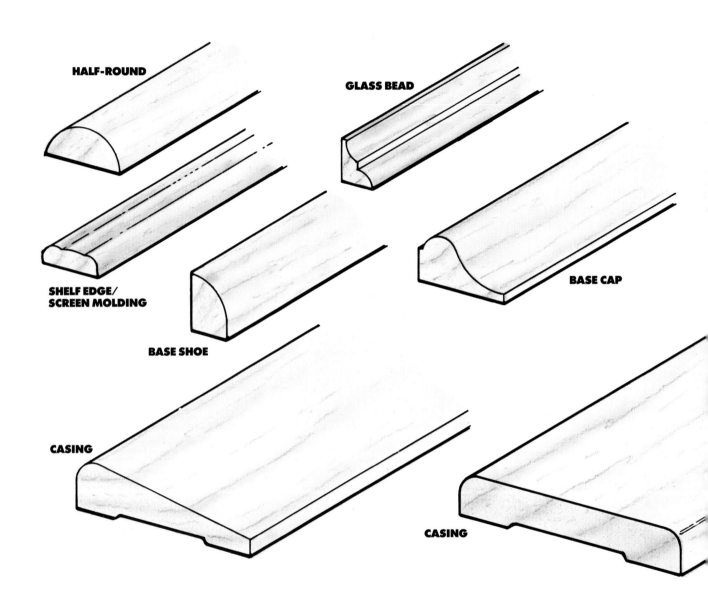

HALF-ROUND

GLASS BEAD

SHELF EDGE/
SCREEN MOLDING

BASE CAP

BASE SHOE

CASING

CASING

Trim & Molding

An often forgotten but essential part of a home

Think of the parts of a house, and you're not likely to think of molding first—or second, third or fourth, for that matter. Yet no other single construction element so strongly influences the look of your home. You doubt it? Next time you glance up from this article, let your eye wander over all the molding in the room: baseboard, ceiling, window and door trim. Now, in your mind's eye, remove it all—or change it to a different style. Molding frames a room, defines its boundaries, accentuates or softens angles, adds depth and presence and to a large extent determines architectural motif—modern, colonial, rustic, traditional, Victorian. Interior designers say that the quickest way to radically alter the appearance of a room is to add, remove or change the trim.

Yet molding is more than mere decorative embellishment. It covers the seams and gaps (and inevitable imperfections) at the junctures of walls and windows, floors, ceilings and doorways. And it protects walls and entrances from bumps and scrapes.

Until the mid-1800s, all moldings were made by hand using special cutting planes,

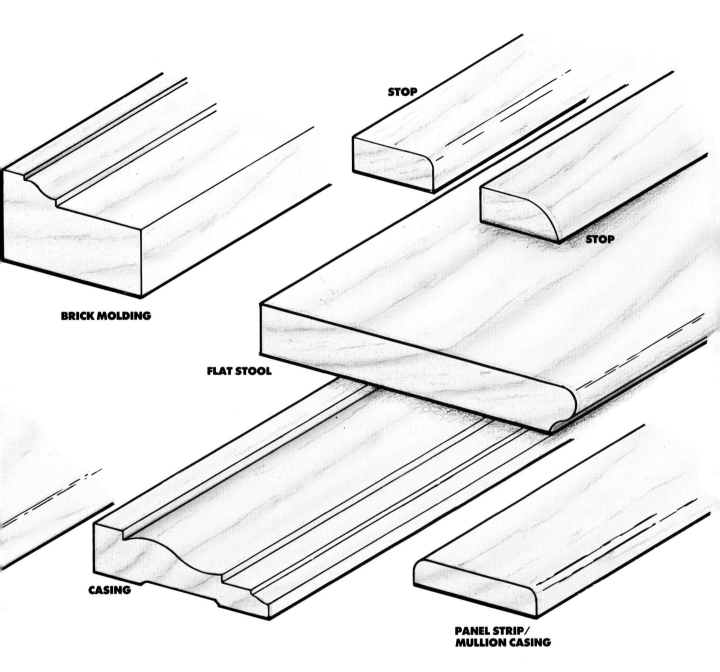

STOP

STOP

BRICK MOLDING

FLAT STOOL

CASING

PANEL STRIP/ MULLION CASING

each designed to produce a different contour or pattern. Trim carpenters carried dozens of different planes in their toolboxes and often spent months finishing the interior of a home. These days the average do-it-yourselfer can choose from several hundred standardized shapes and sizes of ready-made, ready-to-install wood moldings. Few lumber suppliers carry every size and shape, but most offer a good basic selection and can usually show you a book—or display board —of available patterns. In addition, the current trend in home renovation has fostered

millwork shops that specialize in custom moldings—some of which narrow the specialty further to specific period moldings such as Victorian or Greek revival.

Buying Molding

Most lumberyards carry standard molding in clear-grade (also called select, or stain-grade) pine. Some also offer paint-grade pine or fir molding, which has more defects and is sometimes made up of short pieces spliced together with finger joints. Even clear-grade

molding, however, can have defects, so be sure to choose each piece carefully.

Molding is generally made and sold in random lengths from 3' to 20'. Rather than placing an order in terms of the total number of feet you need, it's best to buy individual pieces in the lengths necessary to span each dimension of the room. For example, if you want to install crown molding around the ceiling line of a 12' by 14' room, it's better to order four pieces—two 14'-plus lengths (allowing several inches extra for each miter cut to be made) and two 12'-plus lengths—

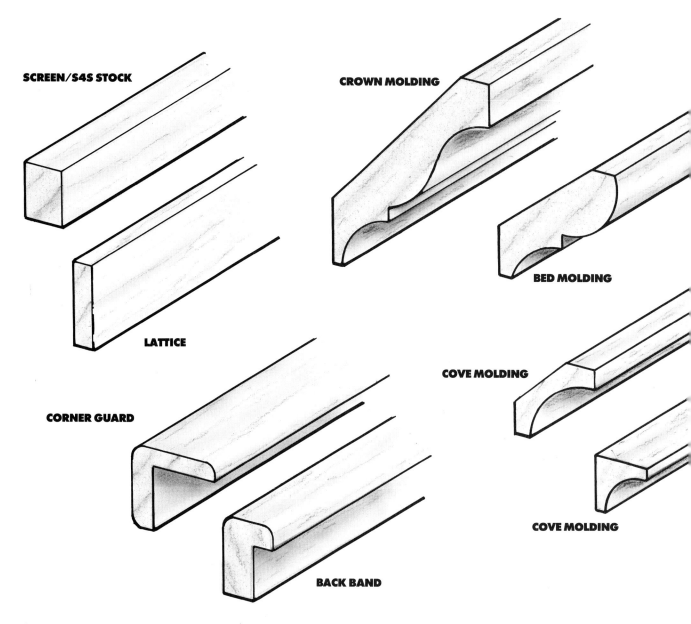

SCREEN/S4S STOCK

LATTICE

CORNER GUARD

BACK BAND

CROWN MOLDING

BED MOLDING

COVE MOLDING

COVE MOLDING

than to ask for, say, 55'. This is because installing a continuous piece of molding on each side of a room is easier (and generally looks better) than butting two or more pieces together. Also, keep in mind that, although pattern books describe molding size in terms of thickness and width, lumberyards generally refer only to the width and style or type: $3^{1}/_{2}$" ranch casing, for example, or 1" half-round. This simplifies ordering but can lead to confusion over minor pattern variations. So be sure the salesperson understands precisely what you want, and when you buy several pieces of a given pattern, check them for possible mismatches.

Molding Types

Although the various patterns and sizes in which molding is available number in the hundreds, they all fall into a dozen or so basic categories of molding types, each intended for specific purposes.

Crown and *bed moldings* are ceiling moldings that bridge the joint between wall and ceiling. Because they are installed diagonal-ly, or *sprung*, from wall to ceiling, rather than fitted flush into the joint, they neatly cover up any irregularities. Sizes range from $1^{1}/_{2}$" bed to $4^{5}/_{8}$" crown.

Cove moldings, though less ornamental, are also often used as ceiling moldings—particularly in ranch-style homes or in rooms that have been paneled. Some types are sprung, while others—more appropriate for rooms in which the joints between paneling or dry wall and the ceiling are virtually perfect—fill in the 90° wall-to-ceiling juncture.

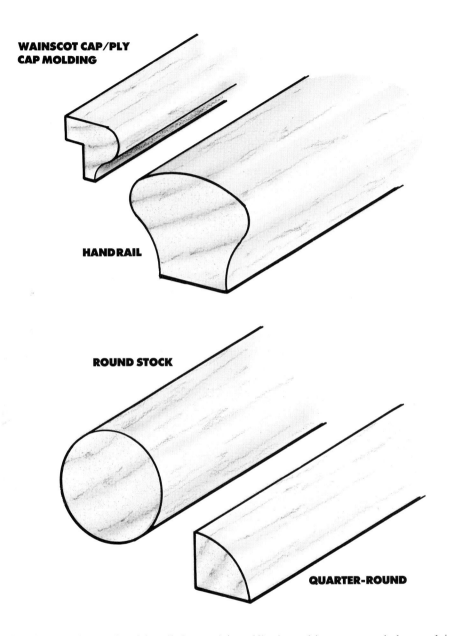

WAINSCOT CAP/PLY CAP MOLDING

HANDRAIL

ROUND STOCK

QUARTER-ROUND

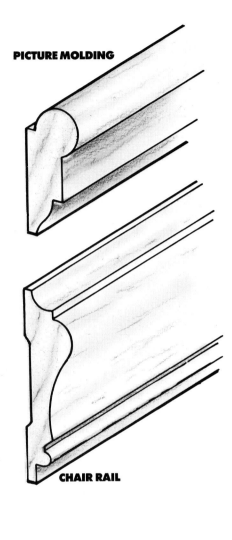

PICTURE MOLDING

CHAIR RAIL

Casing is the woodwork installed around doorways and windows. Because the sizes of both windows and doors are more or less standardized, casing is often sold in standard lengths of 10′, 12′, 14′ and 16′, as well as in random lengths. You can also buy standard-size window and door trim packages that include all the precut molding you need to finish an opening. In the case of a window package, this would include *stool molding*, which forms the interior window sill. *Rabbeted stool molding* is machined to fit over the sloping exterior sill, while *flat stool*

molding is used in casement windows and other applications where the sill surface is level.

Casing for windows and doors is available in more standard shapes (31 in all) than any other type of molding, and in widths ranging from 2¼″ to 4¼″. Regardless of the pattern, the back surface is always partially plowed out, or channeled, about 1/16″, leaving a shoulder on each side. When casing is installed, one shoulder rests on the door (or window) frame and the other on the wall. The channel bridges any high spots or other

imperfections between the two areas and allows just enough "give" for the molding to make good contact with each surface.

Base molding, or *baseboard*, is also channeled at the back to help it fit better against the wall. Like casing, it serves both as a decorative trim and to protect the wall from wear and tear. Most baseboards are finished with *base shoe molding*, which is nailed at (and to) the bottom of the base to cover gaps between the base molding and floor. Furthermore, baseboard is often topped with a strip of *base cap molding*. Base cap is especially

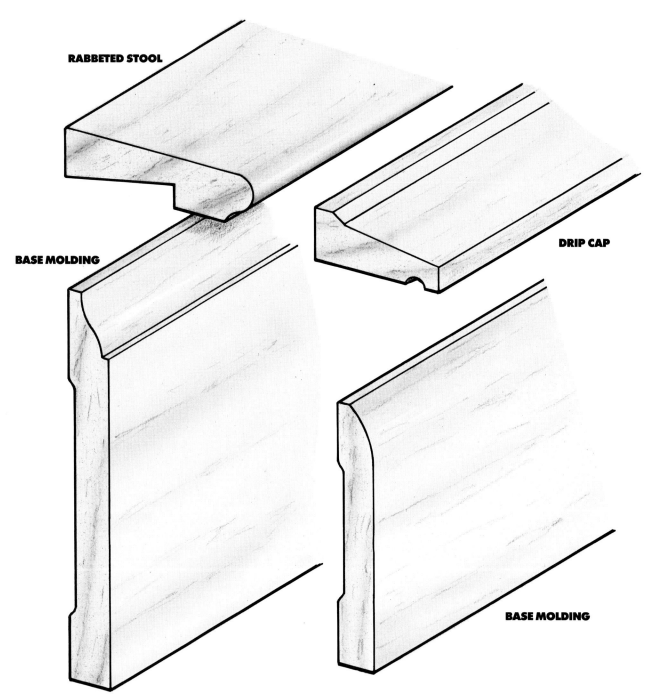

RABBETED STOOL

BASE MOLDING

DRIP CAP

BASE MOLDING

helpful when a wall is not quite straight and true, since it's more flexible than the wider base molding and conforms to (and covers up) minor fluctuations in the wall surface. Base cap is also used to create decorative wall panels.

Base molding is available in patterns ranging in thickness from $1/2''$ to $11/16''$ and in widths from $2^1/4''$ to $5^1/4''$. As a rule of thumb—useful for keeping baseboards in proper proportion to the room as a whole—baseboards in rooms with 8' ceilings should be 3" to 4" high (including base cap, if any),

and baseboards in rooms with higher ceilings should be 5" to 6" tall.

Chair rail moldings are a hallmark of colonial and traditional architecture. Originally intended to protect walls from being bumped by the backs of chairs, chair rail is installed horizontally, usually around all four walls of a room, 30" to 32" above the floor. Today chair rails serve a primarily decorative function, often dividing different wall treatments (such as paneling and wallpaper) to create the effect of wainscoting. *Wainscot cap* and *ply cap moldings* are used to top the

protruding edges of true wainscoting made from solid wood or plywood. They are also sometimes combined with other moldings to create chair rails.

Picture molding is often applied a few inches below crown molding to produce a more ornate or fuller-looking cornice. Its original function, however, was to provide a surface from which to hang pictures; special hooks fit over the molding and support wire for hanging paintings or other framed works. This wall-saving approach, common in Victorian homes, is enjoying a revival.

Miscellaneous Moldings

Handrail moldings are generally made of hardwood and, just as the name indicates, are used for railings in stairwells. Another self-descriptive molding is *corner guard*, applied to either outside or inside corners to cover and protect the right-angle junctures of wallboard or plywood panels. Cove molding also is used to cover joints on inside corners.

Back band molding is similar to corner guard, but is usually applied to the outside edge of window or door casings to further frame the opening and create greater depth.

Mullion casing is installed vertically between side-by-side paired windows to cover rough board edges between the two and to produce the visual effect of a single unit. *Stop molding* is nailed to the inside frame of a double-hung window to keep the lower sash in place. In a doorway, it's nailed to the jambs to prevent a closing door from swinging all the way through.

Brick molding is used for exterior window and door casings. Another exterior molding is *drip cap*, which is installed over window and door frames to keep rain from seeping under the casing and to channel water away from the window or door itself.

Glass bead molding is used in place of putty to hold window glass in place. Though somewhat rare in most modern homes, and not easy to install, this decorative molding creates extraordinarily beautiful windowpanes. *Screen molding* serves the same function for window and door screens; it helps anchor the mesh and covers the rabbet into which the screen is nailed. Screen molding is also called *shelf edge* because it is often applied along the outermost upper edge of shelving as a decorative stop to keep books in place.

Finally, there are several types of moldings that are best described as "utility" or "all-purpose."

Lattice molding, at one time used primarily for building trellises, is $9/32''$ thick and available in widths from $1^1/8''$ to $1^3/4''$. It serves nicely as a simple stop molding and comes in handy in many other applications calling for thin, narrow strips of wood. Even more versatile is *S4S* (surfaced on four sides) molding, rectangular trim made in thicknesses ranging from $1/2''$ to $1^1/16''$ and in widths

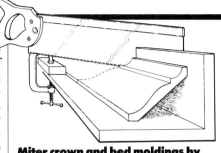

Miter crown and bed moldings by blocking the top edge against the miter box.

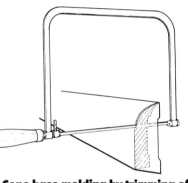

Cope base molding by trimming off the mitered edge.

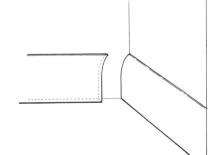

When properly trimmed, the coped base follows the contour on the face of the adjoining molding.

from $3/4''$ to $2^3/4''$. The larger sizes are frequently used in combination with base cap molding to create baseboards and with picture or crown moldings to produce unique ceiling moldings.

Quarter-round molding, available in widths from $1/4''$ to $1^1/16''$, can substitute as glass bead, inside corner or base shoe moldings. *Half-rounds*, ranging from $1/4'' \times 1/2''$ to $1/2'' \times 1''$, are often used as screen or shelf edge molding. *Full-round molding* is sold in $1^1/16''$, $1^5/16''$ and $1^5/8''$ diameters and is used mostly for closet poles.

Make Molding Meet Happily in Corners

Mitering Crown Molding

Mitering most molding is a simple matter of cutting the strip with the molding set square against the back of the miter box and with the saw at the appropriate setting (usually 45° or 90°). But because crown molding is sprung from wall to ceiling at an angle, it must be positioned in the miter box at that angle before it's cut. The best way to do this is to visualize the base of your miter box as the ceiling and the back of the box as the wall. Put the molding in the box upside down, and use a block of wood clamped to the base to hold the strip at the angle at which the molding will be installed.

Making a Coped Joint

When two strips of molding meet at an inside corner, a coped joint often provides a closer fit and better appearance than a simple mitered joint. To make a coped joint, one piece—usually the longest of the two—is cut square at the end and butted flush against the wall. The second piece is then mitered at an open 45° angle. The cut reveals the contour of the molding face. By carefully cutting away the angle with a coping saw, following the contour and cutting slightly more from the back of the molding than from the front, an end is produced that fits tightly over the front of the butted piece. Coped joints work best with relatively simple base molding and least well with ornate sprung crown moldings.

The illustrations you see here provide only a hint of the full range of molding variations available to you. In fact, the most difficult part of working with molding may be choosing from the seemingly limitless number of types, patterns and sizes. The best way to get a feel for the full range of possibilities is to visit local lumberyards, as well as woodworking or millwork shops that produce custom moldings. Then, exercise that mind's eye of yours again. You just may discover an entirely different home lurking within the one you have now.

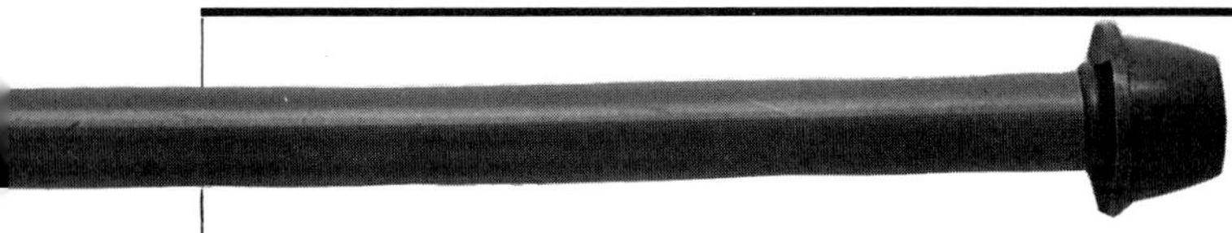

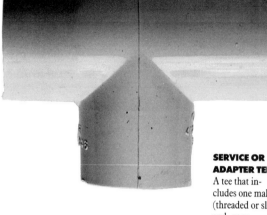

FLEXIBLE FAUCET FIT-TING

A preformed compression fitting and pipe assembly designed to connect a water supply line to a faucet or toilet tank. Made of bendable plastic or brass and formed to match various style fittings.

SERVICE OR ADAPTER TEE

A tee that includes one male (threaded or slip) end, or an internally threaded female end (shown).

90° STREET ELBOW

A "street el" in plumber's parlance, this is a right-angle fitting that includes a male end and a female end in the same piece.

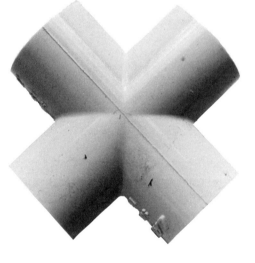

An armchair look at

Plumbing in Depth

Your reference guide to frequently used plumbing fittings

CROSS

A four-way connection used to join pipes at right angles to one another on a single plane.

Household plumbing carries with it no small degree of mystery. In theory, it should all be very simple: Water is sent to a service line in your house. From there, it's distributed to various fixtures through a network of smaller lines, and whatever's not used up is drained through a series of larger pipes to a sewer or septic system.

In practice, it appears anything *but* simple. Upon inspection, the system looks as if the house had been built around it. Plumbing runs twist through places that would accom-modate neither tool nor hand, and if by chance you could snag a maverick fitting, you probably couldn't crack it open anyway.

This, at least, is the way it used to be. Over the past decade, the use of plastic pipe has increased dramatically, making life easier for the plumbers who have to install it, the people who have to live with it and the homeowner who may have to repair it. Plastic weighs a fraction as much as galvanized pipe, can be more durable than copper and is admirably resistant to freeze damage. It's also a great insulator against sound and heat transfer and can be joined in seconds with one application of cement.

Though plastic pipe hasn't changed the intricacies of the plumbing run much, it at least brings it into the realm of reparability. The fittings shown here represent a common sampling of what's available to service household lines. Though polyvinyl chloride (PVC) plastic is the material of choice, these pieces are generally available in malleable iron, copper, and other types of plastic, such as chlorinat-

COUPLING
This straight fitting joins two pipes together and has two female ends.

45° ELBOW
Another common fitting that carries a pipe run through a 45° angle.

TEE
A fitting which allows three pipes to be joined together and which has three female ends.

90° ELBOW
Often called an el, this common fitting is used to make right-angle bends.

NIPPLE
Any length of pipe shorter than 12″. The terminology applies to threaded pipe but can be carried over to plastic plumbing too.

WYE
Available in single or double configurations, with the branch(es) set at a 45° angle. Used to join three (or four) pipes together.

ed polyvinyl chloride (CPVC) and acrylonitrile-butadiene styrene (ABS).

Plumbing's Platitudes

1. Pipe is generally measured by its inside diameter, though the actual measurement is never exactly the same as the nominal size.
2. Pipe grade is based on wall thickness. Schedule 40 is standard, and plastic pipe is graded as equivalent to that standard, or suitable for residential DWV (drain, waste

and vent) or service (noncode) applications.
3. CPVC is a high-pressure (100 psi), high-temperature (180°F) plastic and is a good choice for household supply plumbing.
4. PVC pipe is generally approved for cold-water household supply or drain, waste and vent applications.
5. ABS pipe is most commonly used in drain, waste and vent applications.
6. Some cements are specific to PVC and some to CPVC. Even a universal plastic pipe cement isn't perfect for both.

7. A hacksaw is the best tool for cutting plastic pipe, and a penknife can be used to clean the burrs.
8. Cleaning joint surfaces thoroughly with solvent is the most important step in achieving a sound joint.
9. Trial-fit all pieces before mating them, and try a different fitting if one seems to be too loose.
10. Somewhere there is a fitting that will accomplish what you're trying to do. Seek and ye shall find.

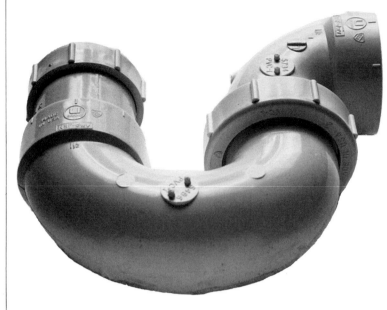

DRAIN, WASTE AND VENT (DWV) TRAP
Available in S, running and P (shown) configurations, traps prevent the odors of waste water standing in the drain line from entering the house. Trap outlets are pitched to provide a drop of ¼″ to the foot.

HUB CROSS
A cross used in drain, waste and vent applications; made with hubs or collars at the four joints.

VALVE
A mechanical fitting that's placed in a pipe run and is used to shut off the flow of water. A valve at the end of a pipe is called a faucet.

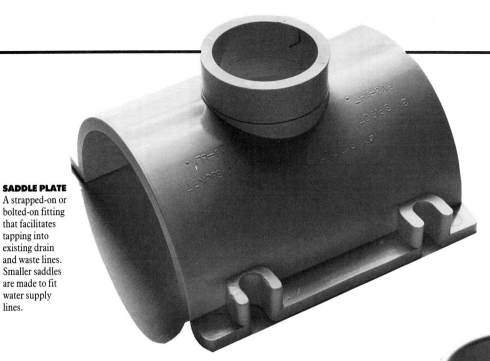

SADDLE PLATE
A strapped-on or bolted-on fitting that facilitates tapping into existing drain and waste lines. Smaller saddles are made to fit water supply lines.

VENT IN- CREASER
A fitting that allows the diameter of the waste vent pipe to be increased at the roof to reduce the chance of blockage and to allow gases to escape more easily.

UNION
Commonly made of iron, copper or brass, a union is a threaded coupling that allows a convenient break in a pipe without disturbing joints preceding or following it. Unions come in a number of configurations to fit several joint types.

SLIP COLLAR
Designed as a temporary repair fitting to join plastic and steel pipe. The collar slides on the plastic neck and seals around the metal pipe with one or more rubber gaskets.

BUSHING
Functions as a reducer, but takes up less space because one end is designed to slip (or thread) inside the larger pipe.

CAP
A fitting used to seal the end of a pipe from the outside.

ADAPTER
A catch-all term for a fitting that connects one kind of pipe to another or one type of joint to another—e.g., a plastic pipe to a threaded pipe. Adapters come in a variety of common configurations.

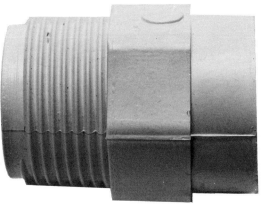

PLUG
A fitting used to seal the end of a pipe from the inside.

REDUCER
Similar to a coupling, but with female ends of different sizes to join two different diameters of pipe.

A Tutorial on Working With Plastic Pipe

There's hardly anything more suited to the occasional handyman than plastic pipe. For unlike copper, iron and other conventional plumbing materials, thermoplastic pipe and fittings require little if any investment in tools and supplies, and ask only that the novice exercise some care in preparing the parts for assembly.

Although there are seven different types of plastic pipe available (they're categorized by application and named by the resins used to make the plastic compound), only two or three of them normally are joined mechanically, either by clamps or by threaded flange-nut couplings. The rest are solvent-welded—a process by which a special primer and solvent actually dissolve the mating surfaces, forming a fused bond that's similar to that of a metal weld.

Solvent-welding is only as effective as the procedure used in completing it. To start, both the primer and solvent must be formulated for the type of plastic they're being used on. Though it's true that "universal" solvents do exist, none are completely adequate for the variety of molecular structures present in different plumbing materials. And though it's also true that a joint will form using solvent alone, the priming step is an important one because it cleans and softens the plastic surfaces. One warning: The solvent chemicals can be very hazardous to your eyes, so always wear eye protection.

Proper fitting is also critical to the strength of a joint. Plastic parts are *interference-fit*—the sockets are tapered so the pipe starts to seat before it's fully in place. Sometimes—especially if the joining parts are made by different manufacturers—the joint will be too loose. If that's the case, it may be necessary to try other fittings in search of one with a better-matched socket.

Finally, it pays to follow proven installation techniques. These include cutting the pipe squarely; deburring the cut; trial-fitting the joint; using fresh, clean solvent within the suggested temperature range; seating the pipe to the fitting and allowing an undisturbed set; and checking the cement bead for consistency.

Patience and a bit of practice will go a long way toward making your plastic plumbing debut a success. Just don't let the simplicity of the process deceive you into thinking that a sloppy job is impossible.

1. Use a hacksaw and a miter box to make a square cut through the pipe. Roller-type pipe cutters designed for plastic make an even cleaner cut.

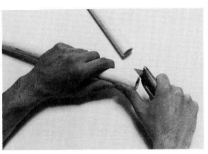

2. Clean the ragged burrs from the cut with a penknife or a deburring tool. Sandpaper works, but may remove too much material. Even one burr can cause a mark that paves the way for a leak.

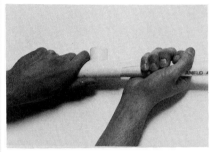

3. Dry-fit joint to check for snugness. If the pipe goes fully into its seat, it's too loose; try another fitting.

4. Apply primer to the clean, dry mating surfaces, using a product formulated for the type of pipe you're working with. First prime the inside of the fitting, then the outside of the pipe.

5. Wait 10 seconds, then brush an even coating of solvent over the inside of the fitting. Follow with a continuous coat over the pipe. Don't daub with little strokes—it causes premature drying.

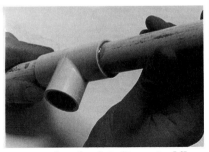

6. Force the pipe into its seat while the solvent is wet, giving the fitting a quarter-turn as you align it to eliminate insertion marks. Hold the joint together for 15 seconds—longer in cooler temperatures—to give the cement time to set. Examine the bead of cement pushed out of the fitting—it should be visibly even all the way around. Don't bother to wipe the excess off, because you may disturb the setting cement.

ACETAL ½" X ½" X ³/8" COMPRESSION TEE
Connects individual ³/8" fixture supplies to a ½" PB tubing.

BRASS ½"-COMPRESSION-TO-½"-MALE-PIPE-THREAD 90° ELBOW
Connects plastic, copper or steel female threads to PB through an el.

Polybutylene—the Plumber's Miracle

About 20% of the water supply systems in homes built during 1987 were plumbed with neither copper nor PVC; they were fitted with plumbing's new miracle plastic, polybutylene. PB appeals to the professional for two main reasons: Its flexibility reduces the number of joints that have to be made at turns, and its cold-or-hot rating eliminates the need to carry two types of pipe, fittings and adhesives. Though PB costs more than PVC, it can be installed so quickly that a contract plumber can still bid competitively on a major job.

Polybutylene tubing has further advantages over its competitors. It is resistant to many corrosive compounds. (PB's main enemies are hydrocarbons, concentrated chlorinated mixtures such as household bleach and swimming pool water, and ultraviolet light.) Because of its flexibility, PB is practically immune to water hammer—pounding caused by pressure waves generated when a faucet is turned off quickly—and freezing won't damage it (though fittings may suffer). PB is also resistant to scale and has excellent flow characteristics. Common household sizes are ³/8", ½" and ³/4". The dimensions used for nomenclature are internal, so you might find ½" vernacularly referred to as ⁵/8"—its outside diameter.

When pros install polybutylene runs, they use either crimp or heat-fusion fittings. These may be made of plastic, copper or brass, depending on the application. Metal fittings and PB tubing are an increasingly popular combination for running lines in a heated concrete slab.

All the professional PB joining systems require tools costing hundreds of dollars, placing them well out of reach of the home handyperson. There are, however, a number of compression fittings suitable for repairs in residential plumbing systems. The only tool needed to install compression fittings is a wrench to tighten nuts.

PB tubing and compression fittings are particularly well suited to replacing sections of copper or PVC supply lines that have been damaged by freezing. You simply cut out the offending section, sweat or glue pipe-thread adapters to each end of the broken line, and connect a replacement section of PB with pipe-thread-to-compression adapters.

Polybutylene and its array of fittings are just beginning to make it out to the hinterlands, so you may get blank looks when you ask for it at your local hardware store. You may have to shop at a wholesale plumbing supply store to find what you need. The compression fittings shown in the accompanying photos are representative of the ones that are commonly available.

BRASS ½"-COMPRESSION-TO-½"-FEMALE-PIPE-THREAD ADAPTER
Connects plastic, copper or steel male pipe threads to PB tubing.

½″ X ½″ COMPRESSION UNION
Used to splice two sections of PB tubing of the same size.

BRASS ½″-COMPRESSION-TO-½″-MALE-PIPE-THREAD ADAPTER
Connects plastic, copper or steel female pipe threads to PB tubing.

ACETAL ½″-COMPRESSION BALL VALVE
Shut-off valve for PB pipe; works in one direction only.

½″ PB ACE-TAL FITTING COMPRESSION SEAL
Fits inside the compression nut; a different seal is used for brass compression fittings.

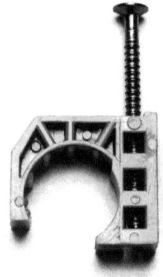

½″ PB TUB-ING HANGER
Used to hang PB tubing from floor joists or other wooden members.

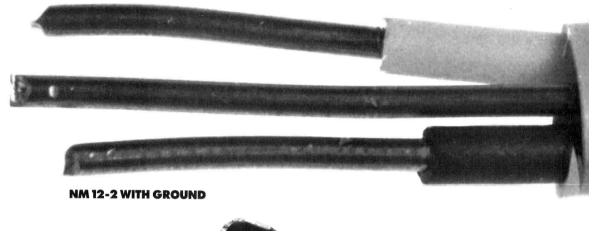

NM 12-2 WITH GROUND

HANDY BOX   **GEM BOX**

Electrical Home Tour

Join us for a sojourn through residential wiring, complete with studs and hickies.

A favorite analogy used to explain electricity moving in wires—a phenomenon that's often considered inscrutable, probably because it's hard to witness in action—is water flowing in pipes. Voltage equals pressure, amperage equals flow, resistance equals friction—a tidy set of metaphors to make the invisible understandable.

Apt as those theoretical associations may be, plumbing makes a lousy mechanical analogy to wiring. A plumbing system has entirely separate supply and drain systems, with distinct hardware and design requirements. But a residential electrical circuit has a bundled cable that handles the in-and-out in one path.

Plumbers aren't electricians, and the twain seldom meet. Just like every department at the hardware store, there's a special jargon spoken on the electrical aisles, and the most intimate knowledge of plumbing Ls and unions won't get you far talking wires. Once

you get to know it, though, you'll probably discover that the common, household electron isn't nearly as mysterious as you may have supposed.

Conductors

An electrical conductor may be either a wire or a cable (a bundle of wires) made of copper, aluminum or aluminum clad in copper. Around the house, most wiring contains at least two conductors, with single wires relegated mainly to the insides of appliances. Lamp (or zip) cord, the ubiquitous hookup for everything from electric fans to stereo speakers, has a pair of stranded (composed of many small wires, for flexibility) conductors. Though lamp cord usually isn't color coded, one of the insulators will have a ridge to help you keep pluses with pluses.

Common interior household wiring usual-

SQUARE BOX

OCTAGONAL BOX

ly consists of two or three conductors housed in a plastic (or cloth, in houses over 50 years old) sheath to form a cable. Under the covering, you'll find single-strand wires with black, white and, in some situations, red plastic insulation. If the cable is described as "with ground," there will also be an uninsulated wire (or, rarely, an insulated one in green or green with yellow stripes).

Material. Copper is the preferred metal for conductors, but aluminum has achieved some acceptance in the building industry. Copper's main advantage is that, for a given size, it can carry more current than aluminum. In residential wiring, aluminum must be a full size larger than copper, and the difference is even greater in larger wires. Aluminum's claim is economy: It is less expensive even though it must be larger for a given application.

Devices and connectors designed for cop-per wire cannot be used directly with aluminum wire, unless it's copper clad. An electrolytic reaction between the two metals at connections produces an oxide that resists current flow, causing overheating and subsequent loosening. Disastrous house fires have occurred because of this incompatibility. If you have or use aluminum wire, make sure that all devices and connectors are compatible with it (look for the markings AL/CU or CO/ALR).

Gauge. The size of a wire or cable is called its gauge, and, in the U.S., it's assigned according to the American Wire Gauge (AWG) standard—a mighty official name for a set of rules accepted more by default than decree. There are actually a half-dozen wire gauge standards in use around the world, and the only one to be officially recognized by an Act of Congress—the Birmingham (or Stub's Iron Wire) Gauge—is obsolete.

Anyway, bigger AWG numbers mean smaller wires: Fourteen is the smallest general-use wire for residential applications; 12 is larger and handles heavier loads; and the cable between the power company's transformer and your meter may be 2, 1, 0 or even 00 (called double aught). Lamp cord is typically available from 14- to 24-gauge.

How much size difference is there between gauges? An AWG wire of a given gauge is 1.123 times larger than the next smaller wire (one digit larger). For those of you who don't tote calculators, diameter doubles every six gauge numbers: Eight is twice the diameter of 14. In practice, there's no need for a single-digit selection of wires, so it's only manufactured in certain gauges. You'll commonly find wire in even-numbered gauges down to No. 4, after which it proceeds in single digits. **Solid versus stranded.** Residential copper wires larger than 8-gauge and aluminum

DEVICE BOX WITH HANGER

WEATHERPROOF OUTLET BOX

PLASTIC DEVICE BOX

BOX HANGER

larger than 10 are always stranded to make them more flexible, though lamp cord and special-application wires of much smaller gauges may also be stranded. (For trivia buffs: Because of a phenomenon called "skin effect," stranded conductors also have lower resistance than solid conductors of the same cross-sectional area. This is of more practical importance to a utility engineer than it is to a home builder.)

Color codes. There are four main colors used in residential wiring: black, white (sometimes gray), red and green. Green is always "ground," and white (or gray) is always "neutral." Black and red are hot, but the National Electrical Code specifies only that hot conductors may not be white, green or gray. For safety's sake, there is a consistent set of applications for the various colored wires. If you get involved in running circuits, be sure you understand and observe the rules.

Insulation types. Different sheaths and insulators are rated for different temperatures and environments. There are several dozen different combinations, but in most residential applications, you'll find one of three labels: NM, UF or SE. NM (nonmetallic) cable is the standard cable for residential wiring and is often referred to by one manufacturer's trademark: Romex. It can be used in any branch circuit (not a main service) application that doesn't expose it to moisture, corrosion or temperatures greater than 140°F. UF (underground feeder) is used specifically for buried service to outbuildings but, in practice, is the usual alternative when NM won't do. (Occasionally, you'll find NMC, which is NM rated for moist and corrosive environments.) UF is also available with an ultraviolet light-resistant sheath for exposed applications. SE (service entrance) is the big cable connecting the meter to the

service panel (fuse or breaker box, in layman's parlance).

Reading the label. A typical residential cable will have a label (printed or engraved) that looks like this: NM 12-2 with ground 600 V. That's a nonmetallic cable with two 12-gauge wires and a grounding wire that are rated for up to 600 volts. You'll also find the manufacturer's trademark. A typical variation is 12-2G (or 12-2W/G) Type NM 600V. Lamp-cord and single-wire labels aren't so standardized but will always have indications of size and suitable applications. One example is HPN heater cord, which looks like lamp cord but has neoprene insulation rated for electrical heating devices.

Boxes

All electrical connections, devices and fixtures go in or are attached to boxes—lots of

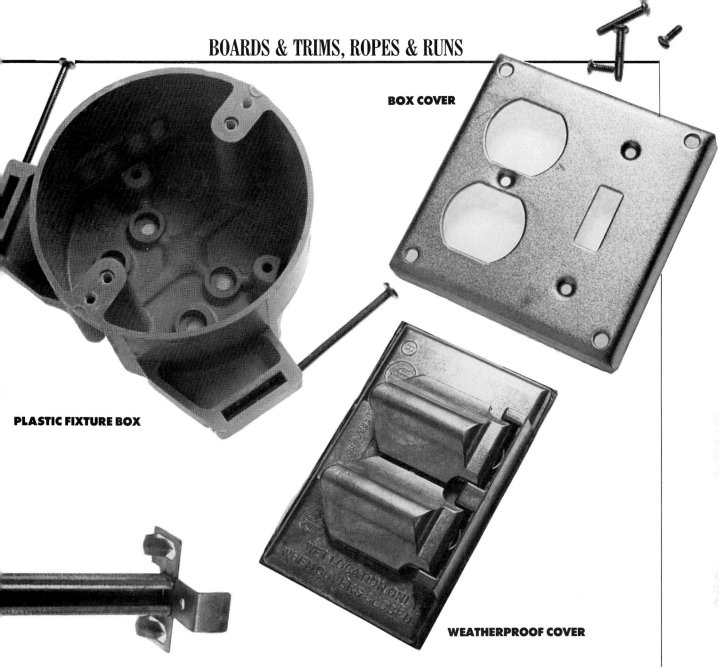

BOX COVER

PLASTIC FIXTURE BOX

WEATHERPROOF COVER

different types and sizes of boxes—made of metal or plastic. Metal is considered more durable (it can survive a misplaced hammer blow), but plastic boxes are often less than half as costly. Before installing one or the other, be sure to check with your electrical inspector. Some local codes—which are usually fashioned after one of several national codes— restrict what kind of box can be used.

Boxes can be divided by function: junction, where electrical connections occur; outlet, to which something that uses electricity (a light fixture, for example) is connected; and device, in which hardware that carries but doesn't consume electricity (such as switches and receptacles) is fitted. Or they can be divided by shape: square, rectangular, octagonal and round. Unfortunately, the two sets of classifications don't correlate exactly. In practice, you might find any combination of function and shape. With that

caveat, we can go on to make a few brash generalizations.

Boxes come in different sizes and depths to accommodate different amounts of electrical paraphernalia. Code is quite specific about how many conductors and devices may be installed in a certain size of box, and one of appropriate volume must be used. This might seem like a fairly esoteric concern to a home handyperson who has no intention of wiring a building. However, horror stories of ineptly installed original wiring (often done before the days of pervasive code influence) make favorite cocktail conversation for remodelers. Lift the cover off a receptacle, and you might be surprised (and appalled) by what you see.

To allow a cable to enter a box, square, octagonal and round metal boxes have *knockouts*—punched circles that can be knocked out with a hammer. Metal device

(rectangular) boxes have knockouts and *pryouts*—smaller circles similar to knockouts but with slots so they can be pried out with a screwdriver. To secure the cable to the box, an *external cable* (or *Romex) connector* can be inserted into a knockout and secured with a nut. Then the cable is clamped by tightening two screws on the outside of the box. (Don't confuse cable clamps with BX or Greenfield clamps, which have round jaws for round armored cable.) An internal cable clamp secures nonmetallic cable fitted through pryouts in switch and octagonal boxes.

There are a variety of other widgets to attach to boxes. *Covers* come solid for junctions, slotted for a switch or receptacle and even with openings for TV and telephone connections. *Extensions* increase a box's capacity or allow it to reach the surface of an added layer of finish material. *Brackets* make

DIMMER

**SINGLE-POLE
LIGHT SWITCH**

**SINGLE-POLE
HEAVY-DUTY SWITCH**

mounting a device or square box to the front or side of a wall stud a simple matter. A steel *box support strap* will let you hang a box between framing members. An *internal strap*—bridging between two screws on a round or octagonal box—will let you hang a light fixture. Two *studs* (threaded rods), combined with a *hickey* (a coupler), make the job even easier. A *grounding clip* simplifies connecting a bare grounding wire to a box. The *weatherproof box* is another category of box with a very specific application.

Device boxes. Most often, switches and receptacles are installed in rectangular *switch boxes*. Most common is the recessed box, which fits with the edges of its opening flush to (or within ¼″ of) the finished wall surface. *Gem*, a trademark for switch boxes with adjustable *mounting ears* and sides attached with screws so that they can be *ganged*, is a common nickname for this type of box. For surface mounting (such as in a garage) of a switch or one duplex receptacle, use a *handy box*.

Junction boxes. Junctions occur in octagonal, round and device boxes when there's some other wiring application going on. But for straight connections—no devices or fixtures—*square boxes* get the nod. Square boxes generally come only with knockouts, so cables must be secured with knockout clamps. Bear in mind that all wire connections must occur within a box and that all boxes must be accessible.

Outlet boxes. The most common box for fixtures is the *octagonal box*, often called a ceiling box because it's so often used for ceiling fixtures. The threaded tabs on octagonal boxes are set for common light mounting (such as ceramic threaded bases), and they're also easily adaptable to straps, studs and hickeys. Octagonal boxes usually have both knockouts and pryouts, allowing use of either clamp type.

Metal round boxes have become less popular in recent years. But at the same time, because they're inexpensive, plastic ones are popular among home builders. Their most frequent application is for light fixtures.

Though the majority of outlet applications will be in octagonal or round boxes, you may occasionally find wall lights emerging from rectangular device boxes or even square boxes (if there are a lot of other connections inside). Other applications are possible; box uses are restricted more by convention and invention than by code.

Devices

There are two main sorts of devices—switches and receptacles—but many different types of each. Besides single and multi-

STANDARD BREAKER

GFCI BREAKER

DUPLEX RECEPTACLE

ple switches, there are quiet switches, lighted switches, delay switches and dimmers—just to name a few. Receptacles come in single and duplex, with different pin arrangements for various voltages and amperages, and with the option of ground-fault circuit interruption (GFCI). Here are a few highlights of each type.

Switches. The standard wall *toggle switch* is meant to control low-power fixtures, such as lights, and has only a 10-ampere rating. To control heaters and other heavy power consumers, look for a switch with an appropriate rating.

Also bear in mind that the amperage rating on the switch doesn't apply to certain types of motors or to direct current loads (unless so labeled). For induction motors, the type often found on stationary power tools with substantial horsepower output, the switch should be derated by 20%.

Switches don't use the ground wire in nonmetallic cable, because they operate only in the hot leg of a circuit. If the connections are in a metal box, the ground wire should be attached to the box with a screw or a grounding clip. A switch is always in line with the black wire or connected directly to the load with a black wire. This is a vital lesson. A light bulb, for example, will work just fine if the switch is in the neutral wire. However, the socket will be hot at all times. Stick a finger in there, and you could become the bulb—even with the switch off.

Though standard switches have only on and off positions, there are different configurations, and you've got to watch out for their nomenclature. A *single-pole switch* has two terminals, and it controls one fixture from one location. A *three-way switch* has three terminals and is used with another three-way to control one fixture from two lo-

cations. A *four-way switch* has four terminals to control one fixture from more than two locations. It is used in combination with three-ways. Mixing three- and four-way switches is probably the most complex (and confusing) aspect of residential wiring. Even experienced electricians resort to head scratching, and they're often reduced to sketching their thoughts on scrap material.

Quiet switches use an internal mercury contact button rather than metal-to-metal contact to "make and break." They're pleasant to deal with but have low capacity and consequently don't tolerate occasional overloading.

Dimmers are switches with rheostats for light intensity control. There are two types: *standard electronic*, only for incandescent lights (generally less than 600 watts in capacity), and *fluorescent*. You'll find it easy to tell the two apart, because the latter costs three

250V-15A RECEPTACLE

250V-30A RECEPTACLE

times as much. When you use dimmers, observe their limited capacity. It's all too easy to overload them.

Receptacles. The shape and arrangement of the slots and holes in a receptacle tell its use. The standard grounded duplex receptacle, for example, has two parallel slots, one larger than the other, and a round hole centered below them. It's rated for 125 volts and 15 amperes. The larger slot is for the neutral line, and the round one is for the ground. A 250-volt, 15-ampere receptacle has its hot and neutral slots in line. Dryer receptacles (250-volt, 30- or 50-ampere) have altogether different patterns. This system is our protection against plugging an appliance in backwards or, more dramatically, the wrong thing into the wrong kind of power.

No doubt you've cursed Big Brother's thoroughness at one time or another. Extension cords and outlets that prevent plugs from being put in upside down or that refuse to accept grounded plugs can be very frustrating. Inconvenient as these safeguards may be, they keep us from overloading extension cords or from inadvertently becoming the ground in an ungrounded circuit. When you understand that a lamp plugged in backwards is dangerous even if it's switched off, it becomes easier to tolerate the inconvenience.

Receptacle terminals are also polarized. The brass screws are for black or red wires, and the silver ones are for white or gray. Down toward the bottom and off to the side a little will be a green screw for the ground wire. (Ungrounded residential receptacles aren't used anymore.) Notice that there's a metal strap spanning the pairs of terminals on each side. If you want the receptacle to be controlled as one unit, you need only connect a wire to one of the screws. If, however, you'd like the top plug to be controlled by a switch and the bottom one not, you can cut the strap and wire the plugs separately.

Ground-fault circuit interrupters. A GFCI is a protection device that senses when a circuit is leaking current to ground. Should more than six milliamperes of current pass to ground—say from an appliance into your hand through your body and to a concrete floor—the GFCI will switch the circuit off within 25 to 30 milliseconds. It's a common misconception that circuit breakers and fuses protect people from shock. Not so. It only takes 50 milliamperes to kill a person; more than 15 amperes is required to open a 15-ampere breaker or blow a 15-ampere fuse.

GFCIs come as receptacles to serve one outlet, as receptacles that can be set up to serve an entire circuit and as circuit breakers that serve an entire circuit. They are required by code for all receptacles in bath-

WIRE NUTS

HICKEY

GROUND CLIPS

TWIST LOCK

CABLE CLAMP

rooms, garages, outdoors and within 15 feet of a swimming pool.

A GFCI receptacle will replace a conventional receptacle in a device box, but it takes up a great deal more room. Make sure there'll be enough space left over for any miscellaneous connections. Once installed, GFCIs should be tested (with a built-in button) once a month.

Making a Connection

Since all electrical connection screws thread inward clockwise, always make wire loops for screw connections in a clockwise fashion. The screw head will then pull the wire in rather than forcing it out. Strip enough insulation to make a 270° loop. More isn't necessary.

Some switches and receptacles now come with push-in connectors in the back. These are very convenient, because you don't have to form a loop in the wire. Somewhere on the switch or receptacle case will be a point where you push to release the wire. Most push-in connections aren't compatible with aluminum wire.

Nearly all residential wire-to-wire connections are now solderless, and all but the junctions in big wires are done with twist-on solderless connectors (often called by the brand name "Wire Nuts"). These are threaded caps that wind two wires together and insulate the bare ends. Twist-on solderless connectors come in sizes to fit specific wire gauges, and they're color coded. However, manufacturers haven't standardized the color coding.

When making connections with a twist-on solderless connector, strip just enough insulation so that the plastic cap will cover all the exposed conductor. If you use a knife instead

of a stripper, angle the blade so you won't damage the wire. If you have chosen the right size twist-on solderless connector, winding the wires together is unnecessary and actually may produce a less-secure connection.

Those are the main elements in residential wiring: wire, boxes, devices and connections. We'll stop short of conduit—metal tube systems for wiring—since they're mainly used in commercial buildings, and we'll leave deep groping in service panels and fiddling with service entrances to electricians and utility technicians. Maybe you'll venture farther when the basics become secondhand.

Chances are you've already gotten the sense that electricity isn't all that intimidating. In fact, we're going to let you in on the well-paid electricians' well-kept secret: All metaphors and analogies aside, wiring is a simpler, cleaner and healthier pastime than plumbing.

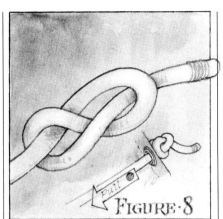

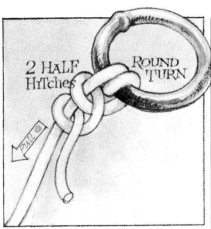

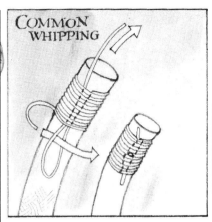

A Few New Twists on Cordage

Lengths of it become everything from lassos and lariats to sheets and spring lines.

Landsmen call it rope. Sailors call it line. It can be as thick and unyielding as a runner's thigh, or as thin and sinuous as birdsong. It has one purpose: tension. Take away the tension and it relaxes into indolent loops that store compactly away. Line is a tool, like a shovel, that can be applied in many ways but serves only one function. Tension.

Line is not wholly passive. Overstress its tension and it bites. During the brief era of the clipper ships, radical rigs stressed ships' rigging beyond previous limits; the low-stretch, tarred-hemp shrouds and stays that held a conventional ship's masts were replaced by iron and steel cable. When the cables parted—they often did, rounding the Horn—the ends slashed through the rigging and across the deck, cutting crewmen in half. Add to that the mindless, malevolent cunning of cordage; with what cobralike aggression loops of passing line snare feet, hands, necks; how predictably a kink of randomly tossed line jams in the smallest crack. Away from tension, line is a mathematical model of random behavior and, as such, it seeks disaster with the Gallic doggedness of an Exocet missile. Cordage deserves a separate section of Murphy's Law: What can be fouled, snared, hung, burned, arrested, wrapped or hog-tied, will be; this, along with structural failure, will occur at the worst possible moment; the results will be worse than you anticipate; amen.

And it will be your own damn fault. Cordage is simple stuff, geometrically uncomplicated. It may be seen as unidimensional, with all its forces acting along its center, a pencil line in space. Theoretically its breaking point is determinable, but you *will* insist on bend-

ing it around screw eyes and making knots in it. You've complicated the simplicity.

An example: You buy, at the hardware, 100′ of Dacron-core, vinyl-clad clothesline. You put a lead anchor and a screw eye in the brick of your garage and another screw eye in the trellis post. Good work. You take a full round turn around one screw eye and lay on two half hitches. You put the clothesline through the other screw eye and haul tight before you hitch it firm, then you stand back to admire your clothesline, tight as a tax man's smile, as if it were drawn with a straightedge. You can't stand it. You walk up and heave down the line to see how it holds. Do not blame me if the screw eye and the lead anchor come rifling at your head. Work out the vectors sometime, and see how astonishingly the point-to-point tension builds with a side pull on a line.

Get half again as much line as you need; extra is no burden. Though the breaking strength of a line may be within the limits you intend, get larger-diameter rope for two reasons: Stresses build up in complex ways when line is knotted or is pulled sideways or crosses sharp corners; the "hand"—the feel of the line and your ability to really grab and tug—is more amenable in larger sizes.

Dacron has a low stretch factor. It is strong, resistant to decay and has a soft hand. If you are holding something that bumps about and needs a gentle restraint, get nylon. Polypropylene has two virtues: It is often colorful and it floats. Manila, a natural fiber, looks nice but is not as strong or as lasting as Dacron or nylon.

What should you have around? One hundred feet of ³/₈″ Dacron will be handy

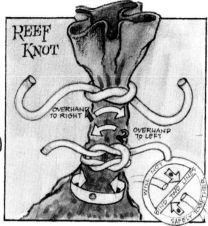

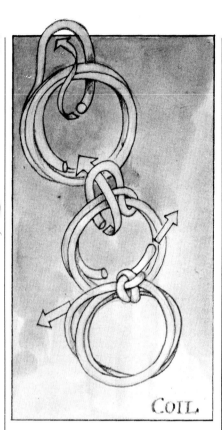

COIL.

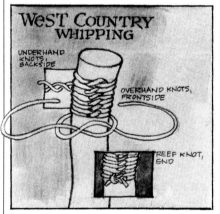

100 times over. Fifty feet of ¹/₄" nylon braid, for lashing trip gear or lumber to the car, will be a blessing. Keep a spool of what Maine men call "pot warp," colored ⁵/₃₂" braid; you can nibble away at it in 10′ or 15′ lengths for incidental work.

If you're going to keep line you should learn a few things. Learn to whip the ends of the line, laid (three twisted strands) or braided. The ends of nylon and Dacron line can be heat-fused with a lighter (go gently and beware of burns from dripping melt) but they still need to be whipped. Manila always does. Tree trimmers and linemen whip with electrician's tape, a vile practice; tape comes loose in strict accordance with Murphy's Law and leaves a sticky, frayed end. Lay on a "Boy Scout whipping" or West Country whipping or, best, a needle-and-twine sailor's whipping. Learn six knots: the half hitch, the figure eight stopper, the clove hitch, the rolling hitch, the bowline and the sheet bend (the last two are identical and differ only in usage). The first of these, the half hitch, absorbs most of the strain from a tugging weight (a nervous horse, a rolling car, one of Her Majesty's ships), leaving the knot to simply secure the end. When you have tied one of your six knots, you must shape the knot into its most stable form before it's ready to take a strain.

Using line is a kind of art, a geometry of tension, a skill with a prerequisite: that your line be clean, coiled and ready when you need it, the right line maintained well.

—*Jan Adkins*

Jan Adkins is an art director in Washington, D.C.

Sorting Out the Rope Fiber Choices

Over the last 20 years, the once simple act of picking out and using a length of rope has become pretty complicated. A profusion of new synthetic lines has joined the natural varieties on hardware store shelves, forcing baffled buyers to choose among well over a dozen combinations of fiber and twisting style.

Of course, each of the numerous ropes that are available is better suited for some tasks than it is for others, and the material that the cord is made of will likely require specific care. So we decided that it might be helpful to describe several of the more common ropes, tell you what they're good for and list steps that should be taken to get the maximum life from each type.

Twisting the Right-A-Way

In its most simple form, rope consists of long fibers that are first twisted (usually in a clockwise fashion) to form *yarns*. Then a number of the wound strings are spun together, in the opposite direction, to yield *strands*, which are in turn twisted back in a right-hand direction (in groups of three) to make *hawser-laid rope*.

The combination of these counterdirectional twists gives the finished cord more strength than that of the individual fibers composing it, since the friction between the fibers, yarns and strands increases the line's resistance to stretch. Furthermore, the wind-

ing process prevents the material from unraveling. (In fact, if you take a good piece of three-strand rope and attempt to untwist it in the middle, you'll notice that, after about one quarter-turn, it vigorously resists unwinding.)

There are, however, a number of other ways to "lay-up" a rope. Although they are somewhat rare, it's possible to locate left-hand-laid three-strand ropes, and even four-strand ropes. But braiding is by far the most

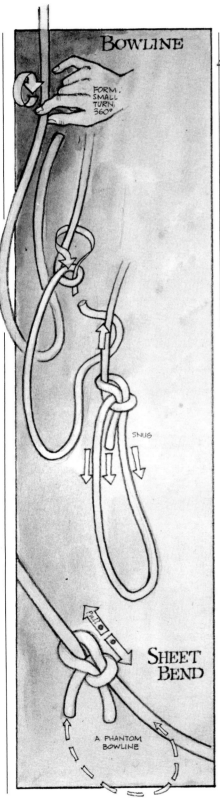

BOWLINE

FORM SMALL TURN 360°

SNUG

A PHANTOM BOWLINE

SHEET BEND

PULL

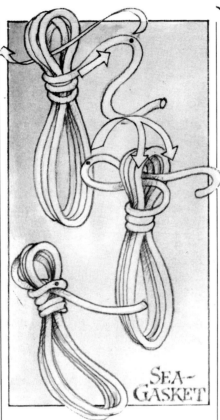

SEA-GASKET

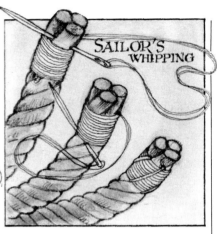

SAILOR'S WHIPPING

common of the alternative twist techniques. It's accomplished by weaving eight (or more) strands together in a diamond pattern, and produces a rope that's very flexible, doesn't tend to curl, and stretches even less than a twisted rope made of the same material and of equal diameter. (Not surprisingly, braided—sometimes called plaited—line's superior qualities result in its having the highest average price tag of all ropes.)

Synthetic vs. Natural

From a utilitarian point of view, synthetic fiber ropes have a number of advantages over natural lines. For a given diameter, they are stronger, more resistant to most types of decay and only slightly more expensive than the nonsynthetics.

Such "artificial" lines are, for the most part, manufactured from by-products of the oil-refining process, and therefore depend upon nonrenewable raw materials. (In fact, polyethylene ropes are made from ethylene, a petroleum substance that can also be used to produce ethyl alcohol, or fuel ethanol.)

Compounds obtained from the hydrocarbons are extruded and drawn, and—depending upon the fastidiousness of the production process—can be formed into threads that extend for the entire length of a rope (a feature not possible with natural fibers). The finest nylon lines are made by this "continuous filament" method, and are easy to distinguish from the fuzzier "spun" nylon ropes.

Despite the advantages of synthetic fibers, many folks still prefer the relatively strong, easy-to-handle, economical natural lines. Manila is the most popular of the plant-derived ropes (it comes from abaca, a banana-like plant). In fact, among seafarers (and landlubbers) who do fancy work with rope, manila is considered the only choice. A less preferred—and less expensive—option is sisal, which takes its raw materials from a species of Mexican cactus. And hemp, which was once a common top-quality rope made from fibers in the stems of *Cannabis* (marijuana) plants, has become quite difficult to find.

The relative strengths of the common natural and synthetic ropes (as well as their resistance to the elements and their stretch, cost, etc.) are compared in the chart that accompanies this article. (It is important to note that the performance of two firms' versions of the same kind of rope is likely to vary more than will the performance of two different kinds from the same manufacturer. Be sure to check the factory specifications, which will be available for many quality ropes.)

For general purposes, the two most useful types of line are manila and nylon. The former has very little stretch, takes knots well without slipping and can easily be spliced

and employed in permanent applications. Nylon, on the other hand, has a significantly higher breaking strength than any other common rope, and has a tremendous ability to stretch and absorb shock loads. In addition, it's unaffected by water, sunlight and alkaline chemicals and is very easy to handle.

Rope Care

Whatever a particular rope's durability and resistance to the elements may be, the line won't last long at all if it's abused. And proper care begins with putting it away after each use.

Ropes—whether they are synthetic or natural—should always be coiled up and hung in a dry place for storage. Of course, when a line is brand-new, you'll find that it won't stay in a neat coil. One way to convince an unruly rope to cooperate is to coil it once or twice in a left-hand direction (for hawser-laid ropes) and then coil it in a clockwise fashion. (If, however, you invest in a braided rope, you'll find it easiest to coil it in a figure-eight pattern.)

One should never leave frayed ends on a good piece of rope. Once the line has begun to unravel, that unwound portion will have to be discarded. Natural fiber ropes should be whipped (a method of binding the line's tips) with either a good synthetic whipping twine or a natural fiber such as waxed linen. There are a number of different ways to whip a rope's end, but common and sailor's whipping (shown in the photos) are two of the more popular approaches.

Yet another way to prevent unwinding in a natural fiber rope is to back-splice it (again, see the accompanying photos). Back splicing, however, is feasible only in circumstances where the rope will not have to pass through a restriction—such as a pulley block, for instance—the doubling up involved in a

1. Seven ³/₈" candidates. From left to right: three-strand nylon, braided nylon, three-strand polypropylene manila imitation, three-strand polypropylene, three-strand manila, three-strand sisal and three-strand cotton. 2. A short splice is well-suited to the permanent joining of two natural fiber ropes that won't have to pass through a pulley. 3. Sailor's whipping follows the strand pattern of the rope. It's a good way to protect natural fiber ends. 4. A back splice will permanently protect the end of a natural rope but can be used only if you won't need to slip the line through a small restriction such as a pulley or eye, since the splice increases the end's diameter significantly. 5. The ends of synthetic ropes can be melted to prevent unraveling. 6. Common whipping holds together the end of a length of cotton rope.

splice increases the end's diameter quite significantly.

Synthetic lines are generally protected from unraveling either by melting the fibers in their tips or by applying a length of shrink tubing to their ends. (Alternatively, it's possible to apply whipping to the ends of synthetic rope, just as you would when dealing with natural fibers.) Whichever method you choose, it's particularly important that the binding be secure, since synthetics seem to be more inclined to unravel than are the natural ropes.

Finally, you should know that some lines are more resistant to certain environmental conditions and uses than others. The accompanying chart sets forth the basic considerations, but manufacturers' specifications should also be looked over carefully. For ex-

ample, most polypropylene and polyethylene ropes can't be used where they'll regularly be subject to direct sunlight, but some factories do apply ultraviolet inhibitors to such lines, eliminating or alleviating that problem.

Application

When you're trying to decide which rope to use for a particular job, it's important to consider both the working load and the breaking strength of the cord in question. While all natural fiber lines are rated for regular working loads of about 20% of their breaking strength, nylon is usually rated for a working load that is 11% of its breaking strength, because of its tendency to stretch. Hence, nylon might be perfect for a towing application where the rope needs to flex and the load will vary considerably. But in a situation where an object needs to be held in position—such as when a rope is used to temporarily guy a tower—a low-stretch manila might be a good choice.

Furthermore, there are a few basic rules for the use of any rope. When you're bending a rope around pulley blocks, for example, the diameter of the pulley should be at least eight times that of the rope. In any application where a line is permanently affixed either to another line or to some object, use a splice rather than a knot, since it places less stress on the fibers. But there are times when a knot is the only practical choice. In such cases, find out what the right "tie" for the job is and use it. You'll insure your own safety, and your rope will last longer as a result.

Even under the best of conditions, all fibers—either natural or synthetic—will wear out. You should learn to recognize the symptoms and put a deteriorating line out of service before an accident happens. Most natural ropes tend to become quite limp when they're nearing the end of their useful career.

The surface will become soft and fuzzy, the color will turn to a dull gray, and the inner filaments will have crumbled to dust. Synthetic fibers, however, don't offer such clear warnings. Generally, they will become limp and soft—and, in the case of the ropes affected by ultraviolet light, the color may change (they will usually fade significantly)—but the interior fibers may, to the eye, appear unaffected. To inspect such a rope, bend the material in your hands and study the condition of the surface fibers. If they're excessively frayed, it's time to retire the line.

But don't throw away rope that's a little too old to be trusted. There are likely to be many short sections that can be turned into all manner of useful objects. Sailors have fashioned everything from handles to door mats out of old lines, and there are numerous working applications for tired rope, too:

It can be used to make bumpers and grommets, for instance.

As you pay more attention to the lines you use, you may find yourself becoming more interested in the time-honored art of ropecraft. There's a real pleasure in working a quality section of rope, savoring the suppleness of manila in hand, and the results of an expert's handiwork can often teeter on the boundary between function and art.

SPECIFICATIONS FOR COMMON ⅜″ ROPES

	Working Load	Breaking Load	Enemies	Stretch	Handling	Price*	Comments
Hemp	270 lb.	1,350 lb.	Moisture, chemicals	Low	Good	2	Becoming difficult to find
Sisal	225 lb.	1,125 lb.	Moisture, chemicals	Low	Fair	1	Tends to fray, has barbs that poke hands
Cotton	150 lb.	750 lb.	Moisture, chemicals	Medium	Excellent	1	Very easy to handle, swells with moisture and grips
Manila	270 lb.	1,350 lb.	Moisture, chemicals	Low	Good	3	The standard natural fiber rope
Nylon	410 lb.	3,725 lb.	Acids	High	Excellent	5	Tends to slip, very flexible if braided, unwinds easily
Polyester	420 lb.	3,600 lb.	Ultraviolet light	Medium	Good	5	Floats, doesn't absorb water, often used braided or pre-stretched for rigging on yachts
Polypropylene	400 lb.	2,350 lb.	Ultraviolet light	Medium	Fair	2	Floats, stiff, may have barbs, subject to chafe, unwinds easily

*Numbers indicate relative cost—from least to most expensive—on a scale of 1 to 5.

PART FIVE

The Finished Product

With a grounding
in tools, techniques and materials,
all that remains
to complete the handiwork
is a pair of
able hands.

A Cedar Heirloom

In a world full of moths, every fine woolen deserves a cedar lining.

Cedar has—for hundreds of years—been known for its insect-repellent qualities and its pleasant aroma. It's no wonder, then, that the wood has long been a mainstay for anyone building chests, wardrobes or closets.

Unfortunately, aromatic cedar—in board form—is increasingly difficult to come by, and if you are fortunate enough to locate some, you'd better be prepared to pay dearly for it.

Still, the lure of the wood's natural fragrance is difficult to ignore, so Clarence Goosen, a research associate at *Mother Earth News*, decided to combine practicality with luxury and build a chest of pine and plywood with a heart that's pure cedar.

Go Shopping, or Scrounging

Clarence suggests starting the project by collecting your tools and materials. You'll need all the lumber and hardware called for in the accompanying list, plus some yellow carpenter's glue; a table saw to make accurate cuts; a power drill with several different-sized bits and a countersink. You'll also need sandpaper in a variety of grits; some shellac (and pumice), clear varnish or tung oil; a tape measure; a screwdriver; and because you'll need to do some fancy finish work, a router.

To make your lumber shopping less of a chore (if, that is, you don't have enough usable scraps around to piece your project together), notice that the list indicates specific board lengths that will allow you to arrange your cuts to produce a minimum of waste. Also, though Goosen opted to use tongue-and-groove strip cedar for the lining of the chest, the cost of such lumber may motivate you to substitute the less expensive cedar particleboard.

Take a Few Tips

The cabinet isn't difficult to assemble, but there are a few tricks you ought to be aware of that will make its construction easier. For one thing, the pedestal should be assembled first, and that entire support can be cut from your 12' length of 1 X 4. Notice, though, that it's only $2^{3}/_{4}$" tall, so you'll have to rip the entire $3^{1}/_{2}$"-wide board down to size before going on to make the miter cuts for the joints and gussets. (Save the leftover strip, since you'll need it later.)

Each of the four identical sides starts with a $3/_{4}$"-thick, 21" X 21" perimeter frame that consists of two 14"-long vertical stiles and full-width top and bottom rails. These four components are held together at the joints with $1/_{4}$" X $1^{1}/_{2}$" X 3" splines that are glued into kerfs sliced across the mating surfaces of the seams.

A $3/_{8}$"-wide by $5/_{8}$"-deep rabbet, cut into the inner face of the bottom rail, will accommodate the $5/_{8}$" X $20^{1}/_{4}$" X $20^{1}/_{4}$" plywood base once everything's assembled; a similar groove (this one $1/_{2}$" deep and $1/_{2}$" wide), routed into the inside edges of the framework, provides a seat for the $1/_{2}$" X $3^{1}/_{2}$" X 16" pine strips that make up the side panel inserts. Furthermore, the side edges of each complete square are 45°-mitered to the inside to form clean finish joints.

Here's a helpful hint: Cut the stiles from the 1 X 4 X 10', and the rails from the 14-footer. Notice that Clarence has routed those boards—with the help of the shaper table, although a straightedge clamped to the work would do in a pinch—to a 3" width. He's also added contoured corners and decorated the frame adjacent to the panel inserts with a shallow fluted edge.

The sides are locked together with glue and No. 8 X $1^{1}/_{4}$" flathead wood screws (in-

LIST OF MATERIALS

Item	Length/Size	Purpose
$5/_{8}$" plywood	(1) 21" X 21"	Box bottom
1 X 4 pine	(1) 10'	Side panel stiles
	(1) 12'	Pedestal, gussets, corner braces
	(1) 14'	Side panel rails
1 X 6 pine	(1) 8'	Lid
Doorstop pine	(1) 7'	Panel inserts and molding
	(3) 8'	Panel inserts
$1/_{4}$" lattice strips	(1) 8'	Joint splines
$3/_{8}$" cedar	(1) 16 sq. ft.	Lining
$3/_{8}$" dowel	(1) 4"	Screw-hole plugs
Flathead wood screws	(56) No. 8 X $1^{1}/_{4}$"	Sides and bottom
	(12) No. 8 X $3/_{4}$"	Molding
Brass-plated piano hinge with screws	(1) $1^{1}/_{16}$" X 20"	Lid
Brass-plated friction lid support with screws	(pr.) $5^{1}/_{2}$" overall	Lid

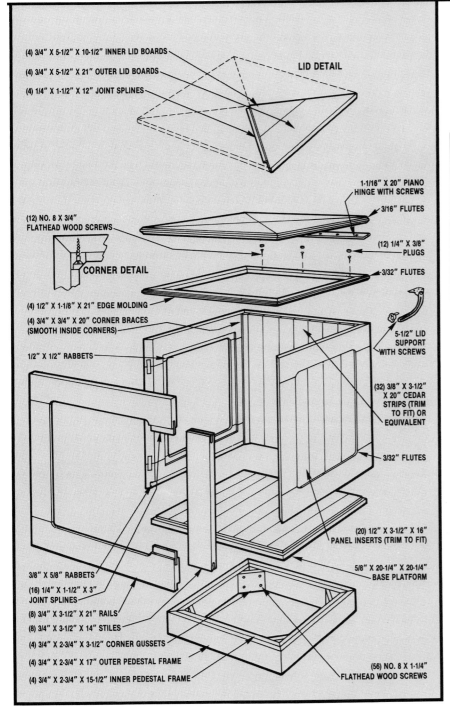

LID DETAIL

(4) 3/4" X 5-1/2" X 10-1/2" INNER LID BOARDS

(4) 3/4" X 5-1/2" X 21" OUTER LID BOARDS

(4) 1/4" X 1-1/2" X 12" JOINT SPLINES

1-1/16" X 20" PIANO HINGE WITH SCREWS

3/16" FLUTES

(12) NO. 8 X 3/4" FLATHEAD WOOD SCREWS

(12) 1/4" X 3/8" PLUGS

CORNER DETAIL

3/32" FLUTES

(4) 1/2" X 1-1/8" X 21" EDGE MOLDING

(4) 3/4" X 3/4" X 20" CORNER BRACES (SMOOTH INSIDE CORNERS)

5-1/2" LID SUPPORT WITH SCREWS

1/2" X 1/2" RABBETS

(32) 3/8" X 3-1/2" X 20" CEDAR STRIPS (TRIM TO FIT) OR EQUIVALENT

3/32" FLUTES

(20) 1/2" X 3-1/2" X 16" PANEL INSERTS (TRIM TO FIT)

3/8" X 5/8" RABBETS

(16) 1/4" X 1-1/2" X 3" JOINT SPLINES

5/8" X 20-1/4" X 20-1/4" BASE PLATFORM

(8) 3/4" X 3-1/2" X 21" RAILS

(8) 3/4" X 3-1/2" X 14" STILES

(4) 3/4" X 2-3/4" X 3-1/2" CORNER GUSSETS

(4) 3/4" X 2-3/4" X 17" OUTER PEDESTAL FRAME

(4) 3/4" X 2-3/4" X 15-1/2" INNER PEDESTAL FRAME

(56) NO. 8 X 1-1/4" FLATHEAD WOOD SCREWS

stalled six to a corner and perpendicular to one another), which are fastened through $3/4'' \times 3/4'' \times 20''$ corner braces (these can be cut from your leftover strip of $1 \times 4 \times 12'$). Once they're joined, the plywood bottom of the box can be glued into its rabbet, and the pedestal glued underneath and screwed in place from the inside.

To make the lid, you'll need to cut your 1×6 into eight pieces, four of which should be 21" and the other four $10^{1}/_2$" on their longest edges. Because these sections' ends meet each other in 45° joints across their

widths (and because you'll naturally want to make the most efficient use of your wood), you'll have to plan your cuts carefully so the angled faces butt against each other—thus eliminating the wasteful wedges that'd otherwise be left between the slices.

These sections are, like the side frames, fastened together with $1/4'' \times 1^1/2''$ splines set and glued into the mating surfaces of each miter face. The straight edges of the boards are cemented at their joints, too. When the lid's completed, $3/16''$ flutes can be added—with the router—to its outer periphery.

You're not quite ready to install the lid, though. First, the cedar lining (whether it's strip or composition board) must be glued in place within the box. Then the edge molding should be rip-cut (from the leftover piece of $1/2''$ doorstop pine) into two $1/2'' \times 1^1/8'' \times 42''$ pieces; one edge of each of them fluted, with the router, to match the lid; and those two lengths sliced in half to create four 21"-long sections, each with mitered ends. A dozen No. 8 X $3/4''$ flathead wood screws hold the trim in place, and the heads should be countersunk so that short plugs—made from $3/8''$ dowel—can be glued over them and sanded flush.

Finally, the hinge can be recessed into the lid and into one of the molding sections (here's another job for that router), and the hinge and cover can be fastened in place with the screws provided. A lid support, placed between one side of the box and the hinged top, will keep the chest open for access when needed.

With everything together, apply shellac to the box's outside, and then smooth it with pumice to provide a glossy finish. If you'd prefer a more subdued appearance, oil can be rubbed into the wood. No matter how you dress it, though, your homemade chest is sure to be a source of satisfaction, either to you—the builder—or to any lucky person who might receive it as a gift.

A Child's Play Center

This workshop-made toy should please any child.

Everyone—young or old—needs a place to call his or her own, and for the tyke of the house, what could be better than a toy chest that also serves as a desk or bench? This convertible piece of furniture will offer a cavernous storage space for treasures, a bench (complete with arms and back) for contemplation and—if the young owner simply folds the back down—a broad desk for developing those free-form works of art. (Who knows, with supplies so close to where they'll be used, maybe the crayons will even be put away.)

All of the major wooden parts for the chest/bench/desk can be trimmed from a 4' X 8' sheet of ³/₄" plywood. In addition, if the child you imagine enjoying this work-and-play station happens to live some dis-

tance away, you'll be pleased to know that the whole thing can be broken down into an 8" X 18" X 36" package for shipping. Then, once the carton arrives at its destination, the installation of 26 flathead machine screws turns the parts back into a youngster's delight on Christmas morning.

Come Ply With Us

The entire unit could be built with hand tools, but if you have access to a band saw and/or a drum sander, your work will go much more quickly. All of the panels that make up the chest should first be cut to the sizes indicated in the list of materials (check the drawings, too, for angled cuts). Then the details—such as the relieved areas on the bottoms of the box ends and the profiling along the tops of these ends—can be added to the more easily managed small parts. Feel free to deviate from the dimensions we've listed if you can visualize a more attractive profile, but do maintain a 3³/₄" distance between the top of the endpieces and the ledge that supports the bench back when it's in the "up" position.

Pieces of one-by lumber are glued and tacked to the underside of the chest bottom (front and back) and to the insides of the ends. These strips are drilled for the ¹/₄" screws and have T-nuts embedded in them.

T-nuts are also used to attach the ends to the front and back, but—in these cases—they're set in reliefs that have been chiseled into the boards, as shown in the drawings. When you form the slots, chisel through to—but not into—the last ply of the ³/₄" birch material.

The box lid incorporates a strip of one-by lumber—which runs along the hinged edge—to add support. This piece should be glued and tacked in place before the edges of the box lid are sanded, to assure that the two parts can be blended together well. The hinges themselves consist of ¹/₄"-20 X 2¹/₄" flathead machine screws set through T-nuts, through the box ends and into the joint between the lid and its one-by support—with flat washers positioned between the threaded fasteners and the lid to serve as spacers. However, it's very important that the lid have more support than these mere pivots. So, to protect a diminutive future owner from trapping his or her appendages between the heavy lid and the box front, we installed a pair of lid supports with adjustable friction points. (If you can't find these locally, you can request two straight friction lid supports, order number D1205, from The Woodworkers' Store, 21801 Industrial Boulevard, Rogers, Minnesota 55374.)

Before moving on to the desk portion, you should install the two lid rests, making certain that their upper surfaces are level with the centers of the pivot-bolt holes. (Because a good deal of pressure will come to bear on these two pieces of one-by lumber, you should anchor them to the box ends by sinking at least two No. 8 X 1¹/₄" flathead wood screws into each board.)

Taking your measurements from the pattern we've included in the accompanying drawing, sketch the shape of the desk supports (four of them) onto the remaining portion of ³/₄" plywood. Then saw these parts out with a band saw, a jigsaw or a coping saw (and lots of endurance). Glue together pairs of the curved boards, and then sand them until their arcs are smooth and well formed. (You'll no doubt find that a drum sander will be a real boon when you're working on the inside curves.)

Four more T-nuts and ¹/₄"-20 X 3" flathead machine screws are used to hold the desk to its supports, and they in turn are fitted to pivots on the box ends in the same fashion as was the box lid. After you've

LIST OF MATERIALS

Material	Size	Purpose (Location)
³/₄" birch plywood	(1) 14" X 33"	Desk top (a)
³/₄" birch plywood	(1) 13¹/₂" X 25³/₄"	Box lid (b)
³/₄" birch plywood	(2) 15" X 16¹/₂"	Box ends (c)
³/₄" birch plywood	(1) 13¹/₂" X 26¹/₂"	Box front (d)
³/₄" birch plywood	(1) 13" X 26¹/₂"	Box back (e)
³/₄" birch plywood	(1) 14³/₈" X 26¹/₂"	Box bottom (f)
³/₄" birch plywood	(4) 14¹/₄" X 22⁷/₈"	Desk-top supports (g)
Pine	(2) ³/₄" X 1" X 11¹/₂"	Lid rests (h)
Pine	(2) ³/₄" X ³/₄" X 14³/₈"	Bottom rests (i)
Pine	(2) ³/₄" X ³/₄" X 25"	Bottom rests (j)
Pine	(1) ³/₄" X 2" X 25³/₄"	Box-lid hinge (k)
Pine disks	(2) ³/₄" X 2"	Desk stops (l)
T-nuts	(26) ¹/₄"-20	(m)
Flathead screws	(8) ¹/₄"-20 X 1¹/₂"	(n)
Flathead screws	(10) ¹/₄"-20 X 2"	(o)
Flathead screws	(4) ¹/₄"-20 X 2¹/₄"	(p)
Flathead screws	(4) ¹/₄"-20 X 3"	(q)
Flat washers	(8) ¹/₄"	Spacers (r)
Friction lid supports	(2) 6"	(s)

THE FINISHED PRODUCT

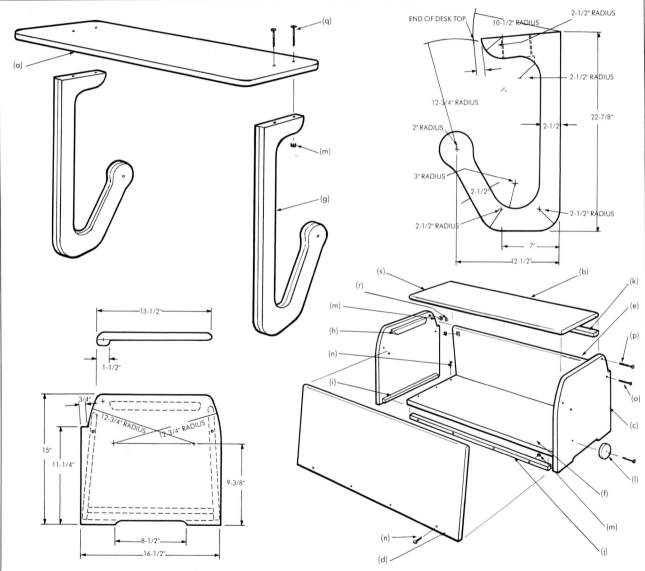

mounted the curved supports to the chest, check to see that the flat bottoms are resting on the floor, and mark the positions for the 2″-diameter stops. (These two disks will prevent the desk from folding beyond its correct position.) Finally, cinch down the desk-top pivot screws to the point where there's enough friction to prevent the work surface from falling by its own weight.

We applied a light golden oak stain to the activity center, and then coated it with polyurethane varnish—the most child-resistant finish we've found. As you can see from the photographs, the chest/bench/desk has been thoroughly approved by our young model. In fact, we've had only one problem with the piece: trying to talk the youngster into giving it up.

The Shaker Lap Desk: Honestly Functional

Woodcraft befitting the correspondent's art

The lap desk is only one of many practical contributions bestowed upon us by the Shakers—members of a communal religious sect active in agriculture and manufacturing since the eighteenth century. In accordance with their lifestyle, the Shakers crafted goods that tended to be straightforward, functional and devoid of any frills.

This modified version of the original lap desk serves a like purpose: It's designed to hold papers, correspondence and business effects, yet it's portable and lightweight enough to be set on the knees and used as a writing surface. The dimensions are appropriate to the storage of stationery, note cards, writing implements and even a calculator.

To start, we'd suggest using a warp-resistant, straight-grained, knot-free hardwood, such as the walnut we chose. A softwood could be used, but it wouldn't take a stain gracefully and would probably be marred by the pressure of pen points.

The accompanying list of materials will provide you with the finished dimensions for each of the desk's component parts. Since the major pieces are $^3/_8''$ thick, you'll either have to purchase surfaced boards from a quality lumber dealer, or cut and plane the wood yourself from larger billets. A jack plane can be used to dress your stock as required, but you'll also need a table saw, a router, a mortising chisel, a hammer, a drill with an assortment of small bits, some bar clamps and carpenter's glue to complete the project.

Once you've cut all the pieces to size, fine-sand them, then measure and cut the dado grooves in the desk's front and back sections. With this done, cut the matching rabbets on the sidepieces and check to see if the outside edges of the corners come out flush. (To guarantee accuracy, consider making a few practice joints using wood scraps; they'll allow you to establish your technique and to set your saw at the same time.)

Next, prepare to assemble the right and left accessory trays by cutting dadoes into the bottom pieces to secure the dividers. We've located the right- and left-hand dividers $5^1/_2''$ and $8^1/_2''$ from the back edges, respectively, but you should measure your calculator (if you use one) and reposition the appropriate grooves if necessary. Glue the dividers in place, then glue and screw the sides against the mated assemblies, using No. 2 X $^3/_8''$ roundhead fasteners.

The finished trays should have a $^1/_8''$ lip at each end. These will fit into the dadoes which you'll cut into the front and back frame pieces. Once you've trial-fit the parts and made any necessary adjustments, spread glue on the joining components and clamp the box and trays together, assuring squareness by laying the assembly on a flat surface.

If you want to be especially meticulous, you can use $^1/_8''$ X $^3/_4''$ dowel pins to secure the desk's base to its frame. This requires careful measuring, but it'll result in a "hidden" joint and will help to true the frame if it's slightly out of square. Alternatively, you can fasten the pieces using No. 4 X $^3/_4''$ countersunk flathead wood screws and a glue bead.

Before making the final fit, you'll want to attach the letter-holder lip to the inside face of the base, $1^1/_4''$ from the back. This, too,

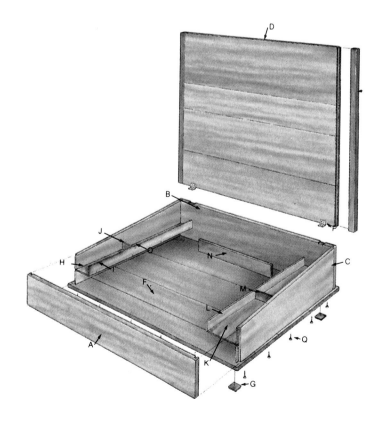

LIST OF MATERIALS

Part		Dimensions	Purpose
A	(1)	$^3/_8$" X 3" X $18^3/_4$"	Front
B	(1)	$^3/_8$" X $4^1/_2$" X $18^3/_4$"	Back
C	(2)	$^3/_8$" X 3" X $4^1/_2$" X $13^1/_4$"	Sides
D	(1)	$^3/_8$" X $14^1/_4$" X $18^1/_4$"	Top
E	(2)	$^3/_8$" X $^5/_8$" X $14^1/_4$"	Breadboard edges
F	(1)	$^3/_8$" X $14^1/_8$" X 19"	Bottom
G	(4)	$^3/_{16}$" X $^3/_4$" X $^3/_4$"	Feet
H	(1)	$^1/_8$" X $1^7/_8$" X $13^1/_4$"	Left tray bottom
I	(1)	$^1/_8$" X 1" X $12^7/_8$"	Left tray side
J	(1)	$^1/_8$" X $^3/_4$" X $1^7/_8$"	Left side divider
K	(1)	$^1/_8$" X $3^3/_8$" X $13^1/_4$"	Right tray bottom
L	(1)	$^1/_8$" X 1" X $12^7/_8$"	Right tray side
M	(1)	$^1/_8$" X $^3/_4$" X $3^3/_8$"	Right tray divider
N	(1)	$^1/_4$" X $1^1/_2$" X 9"	Letter holder
O	(10)	No. 2 X $^3/_8$" roundhead screws	Tray fasteners
P	(2)	1" X 1" butt hinges	Lid hinges
Q	(24)	No. 4 X $^3/_4$" flathead screws	Bottom fasteners

can either be doweled or screwed in place. Finally, the four feet can be added to the bottom. First, mortise square sockets in the base, centered $1^3/_8$" from each corner. Then round the edges of the feet slightly and glue them, shaped side out, into the shallow niches.

The lid incorporates a breadboard edge at each side to protect the exposed end grain of the writing surface. Cut the dadoes into the edge pieces first, then make a sample tongue using a scrap of wood the same thickness as the top. Now, with your saw set, carefully cut the actual tongues and trial-fit the joints. If you're satisfied with the match, fasten the pieces by gluing only the middle section of each joint; a 1" bond will allow the wood to move with changes in humidity. (If you wish, you may use this edging technique on the base, as well.)

At this point, you're ready to attach the lid. First, plane the upper edges of the front and back pieces to match the angle of the sides. With that done, mortise an area on the back edge for the two hinges, and fasten them flush to the box with the screws provided. Align the lid, mark the hinge positions, then mortise reliefs in the top, as well. When fastening the upper hinge leaves, take care not to pierce the writing surface with either the drill bit or the screws.

Finally, give the wood a last sanding and apply a multilayered finish of varnish, lacquer or shellac (try to avoid oils, since they might stain stored papers). And if you like to combine beauty and function—as the creators of the lap desk did—you might want to cover a single coat of satin varnish with two successive layers of gloss varnish, thereby imparting an appearance of depth and offering a good, hard writing surface.

High Chair

An attractive, stable dinner-table boost

Ask experienced parents what qualities they'd most appreciate in a high chair, and there's a good chance you'll hear three points mentioned over and over: stability, ease of cleaning and a tray that is secure but simple to install. Unlike many commercial models that the parents among us have known, the high chair you see here has survived the assault of a two-and-a-half-year-old without tipping, has shed flying applesauce and sports a tray that comes and goes with ease. What's more, the construction involves no turnings or exotic joints; it would be possible, in fact, to build it solely with hand tools.

Most parents find it handy to be able to get the arms of a high chair—without the tray—under the kitchen or dining room tabletop, so the child can eat with the rest of the family. For that reason, consider measuring to the underside of your table and adjusting the leg dimensions in our drawing accordingly.

All told, you'll need about 24 linear feet of ³/₄" X 2¹/₈" framing stock and another 4' of wider material for the seat, seat back and tray. We used locally milled red oak, but there are certainly lots of other good options. Bear in mind, though, that softwoods will be more likely to splinter when jointed.

All but one of the chair's joints are cross- or end-lapped, and made 7° off perpendicular. The taper gives the chair a sturdy footing at the floor and a child-proportioned seat. Don't be intimidated by the off-square construction; a simple jig for a router or a carefully set table-saw miter gauge will allow you to repeat the cuts with accuracy. If you do decide to use a router, leave about 2" of extra length for each end-lap joint. The extra material will brace the router while you cut the joint, and it can be trimmed off later.

The Seat

To keep the chair's construction uncluttered and to prevent warping, the seat is let into a ¹/₄"-deep, ³/₄"-wide mortise in each side frame. Just cut the mortise square to the frame, and relieve the top of the slot about ¹/₃₂" with a chisel to accommodate the off-perpendicular angle. When it comes time to crosscut the seat, however, it's worth the trouble to tilt the saw 7° off perpendicular so that the tenon will seat squarely in the mortise for good glue adhesion.

It's probably easiest to cut the mortise on a router table by drilling a lead hole for the bit. Unless you have a very powerful router, though, don't expect to remove all the material in one cut. As an alternative, you could do the job on the table saw by lowering the stock onto a dado and then cleaning out the ends with a chisel. This is a fairly hairy operation that shouldn't be attempted without appropriate jigs and feather boards. In the end, it might be quicker to cut the mortises by hand with a chisel than to set up for either the router or the table saw.

Side Frames

Glue the side frames together first, clamping each joint to ensure a good bond. (There's plenty of surface area so no screws are really necessary.) Once the glue has had time to set, round the front and back of the arms with a coping, saber or band saw.

Next, round over all the edges to protect small hands from splinters. The quickest method is to use a router. And a ³/₈" rounding-over (or corner-bead) carbide bit with a pilot bearing is highly recommended for this job.

Final Assembly

The last component you need for assembly is the seat back. Use the bottom dimension provided in the drawing, with your table-saw miter gauge set at 83°, to cut out a polygon. Then, in the top of the piece, saw an arc that pleases your eye. Sand out the major irregularities your saw left in the curve, and round over the front and back, stopping short of the sides by about ¹/₄". It's safer to sand this last bit of curve to blend well with the flat, butted sides.

Set the seat and cross braces in place temporarily, and locate the position of the chair's back. Then clamp everything temporarily while you drill and countersink the screw holes for the butted back, the mortised seat and the cross braces. Pop the clamps back off, apply glue, reassemble, reclamp, set the screws, and let the assembly sit overnight.

For the sake of appearance and to avoid traps for mini-compost piles of spilled food, all of the screw holes should be plugged. Be sure you don't countersink any deeper than about ¹/₈" on the cross braces or you'll come through the joint. If you use Phillips-head No. 8 X 1¹/₄" screws, you should be able to apply enough torque to seat them firmly into the bottom of the screw holes. Nonetheless, commercial screw-hole plugs will have to be trimmed flush with a sharp chisel.

The dimensions we used for the tray were acquired by tracing around a commercial unit; you might find it easier to do the same, rather than try to work from the drawing. The catches are made from filed-down ¹/₄" carriage bolts with nuts and compression springs. The ³/₄" stock in which they ride also helps brace the tray and limit warping. When drilling the braces, first bore the ⁹/₁₆" hole. Then use the center hole left by the ⁹/₁₆" bit to start the ¹/₄" hole. The chair arms make a handy jig for positioning the braces on the underside of the tray.

Once you've assembled the tray, you can use it to locate the holes in the arms. Remove the carriage bolts from the braces, and set the tray down on the arms so that the holes are 9" in front of the seat back. Push a 16d nail through each hole, and give it a light tap to mark the spot. You can repeat the process three more times at 1" intervals, and then bore the ¹/₄" X ³/₈"-deep holes.

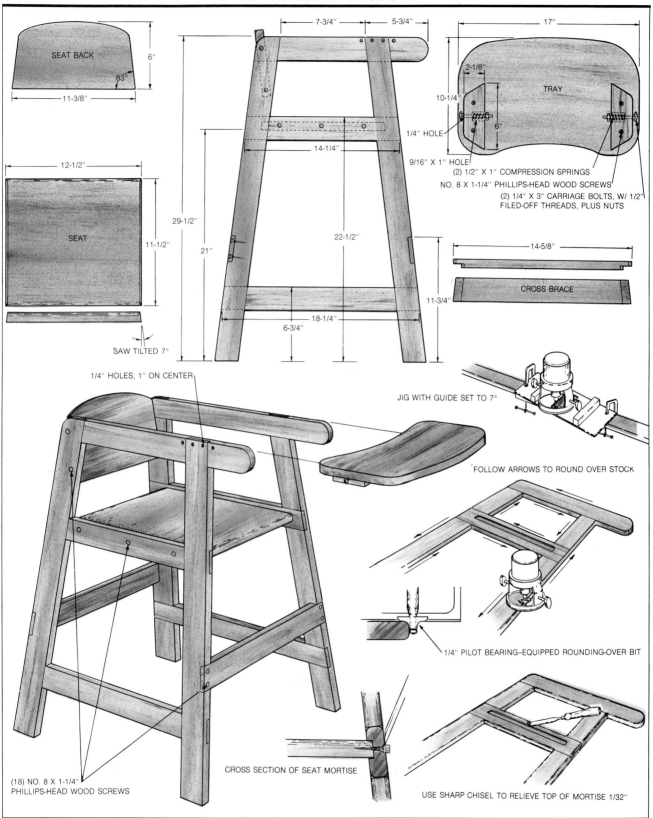

SEAT BACK

6"

83°

11-3/8"

7-3/4"   5-3/4"

17"

2-1/8"

10-1/4"

TRAY

1/4" HOLE

6"

9/16" X 1" HOLE

(2) 1/2" X 1" COMPRESSION SPRINGS

NO. 8 X 1-1/4" PHILLIPS-HEAD WOOD SCREWS

(2) 1/4" X 3" CARRIAGE BOLTS, W/ 1/2"
FILED-OFF THREADS, PLUS NUTS

12-1/2"

SEAT

11-1/2"

29-1/2"

21"

14-1/4"

22-1/2"

14-5/8"

CROSS BRACE

11-3/4"

18-1/4"

6-3/4"

SAW TILTED 7°

1/4" HOLES, 1" ON CENTER

JIG WITH GUIDE SET TO 7°

FOLLOW ARROWS TO ROUND OVER STOCK

1/4" PILOT BEARING–EQUIPPED ROUNDING-OVER BIT

(18) NO. 8 X 1-1/4"
PHILLIPS-HEAD WOOD SCREWS

CROSS SECTION OF SEAT MORTISE

USE SHARP CHISEL TO RELIEVE TOP OF MORTISE 1/32"

Fini

Finish is a matter of personal preference, but the abuse that a high chair sees offers a compelling argument for polyurethane var- nish. A coat of natural stain beforehand will help make up for the finish's lack of grain en- hancement. We used three coats of hand- rubbed (with 0000 steel wool) satin poly- urethane varnish over the stain.

If you're just starting a family, now's the time to put your youngster in a high chair of your own crafting. This design should be durable enough to survive a growing brood. And if you wait till the younger brothers and sisters arrive, you'll no doubt be hard-pressed to find the time to build it.

Medicine Cabinet

Here's an addition to your bathroom that will reflect good taste.

Whether you rent or own your home, you probably have a particular something in common with the rest of us: an ugly medicine cabinet. In fact, if you were to run a survey of new construction, you might be convinced that there's no reasonable alternative to the stamped-steel, refrigerator-white box.

One contribution to the war against "hospital decor" is made from oak and has enough storage space to cache a lifetime supply of pills, blades and toiletries. The two outer mirrors hinge on the inside, so they can be swung inward for proper primping. And—unlike some three-mirror models—the center door is also hinged to allow access to the compartment behind.

Though this cabinet was designed to be mounted on the surface of a wall, the 44″ width makes it comparatively easy to recess the unit into a conventional 2 X 4 stud wall.

One or two studs must be cut, and headers have to be installed above and below the cabinet. (To meet your local code, you may need to double-frame the jambs and headers in load-bearing walls.) Then the gap on each side of the cabinet will allow shimming to correct for out-of-plumb studs. (If you don't get the cabinet plumb, the doors will swing open to remind you.) Although the $3^7/8''$ stock width on the cabinet frame may seem a little odd at first, it will allow the main frame to recess into a standard $3^1/2''$ wall with $3/8''$ dry wall so that the rear of the cabinet is flush with the adjoining wall. However, if you are recessing the cabinet into a wall with a thicker dry wall or into a plumbing wall (which has thicker studs), you'll want to back the cabinet with $1/8''$ lauan or tileboard, instead of installing the cleat shown in the illustration. (Otherwise, your aspirin may be swallowed up by your stud wall.)

A Couple of Tips

There are several possible approaches to cutting the joints for the cabinet, but a table saw with an adjustable dado really makes the work go quickly. You'd set the dado for a $3/4''$ width to cut the frame grooves, $5/8''$ for the shelf track grooves and $1/2''$ for the mirror recesses and the mortises and tenons at the door corners. Don't let the door joints intimidate you; they're much easier to make than they seem to be at first glance. One hint, though: If you use softwood, make the ripped

mirror recesses after doing the crosscutting, because there's a greater likelihood of tearout when crosscutting.

Also, if you decide to surface-mount the medicine chest, check the wall to see if it's flat before you hang the cabinet; many a dry wall has bows or waves that are hard to see until something flat is set against it. If your wall does turn out to have this problem, try installing a second cleat at the bottom of the cabinet—between the frame members for the center compartment will be sufficient—so that you can pull the bottom and the top of the frame firmly against the wall. Locate the studs, and anchor the cabinet to them with No. 12 X $2^1/4''$ screws.

Off the Shelf

You might have a tough time settling on a material to make the shelves. Many commercial cabinets have beveled, double-strength glass shelves, but even these might shatter. Tempered glass, which is cut before tempering, is ideal though expensive. The cost of materials can be cut by using clear $1/4''$ acrylic glazing (often known by the brand names Plexiglas or Lucite). The plastic will scratch in time, but it's safe.

Finish

The humid environment of a bathroom can produce dramatic expansion problems in woodwork. With this in mind, set aside your favored oil finish and apply polyurethane varnish to the medicine cabinet. Natural stain helps accentuate the grain of the oak, and three thorough coats of the plastic finish can be applied on top of that. The goal of finishing, in this case, is to seal the wood as much as possible, so that changing humidity won't alter the wood's moisture content and loosen joints from the continual expansion and shrinkage encountered in the ever-changing bathroom environment.

"Good Morning, Mirror"

For many of us, the first few minutes of a new day aren't the easiest. If you're a member of the morning fog clan, perhaps it will help to contemplate a fine example of your own handiwork when you reach for your toothbrush.

Full-length continuous hinges are attractive and support the door frames evenly; they're fastened to the inner stiles. Cutting ½″ X ½″ rabbets into the door frames creates enough recess to accommodate the mirror glass, the backing and the retaining strips. A full-width cleat recessed into notches cut into the upper corners of the inner frame members supports the cabinet for surface mounting. The cleat is fastened to the two inner uprights and through the outer frame members with countersunk wood screws. Through mortise-and-tenon joints at the door corners are easy to make and offer a pleasing contrast between side and end grains. The joints are pinned with short wire brads. Magnetic catches are used because they're inexpensive and self-aligning. The shelf tracks fit into ³/₁₆″ X ⁵/₈″ dado grooves cut into the vertical frame members. Notice that the rail and stile facer strips are merely butt-jointed, and fastened to the cabinet frame with deep-set casing nails. The holes are filled and sanded flush.

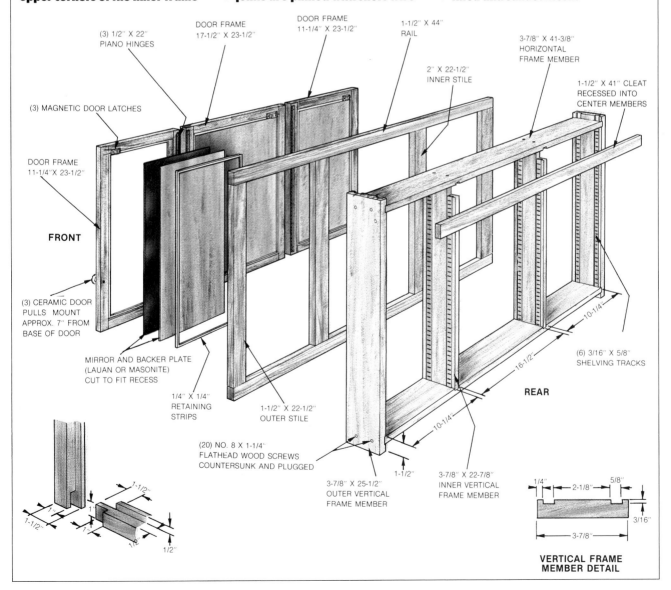

(3) 1/2″ X 22″ PIANO HINGES

DOOR FRAME 17-1/2″ X 23-1/2″

DOOR FRAME 11-1/4″ X 23-1/2″

1-1/2″ X 44″ RAIL

3-7/8″ X 41-3/8″ HORIZONTAL FRAME MEMBER

2″ X 22-1/2″ INNER STILE

1-1/2″ X 41″ CLEAT RECESSED INTO CENTER MEMBERS

(3) MAGNETIC DOOR LATCHES

DOOR FRAME 11-1/4″ X 23-1/2″

FRONT

(3) CERAMIC DOOR PULLS MOUNT APPROX. 7″ FROM BASE OF DOOR

MIRROR AND BACKER PLATE (LAUAN OR MASONITE) CUT TO FIT RECESS

1/4″ X 1/4″ RETAINING STRIPS

1-1/2″ X 22-1/2″ OUTER STILE

(20) NO. 8 X 1-1/4″ FLATHEAD WOOD SCREWS COUNTERSUNK AND PLUGGED

3-7/8″ X 25-1/2″ OUTER VERTICAL FRAME MEMBER

3-7/8″ X 22-7/8″ INNER VERTICAL FRAME MEMBER

REAR

(6) 3/16″ X 5/8″ SHELVING TRACKS

10-1/4″

16-1/2″

10-1/4″

1-1/2″

1-1/2″

1-1/2″

1/2″

1/4″

2-1/8″

5/8″

3/16″

3-7/8″

VERTICAL FRAME MEMBER DETAIL

Butler's Tray Table

This design from the past adapts to the self-serve world.

The butler's tray table was designed hundreds of years ago—no doubt to make it easy for "the help" to deliver milord and milady's teatime victuals. It was, after all, a simple matter to load the removable tray with goodies in the kitchen, and then deposit it—atop its waiting legs—before a hungry group of nobles.

Even today, in our self-serve society, antique reproduction butler's tables are often found in American households. And, when you think about it, the convertible furnishings actually have dozens of potential uses, from serving breakfast in bed to transporting bowls of midnight popcorn. What's more, we believe you'll find that this mini-mobile groaning board is an uncomplicated but satisfying shop project, as well as a treat for the eyes.

Money-wise woodworkers buy large boards and divide them, instead of paying the added board-footage charge for cut-to-size lumber. For example, if you're willing to rip two 1 X 8 X 8' boards as shown in the cutting diagram, you can avoid the additional expense of having to buy two (closer-to-size) 1 X 4s *plus* one 1 X 8.

Take It From the Bottom

The table's legs and braces are held together by $5/16$" X $1 1/2$" fluted dowels. (Note: Since the wooden pegs enter the corner posts from two different directions, the $3/4$"-deep holes must be staggered or the pairs of plugs will run into each other.) The dowels should be glued into the holes, and the contact surfaces between the boards must also be bonded. Once all the pieces are glued and slipped together, apply pressure to the assembly with either four bar clamps or a strap clamp. (If you have trouble keeping the legs square, just tack thin strips of wood—such as split lath or $1/4$" dowel—between the feet to hold them in position until the adhesive has set.)

And Continue on Top

The holes for the $1/4$" X $1 1/4$" fluted doweling—which holds the various parts of the table's top together—must be very carefully aligned, or the ends of the boards won't square up. So, before you do any drilling, lay out the various sections and mark them, al-lowing for two dowels in each long dimension and one in each of the shorter sides.

Start assembling the tray section by joining two $6 1/4$" X $10 1/4$" boards with a 2" X $10 1/4$" section between them. Now secure a 2" X $14 1/2$" segment to each side of the three-piece unit. Then construct another three-board assembly, attach it to the already assembled five-piece portion, and affix the last 2" X $14 1/2$" plank to your platform's "unoccupied" edge. Complete the table-top by adding the 2" X $26 1/2$" side boards, and clamp the assembly securely while the glue dries.

Once the glue has set sufficiently, remove the clamps and lay the joined boards upside down on your workbench. Position the base unit, legs up, on the top (leaving about $1/4$" space all around), and scribe a line—on the underside of the platform—around the inside of the base's boards. Then, using leftover scraps of wood, make $3/4$" X 1" X 2" cleats and fasten them along the pencil line with wood screws—two to each corner. (These pieces will prevent the top from sliding on the base, while still allowing for its easy removal.)

Handles

One simple way to form an accurate curve for the fold up handles is to make a template from a piece of cardboard. Cut out a $3 1/2$" X $18 1/2$" chunk of the paper product and another that's $3 1/2$" X $26 1/2$", and fold each one in half, end to end. Once you slice out a suitable curve on both templates, the un-folded cardboard pieces will provide symmetrical arcs.

To make the hand grips, just locate the center of each board's long dimension, move in $1 1/4$" from the curved side and bore a 1" hole. Drill another 1" opening on each side of the centered one, then file out the rest of the finger slot with a rasp.

Finishing

Attach the handles to the tabletop with four pairs of brass hinges (the locking type is best), sand to an even surface, apply poly-urethane varnish, and rub the whole thing out with 0000 steel wool. Now you're ready for some high-class serving; don't forget the white towel and ice bucket.

Butler's Tray Table

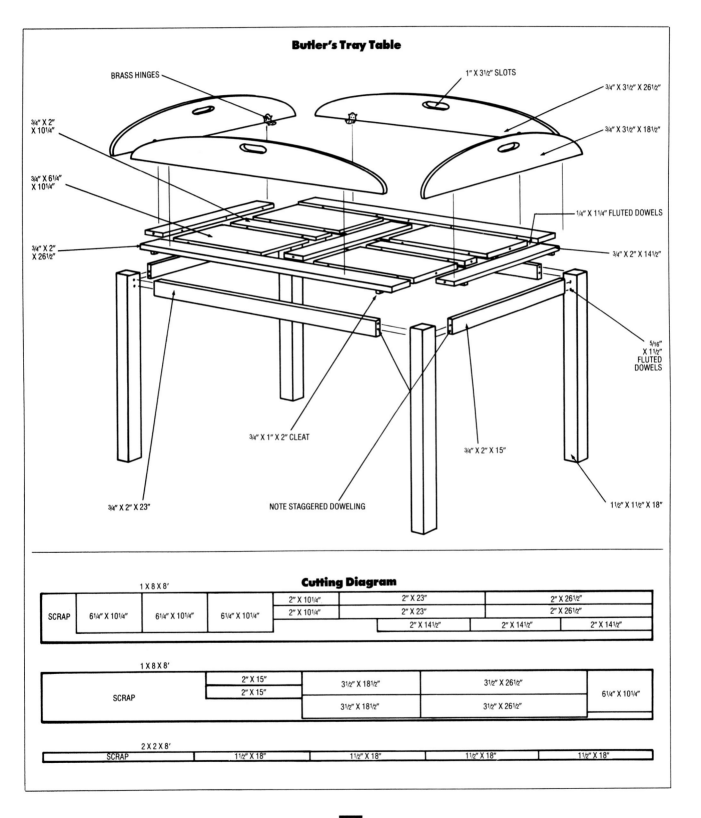

BRASS HINGES

1" X 3½" SLOTS

3/4" X 3½" X 26½"

3/4" X 3½" X 18½"

3/4" X 2" X 10¼"

3/4" X 6¼" X 10¼"

1/4" X 1¼" FLUTED DOWELS

3/4" X 2" X 26½"

3/4" X 2" X 14½"

5/16" X 1½" FLUTED DOWELS

3/4" X 1" X 2" CLEAT

3/4" X 2" X 15"

3/4" X 2" X 23"

NOTE STAGGERED DOWELING

1½" X 1½" X 18"

Cutting Diagram

1 X 8 X 8'

SCRAP	6¼" X 10¼"	6¼" X 10¼"	6¼" X 10¼"	2" X 10¼"	2" X 23"	2" X 26½"
				2" X 10¼"	2" X 23"	2" X 26½"
					2" X 14½"	2" X 14½"	2" X 14½"

1 X 8 X 8'

SCRAP	2" X 15"	3½" X 18½"	3½" X 26½"	6¼" X 10¼"
	2" X 15"			
		3½" X 18½"	3½" X 26½"	

2 X 2 X 8'

SCRAP	1½" X 18"	1½" X 18"	1½" X 18"	1½" X 18"

Make an Easy Chair

A structural design and the proper jigs make building "truss-worthy" chairs as simple as sawing and nailing.

The chair is a common piece of furniture, yet it's probably one of the most difficult home furnishings to make. Why? Because these usually delicate-appearing seats must be built to withstand the stress of people leaning back on the rear legs, and often rely upon some complicated joinery techniques.

However, even a novice should be able to cobble together this alternative design fairly quickly, using nothing more than a hammer, a saw, some nails, a punch and a bottle of glue. It incorporates simple joinery—lap joints—and the structural strength of a truss framework to make a truly durable chair.

The Jig

First, you'll need to make a jig: a guide that will help you position the components accurately to assure that all of your chairs will be identical in design. To build one, just round up some scrap plywood and a few pieces of 1 X 2 lumber (the actual measurements will be $^3/_4$" X $1^1/_2$"). Now, keeping an eye on Fig.1, proceed as follows:

Use an approximately 24"-square piece of plywood—almost any thickness will do—for the jig's base (part Q in the diagram). Nail a 20" 1 X 2 (part R) flush with, and centered along, one edge of the base. That'll be the jig's bottom edge. Then cut a piece of $^3/_4$" plywood to form a trapezoid (part S) measuring $9^1/_4$" at its top, $15^1/_4$" at its bottom

and $14^1/_4$" on each side. The sides should each form a 78° angle to the base of the jig's bottom edge (make sure that both angles are identical).

Now nail the trapezoid in place so that its bottom is flush against, and centered along, part R. Nail a 12" 1 X 2 (part T) parallel to, and $4^1/_2$" above, the trapezoid's base. Then affix a 9" 1 X 2 (part U) across, and flush with, the top of the trapezoid.

Finally, cut a triangle of $^3/_4$" plywood (part V) to measure $7^1/_2$" at its base and 11" on each side. Then saw the point straight off, about $1^1/_4$" from the tip, so that the resulting snub-nosed isosceles can be nailed flush—upside down—with cross members T and U as shown in Fig. 1. There. Your jig is now complete.

The Chair

The chair itself is made entirely of 1 X 2s: You'll need about 34 linear feet in all, cut to the lengths indicated. (The components are keyed to Fig. 2.)
A: Four $15^1/_2$" legs
B: Two 18" bottom rails
C: Two 16" top rails
D: Two 30" back rails
E: Two $12^5/_8$" front supports
F: Ten 15" seat and back slats
G: Two (one front, one back) 15" bottom braces

If you're purchasing dimensional lumber, one 8′ piece will cover parts A and C; another 8′ board will make parts B and D; a 6′ length will supply parts E, G and one slat from F; and a 12′ plank can be cut to yield the nine remaining F slats.

Basically, the chair consists of two side frames (which you make, one at a time, on the jig) connected by seat slats, back slats and two cross braces.

Begin by constructing the left side frame, using Fig. 2 as a guide. Lay your jig flat on a worktable, and place a leg piece (A) against each of the trapezoid's angling sides so that the ends of each leg butt against the jig's bottom board (R). Now position the bottom rail (B) lengthwise against the bottom edge of the jig's crosspiece (T), and mark where the rail overlaps the legs (each of its ends should extend equally from the outside edge of each leg). Then set the rail aside for a moment, squeeze enough glue (yellow carpenter's or

any resin adhesive) onto the marked areas to cover them thoroughly, and put the bottom rail back into place. Finally, while holding one leg and the rail firmly in position with one hand, drive two $1^1/_4$" 3d finishing nails or wire brads into the joint. Do the same with the opposite leg. With hardwoods, it's best to dip the fasteners in paraffin to keep the wood from splitting.

Next, position, glue, and nail the top rail (C) into place as shown in Fig. 2, making certain that piece is pushed firmly against the jig's top cross member (U). As you can see from the illustration, the top rail's right, or forward, end should extend 2" in front of the front leg. (Note: When you build the right side frame, position the top rail the other way around—with the left end extending 2" outward from what will be its front leg.)

Now you're ready to install the left side frame's final two members. Place the long back rail (D) flush along the left side of the jig's triangle, positioning the corner of D's bottom end flush with the lower edge of the bottom rail (B). The top end of the back rail will then extend across, and well beyond, the joint you just made at the rear leg and top rail. Glue and nail the component in place, using two 2" finishing nails at the top joint and a couple of $1^1/_4$" brads at the bottom.

With that done, position a front support piece (E) along the right side of your jig's triangle, with the outside corner of the part's bottom end flush with the lower edge of B, and the inside corner of its top end flush with the top rail's upper edge. If the support's been cut a bit long, make sure the excess is toward the bottom, where it won't interfere with the slats. Now glue and nail the front support in place, again using a pair of 2" finishing nails at the top and two $1^1/_4$" brads at the bottom.

Remove the completed side frame, put it on a solid work surface, and center-punch all the nails to draw each joint up tightly and to sink the heads below the wood's surface. Now set the frame aside for at least 24 hours to allow the glue to dry. Don't skip this required step. If you do, you'll loosen each glue joint when you hammer the slats and braces in place, and your chair won't last more than a week.

Naturally, once you've assembled the left side frame and stashed it away to dry, you'll

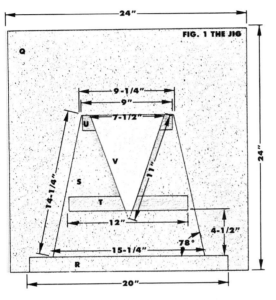

FIG. 1 THE JIG

24"

9-1/4"
9"
7-1/2"
14-1/4"
17"
12"
15-1/4"
20"
24"
4-1/2"
78°

Q U V S T R

A Chippendale it ain't, but the truss-worthy's rustic simplicity, low cost and structural soundness make it appealing and practical.

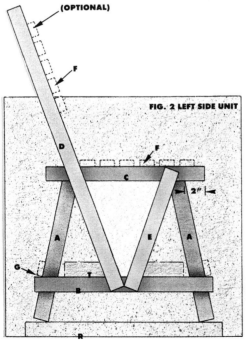

(OPTIONAL)

FIG. 2 LEFT SIDE UNIT

2"

D F C A E A G T B R

By extending the front legs, adding arms and nailing on a pair of rockers, anyone can turn the standard chair into a comfortable and functional rocking model.

be ready to whip together the right side of the chair. Remember, though, to reverse the position of the back rail and the front support. The longer piece (D) should be to the right of the triangle, and the support (E) to the left.

A Day Passes

To finish your chair, just position the seat slats $1/2$" apart across the side frames, mark where the slats overlap the top rails (each end should extend outward by $3/4$" or so), apply glue to the contact areas, and hammer the slats in place, using a pair of 2" finishing nails at every joint.

You'll need some patience when you attempt to attach the first few slats, as you'll have a hard time keeping the side frames upright and aligned while you hold the slat in place, but you'll be OK as soon as the first couple of slats are nailed down and the chair gains some rigidity. Make a point to check each slat with a try square to make sure it's perpendicular to the frames.

Next, go to work on the back crosspieces. Position the first slat with its lower edge 5" above the seat, and space the remaining three pieces $1/2$" apart. The ends should extend $1 1/2$" beyond each back rail.

Before you flop your carcass onto your newly built handiwork, glue and nail the front and back bottom braces (G) in position, as shown in Fig.2. Place each one so that its lower edge is pretty much even with the top edge of the bottom rails (B). Set all the newly sunk nails, give the whole thing another 24 hours to dry, and *then* you and your chair will be ready to meet seat to seat.

The functional simplicity of the furniture seems to call for a natural treatment, so just sand the pieces slightly and apply a penetrating oil. If a conventional softwood were used, a finish made of a medium-dark stain blended with a bit of boiled linseed oil would give some color to the "fresh" wood.

These quick-and-easy chairs could be easily adapted to make other living room furniture in the same pattern. A walnut rocker requires only a few modifications to the original design; and even further variations on the theme (making a larger chair on a larger jig, for instance) are possible and waiting to be discovered by some imaginative soul. Could that person be you?

Indoor Climber

Build a sturdy structure for child's play.

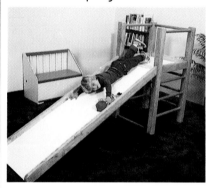

Winter days of indoor confinement can be hard on toddlers and parents alike. When it's too cold and wet to play outside, antsy youngsters are all too prone to make kitchen cupboards their playground.

We won't promise that our climber will return winter peace and tranquillity to a household with several young children, but we can tell you that it's given more than one tot hours of happy, muscle-stretching play. The first version made its debut on Christmas morning a couple of years ago, thrilling a busy one-and-a-half-year-old.

Since then, the details of the design have been improved, but the basic dimensions still hold. Through trial and error, we've found that the spacing of the rungs and rails, and the angle of the slide, suit the reach and physical capabilities of children one-and-a-half to three years old.

Step-by-Step

1. Dado a $^3/_4$" X $^{13}/_{16}$" groove in one face of the 8' 2 X 4 and in one face of one 12' 2 X 4, each groove exactly $^3/_4$" from an edge.
2. Round over all edges on these boards with a $^1/_4$" or $^3/_8$" rounding-over bit in a router.

If you use a $^1/_2$" bit on the edge farthest from the dado on the 8' piece—which will become the three tower rails—little fingers will have an easier time getting a grip.
3. Cut eight 48" lengths from the remaining 2 X 4s. Glue pairs together face to face.
4. Bisect the $^5/_8$" plywood and the hardboard lengthwise. Use a metal-cutting blade to get a smooth edge on the hardboard.
5. Cut a $25^1/_2$" piece from both the plywood and the hardboard. Then cut a 25° bevel across the end of the $70^1/_2$" length of plywood that you just sawed, removing 1" from the "C" side and a little more from the other. Remove 1" from the hardboard with a square cut.
6. Trim the corners of the 24" X $25^1/_2$" plywood and hardboard, as shown in the illustration, to form the tower floor. Glue the sheets together with the hardboard on top and the plywood's good side down.
7. Cut two 21" pieces of 2 X 4 from a 2 X 4 X 12' board, and bevel the long edge of one at 25°.
8. Cut two 21" pieces from the 1 X 2. Glue and nail one to the unbeveled 2 X 4 X 21" and the other to the beveled piece, as shown. Clamp (don't glue) the two assemblies together temporarily, and drill $^5/_{16}$" holes through them, 4" from each end, to accept the 4" carriage bolts.
9. Glue and screw the beveled face of the 2 X 4 to the "B" side of the plywood, so that it's centered ($1^1/_2$" in from each edge) and matches the beveled edge on the sheet.
10. Glue the $69^1/_2$" piece of hardboard to the "C" side of the corresponding plywood.
11. Remove the clamps from the face-glued 2 X 4s, and rip off $^1/_4$" on each side where the joint is exposed, to form 3" X 3" posts. Make a light cut on each end to square them. Round over all edges with the router.
12. Drill $1^1/_4$" holes $^3/_4$" deep in the posts for the $1^3/_8$" closet rod, at the positions noted on the illustration. (Check your layout twice before proceeding; this is an easy place to become confused.)
13. Drill $^1/_4$" holes all the way through the posts at the positions corresponding with those noted on the tower rail illustration. These holes are staggered so they won't intersect inside the two posts.
14. Drill $^1/_4$" holes $1^1/_2$" deep in the ends of the three 2 X 4 tower rails, as shown in the illustration. Note that the holes in the tow-

er rail opposite from the slide are in different locations from the holes in the other rails.
15. Drill two $^1/_4$" X $1^1/_2$" holes in each end of the slide support rail, 1" from the top and the bottom.
16. Fashion V-blocks or some other means of holding the posts on edge while dadoing. Set the dado so that it makes a $^3/_4$"-wide X $1^9/_{16}$"-deep cut into the inside corner of each post, at the position noted on the illustration. Again, check twice to be sure you're cutting the right posts in the right place. Then set the dado for $^3/_4$" X $^{13}/_{16}$", and notch the full inside of the two posts adjacent to the slide.
17. Assemble the left and right sides of the tower separately, gluing the closet rod into the holes and setting the side rails by driving pieces of dowel through the posts and into the ends of the rails.
18. Set one end of the slide-support rail into one of the sides with the $^1/_4$" dowels.
19. Lay that side of the tower flat on the floor, and set the closet rods into it.
20. Apply glue to the exposed ends of the closet rods, set the tower floor into the side lying on the floor (no glue is needed), and lower the other side onto this assembly.
21. Crosscut the 2 X 4 X 12' at a 25° bevel to form a slide rail $70^1/_2$' long. Cut the other $70^1/_2$" 2 X 4 at the same angle, but make sure that the opposite face is up. (One should be cut with the dado up and the other with the dado down.) Round the other ends of both boards.
22. Apply glue to the dados in both slide rails and slip them onto the slide, making sure the bevels match.
23. Trim the ends of any exposed $^1/_4$" dowel with a sharp chisel or a saw with no set. Sand off any glue leaks, stain with a fruitwood or equivalent coloring, and finish with your favorite formulation.

LIST OF MATERIALS

(1)	2 X 4 X 8'
(4)	2 X 4 X 12'
(1)	1 X 2 X 4'
(1)	$^5/_8$" X 4' X 8' B-C plywood
(1)	$^1/_8$" X 4' X 8' tempered hardboard
(2)	$1^3/_8$" X 8' closet rod
(1)	$^3/_8$" X 10' closet rod
(1)	$^1/_4$" X 3' dowel
(3)	No. 10 X $1^1/_2$" wood screws
(2)	$^1/_4$" X 4" carriage bolts and wing nuts

About Materials

The version we're showing here is our economy model—not the cheapest possible but one that accents durability over exotic materials. The first climber we built was framed in clear fir coated with tung oil, and the slide was birch plywood slickened with bowling alley wax. It was truly attractive, until its proud new owner decorated it with an indelible marker.

We used ⁵/₈" plywood on the climber shown, because it's only a couple of dollars more than ¹/₂", and it yields a convenient ³/₄" thickness when combined with ¹/₈" hardboard. Likewise, the 1³/₈" closet rod isn't necessary for strength; it's just less costly than dowel. The 2 X 4s are framing lumber, but it would have been nice to have something a little better when the time came to rout the edges. Knots and rounding-over bits don't mix well.

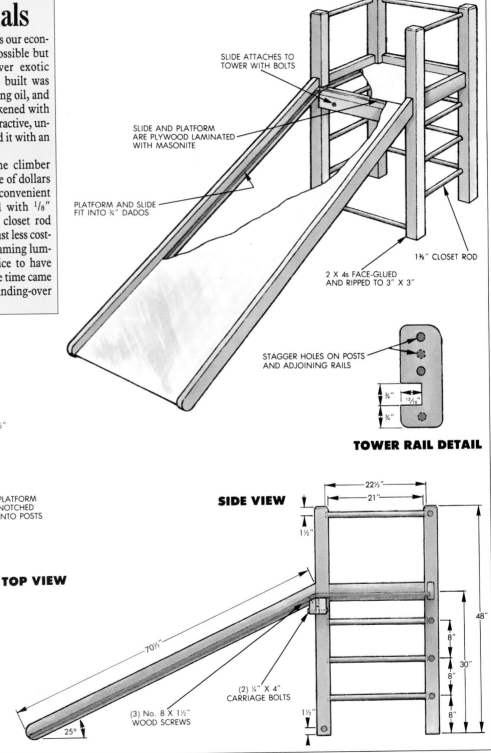

SLIDE ATTACHES TO TOWER WITH BOLTS

SLIDE AND PLATFORM ARE PLYWOOD LAMINATED WITH MASONITE

PLATFORM AND SLIDE FIT INTO ¾" DADOS

1⅜" CLOSET ROD

2 X 4s FACE-GLUED AND RIPPED TO 3" X 3"

STAGGER HOLES ON POSTS AND ADJOINING RAILS

¾"
13/16"
¾"

TOWER RAIL DETAIL

24"

25½"

PLATFORM NOTCHED INTO POSTS

TOP VIEW

27"

SIDE VIEW

22½"
21"
1½"

70½"

(2) ¼" X 4" CARRIAGE BOLTS

(3) No. 8 X 1½" WOOD SCREWS

25°

48"
8"
30"
8"
8"
1½"

Blanket Statements

An elegantly simple rack solves storage problems.

Storage space for blankets—during the "in between" months when it can be cold one night and warm the next—can sometimes be hard to come by, especially when the shelves of many folks' bedroom closets are overflowing with the young'uns' toys, last season's clothing or assorted containers that are "sure to come in handy someday."

A blanket rack can provide an easy solution to the problem—and one that won't crush the down in your comforter or crease the fabric of your favorite bed coverings. Better still, the holder's wooden rods can also be used for drying clothes, hanging towels (when you find yourself besieged by a lot of guests) or racking shoes (they rest against the bottom crossbars).

The attractive piece of furniture can be yours to enjoy for only a few dollars' worth of wood and a couple of hours of your time. And this is one project you just about have to build yourself, because it's not the kind of item you'll find in the local department store at *any* cost.

The handy device you see here is built

from spruce, but you can get almost the same results using white pine or fir. We cut a pair of 32" lengths of 1 X 12 for the rack's ends, and ripped five 1¼" X 1¼" boards from a 20" length of 2 X 8. (You could also use your ripsaw to divide three 20" 2 X 4s, which would leave you with one extra rod.) Our materials list was filled out with 10 No. 12 X 1½" flathead screws, ten ½" wooden cap buttons and some glue and varnish.

As for tools, you'll need a ripsaw, a cross-cut saw, a saber saw, a hand drill with a No. 12 adjustable countersink bit, a screwdriver, a paintbrush and some sandpaper.

After cutting the 1 X 12s to length, you can determine the shape you'd like and cut both pieces with a saber saw—or you could, if you prefer, simply assemble the rack with un-adorned rectangular sides. We decided on the diamond-and-a-half pattern shown in the picture. (The size and shape of the bottom scrollwork and upper cutout are arbitrary.)

The best way to come up with a pleasing end pattern that's symmetrical is to make a template by folding a sheet of wrapping paper—11" wide and 32" long—in half, lengthwise. Draw one edge of your proposed end board; cut both edges of the folded

paper; open it up; and if you like the result (assuming the removal of the wood will leave room for attaching the five crossbars), trace the line on one of the 1 X 12s and then cut the two of them at once.

We elected to place the centers of the two lower rods 4" above the floor line and 6" apart. The ends of the three upper pieces form the points of equilateral triangles with 5" sides—the highest points being 2" below the end pieces' top edges.

We marked the two 1 X 12s and, using a No. 12 adjustable countersink tool, bored the holes for the crossbars. This drill/counter-sink tool not only creates the right-sized hole, but sinks it ³⁄₁₆"—which is the depth you'll need later to install the ½" cap buttons.

Then we glued and secured—with No. 12 X 1½" flathead screws—the ends of the rods to the inner faces of the two 1 X 12s. Note that the 1¼" faces of the lower cross-members are parallel to the floor, while the three upper pieces are cocked 45°.

Next, we glued in the cap buttons and sanded all edges and surfaces. A couple of coats of satin urethane varnish (lightly sanded between applications) and *voilà*: Our blanket rack was complete.

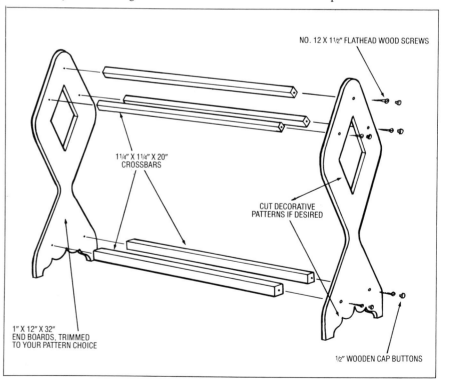

NO. 12 X 1½" FLATHEAD WOOD SCREWS

1¼" X 1¼" X 20" CROSSBARS

CUT DECORATIVE PATTERNS IF DESIRED

1" X 12" X 32" END BOARDS, TRIMMED TO YOUR PATTERN CHOICE

½" WOODEN CAP BUTTONS

Spalted Oak Cradle

It's often best to let nature take its course.

Ever wonder how a truly gifted woodworker creates his or her most attractive pieces? Often enough, it's simply done by letting nature take its course—a practice that isn't beyond the capability of even the more modest home crafters among us.

The infant cradle you see here—built by Dean Davis for a coworker celebrating his family's first child—serves to point up just what we mean: Rather than cutting the wood into intricate shapes and relying on a stain to highlight the grain, Dean took pains to select *naturally* formed and accentuated stock and to let the wood's inherent irregularities define relevant borders.

"I chose the spalted oak for its character, and though the spalting represents early stages of rot, I was careful to select sound slabs caught at just the right stage of decay. Since the cradle's depth precluded using one-piece boards, I had to rip the lumber into random widths and butt-and-glue the pieces together to achieve the necessary dimensions."

The bassinet's finished size came to 14″ X 24″ X 30½″. The end boards are ¾″ thick, and the floor and sides were planed to ⅜″. The taper—from 19½″ at the top to 12″ at the bottom—figures out to 20° from vertical (for those with a geometrical bent). By the same token, the arc of the rockers, which dictates the duration of the cradle's to-and-fro action, is relatively mild and can be established on a cardboard template by swinging a pencil on a 4′ string radius.

To maintain the handcrafted flavor of the piece, Dean insisted on traditional end-to-side and bottom joints. "I went with full mortise-and-tenon joints at the main corners to show the end grain, and kept the tenons to ⅜″ X 2″, with rounded edges. The

mortises—which I made with a router, but which could be fashioned with a drill and chisel—are spaced 2¼″ apart, and a ¼″ hardwood dowel pin, set perpendicular to the tenon's face, secures each of the 12 unions. The only tricky spots were in the rockers themselves, because I had to start the pin sockets about 1½″ from the joints, and then use 2″-long dowels, rather than the shorter one-inchers."

The remaining joints—specifically those between the bottom and the sides and ends—were merely secured with appropriately sized ⅛″ dowels (though wire brads could also be used) that were tapped through the walls and into the edge of the flooring—which, naturally, was beveled at the sides to form a perfect match with its tapered mates.

After giving the entire cradle an even sanding with progressively finer grades of paper, Dean hand-finished the piece inside and out with 100% tung oil—a product containing no petroleum distillates whatever and thus a sound choice for an infant's environment.

Mother Nature provided an exemplary design for the Davis cradle, and we know that both proud parents—and baby Jade Alysen—are pleased that she did.

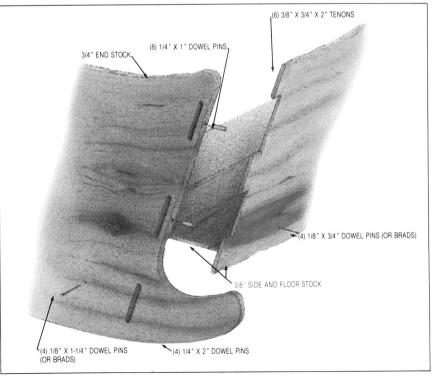

(6) 3/8″ X 3/4″ X 2″ TENONS

(8) 1/4″ X 1″ DOWEL PINS

3/4″ END STOCK

(4) 1/8″ X 3/4″ DOWEL PINS (OR BRADS)

3/8″ SIDE AND FLOOR STOCK

(4) 1/8″ X 1-1/4″ DOWEL PINS (OR BRADS)

(4) 1/4″ X 2″ DOWEL PINS

Credits

Cover: Michael Soluri **Contents:**
Michael Soluri

Part I

p. 9: Joel Popadics **pp. 10-11:**
Berenice Abbott/Commerce Graphics
Ltd. Inc. **pp. 12-13:** Neil Slavin **p. 13**
(**bottom**): © 1987 Drew: Leviton-
Atlanta, Inc. **pp. 14-15:** Jeff Britton
pp. 17-21: Illustrations reprinted
from *The Antique Tool Collector's
Guide to Value* (Windmill Publishing,
El Cajon, CA) **pp. 22-24:** Bill Hay-
ward **p. 25:** Michael Soluri

Part II

p. 29: Joel Popadics **pp. 30-35:** Aaron
Rezny **pp. 36-41:** Michael Soluri **pp.
42-45:** Aaron Rezny **pp. 46-49:** Don
Osby **pp. 50-54:** Ken Forsgren,
photos; Clarence Goosen, illustrations **pp. 56-57:** Michael Soluri **pp.
60-61:** Michael Soluri **pp. 64-65:**
Michael Soluri **pp. 68-69:** Michael
Soluri **pp. 72-73:** Michael Soluri **pp.
76-77:** Michael Soluri **pp. 80-82:** ©
Brad Hess/Black Star **pp. 84-89:**
Michael Soluri **pp. 90-91:**
Don Osby, illustrations
p. 93: Don Osby **pp.
94-95:** Clarence Goosen

Part III

p. 97: Joel Popadics **pp. 98-101:**
Clarence Goosen and Don Osby **pp.
102-103:** Aaron Rezny **p. 104:** By
permission of Sterling Publishing
Co., Inc., from *Gluing & Clamping*,
© 1986 by Patrick Spielman, photos
by Dick Frank & Frank Attardi **p.
105:** Michael Soluri **p. 107:** Furman
Roth Advertising, Inc. **pp. 108-111:**
Michael Soluri **pp. 112-118:** Clarence
Goosen **pp. 120-123:** Don Osby **pp.
124-129:** Don Osby

Part IV

p. 131: Joel Popadics **pp. 132-133:**
Tom Tracy **pp. 134-135:** Michael
Soluri **p. 136:** Tom Tracy **p. 137:**
Giorgio Palmisano **pp. 140-145:** Don
Osby **pp. 146-153:** Michael Soluri **pp.
154-161:** Clarence Goosen **pp. 162-
165:** Jan Adkins

Part V

p. 169: Joel Popadics **p. 171:** Clarence
Goosen **p. 173:** Clarence Goosen,
illustration **p. 174:** Don Osby **p.
177:** Don Osby **p. 179:** Don
Osby, illustrations **p. 181:**
Don Osby **p. 183:** Don
Osby, illustrations **p. 185:**
Don Osby **p. 186:** Don
Osby, illustration **p. 187:**
Don Osby, illustration **p.
192:** Reprinted from *The
Antique Tool Collector's Guide
to Value* (Windmill Publishing,
El Cajon, CA)